CULTURE AND TRUTH

CULTURE & TRUTH

The Remaking of Social Analysis

With a new
Introduction

RENATO ROSALDO

BEACON PRESS

Boston

Beacon Press
25 Beacon Street
Boston, Massachusetts 02108

Beacon Press books
are published under the auspices of
the Unitarian Universalist Association of Congregations.

99 98 97 96 95 94   8 7 6 5 4 3 2

Text design by Linda Koegel

Library of Congress Cataloging-in-Publication Data

Rosaldo, Renato.
    Culture & truth: the remaking of social analysis / Renato
Rosaldo.
        p. cm.
    Includes bibliographical references and index.
    ISBN 0-8070-4623-X
    1. Ethnology—Philosophy. 2. Subjectivity. 3. Discourse
analysis, Narrative. 4. Ethnology—Methodology.
I. Title. II. Title: Culture and truth.
GN345.R667 1993
306'.01—dc20   93-18158
                                                                CIP

For my children, Sam, Manny, and Olivia

Contents

Introduction to the 1993 Edition   ix
Preface   xxi
Introduction · Grief and a Headhunter's Rage   1

Part One · Critique
1   The Erosion of Classic Norms   25
2   After Objectivism   46
3   Imperialist Nostalgia   68

Part Two · Reorientation
4   Putting Culture into Motion   91
5   Ilongot Improvisations   109
6   Narrative Analysis   127

vii

Part Three · Renewal

7   Changing Chicano Narratives   147
8   Subjectivity in Social Analysis   168
9   Border Crossings   196

Epilogue · A Raging Battle   218

Notes   225
Index   247

Introduction
to the 1993 Edition

A NEW EDITION of *Culture and Truth* provides me with a dual opportunity, initially to reflect on recent developments in higher education and then to address the role of anthropologists in these changes. Broadly speaking, such changes require an analysis of cultural citizenship and educational democracy. Working for institutional change requires coordinated efforts and can be guided by a set of principles for achieving diversity in higher education. The rules of thumb set out in what follows should not be taken too literally, however, because under conditions of rapid institu-

tional change today's wisdom can quickly become yesterday's cliché.

The past twenty-five years of increasing inclusion in higher education show a clear pattern: the lower the level in the institutional hierarchies the greater the degree of inclusion achieved. At the present time, changes in student bodies have been greater than those in teaching faculties, and changes in teaching faculties have been greater than those in central administrations. Similarly, less powerful humanities faculties have grown more diverse than their social science counterparts, and less powerful social science faculties have grown more diverse than their natural science counterparts. It is also worth noting that the teaching faculty, a supposedly enlightened group, has often proven to be more a part of the problem than of the solution in efforts to promote diversity.

Processes of institutional change appear to have gone through more or less characteristic phases. Initial efforts concentrated on getting people in the door. Institutions of higher learning appeared to tell those previously excluded, "Come in, sit down, shut up. You're welcome here as long as you conform with our norms." This was the Green Card phase of short-term provisional admission in the name of increasing institutional inclusion and change.

In time, institutions found that they had problems retaining newly admitted students, faculty, and staff. The newcomers entered only to exit shortly thereafter as dropouts. The door of admission turned out to be a revolving one that whisked people out as quickly as they came in. Colleges and universities were not hospitable to their new members. Problems of retention for racialized minority students had to be faced. Such efforts as building a critical mass of minority students, creating ethnic studies centers, establishing positions for minority deans, opening minority student centers, and developing ethnic theme houses helped construct an environment where minority students could become long-term, contributing, more fully enfranchized members of their colleges and universities.

More recently, the issue of institutional responsiveness to educational content has come to the foreground. In one case I witnessed, students stunned a university president by taking over his office and then demanding an education that responded to their concerns, one that recognized their existence and their distinctive goals in pursuing higher learning. Certain changes in institutional norms, curricula, and pedagogies appear crucial for democratizing educational institutions over the coming decade.

At one time students and faculty in women's and minority communities debated intensely about whether their programs should risk dilution by becoming mainstream or retain purity by remaining separate. By now many agree on the need for both, the prime time of mainstreaming and the safe house of separateness. Mainstreaming plays a critical role because of the scope and prestige of prime time. To articulate divergent perspectives and to inspire coming generations, diversity must be present in institutional authority. How otherwise can diverse groups articulate their intellectual visions to greatest effect? How otherwise can diverse groups become full citizens of the Republic of X (supply the name of your college or university)?

Why then do institutions need safe houses? Safe houses can foster self-esteem and promote a sense of belonging in often alien institutions. Such factors have proven critical in the retention of students and should not be minimized. The benefits of creating safe houses also include intellectual contributions. Safe houses can be places where diverse groups—under the banners of ethnic studies, feminist studies, or gay and lesbian studies—talk together and become articulate about their intellectual projects. When they enter mainstream seminars such students speak with clarity and force about their distinctive projects, concerns, and perspectives. The class is richer and more complex, if perhaps less comfortable, for its broadened range of perspectives.

The general goal is to achieve diversity in all rooms, decision-making rooms, classrooms, faculty rooms, rooms of all kinds, shapes, and sizes. In order to democratize higher education, people need to work together to change the present situation where the higher the perceived social status of the room the less diverse its membership. When people leave a decision-making room and one hears that a consensus was reached, remember to ask: "Who was in the room when the decision was made?" Introducing diversity in such rooms will slow down the process. Decisions will be harder to reach and the process will be less comfortable than via the old method, but the decisions made will find broad support and prove more effective in the long run.

Achieving diversity in classrooms follows a distinctive pattern. It produces instant changes and calls for a series of further changes. One reaction is predictable. People who once had a monopoly on privilege and authority will suddenly experience relative deprivation. True to anthropological theory, they will feel diminished and may in certain cases find themselves drawn to nativistic movements, perhaps to the National Association of Scholars or other groups bent on practicing curricular apartheid. When people become accustomed to privilege, it appears to be a vested right, a status that is natural and well deserved, a part of the order of things. In the short run, the transition to diversity can be traumatic; in the long run, it promises a great deal.

Consider the following representative yet hypothetical case. There once was a place where people of the male persuasion gathered. It was called the old boys' room. At times it seemed that men went there only to talk about absent parties, people who were prohibited from entering the room— in short, women. Sometimes their remarks were excessively flattering and astonishingly graphic. More often, they were downright crude, vulgar, and demeaning.

Then one day the old boys' room was integrated. Both men and women began to hold their conversations there. The men had shockingly strong reactions. They felt uncomfortable; some said they were being silenced. One woman asked, "What exactly do you want to say about me? What have you become used to saying about me that you now feel inhibited about saying in my presence?"

My hypothetical case depicts the dynamics of political correctness. The story conveys the psychic reality that political correctness creates for people who report that they feel afraid to say the wrong thing. Have such people become accustomed to saying hateful things with impunity because the people spoken about are not in the room? Alternatively, has the lack of accountability in exclusionary environments led to insensitivity and ignorance about the impact of one's words and deeds? In such cases a person's intentions and the effects of their actions do not coincide, but institutional change requires attention both to intentions *and* to effects. Benevolent intentions do not erase damaging effects. Much as the former exclusive inhabitants of the old boys' room can, in the long run, remake relations between men and women in fuller more egalitarian ways, so too can Anglos and people of color as well as straights and gays remake their relations. The remaking of social analysis called for in *Culture and Truth* was inspired at its heart by such struggles to remake institutions and the social relations of their members.

Diversity in classrooms does more than arouse predictable discomfort and resistance. The moment classrooms become diverse, change begins. There is no standing still. New students do not laugh at the old jokes. Even those teachers who do nothing to revise their yellowed sheets of lecture notes know that their words have taken on new meanings. New pedagogies begin. New pedagogies include new courses and new texts. One crucial ingredient involves affirmative action for course readings (and for works cited in publications). Teachers find new ways to seek out pertinent works of high quality by people of color, women, gays, and lesbians. Looking in the usual places and in the usual ways will not produce change. In a graduate seminar I offered a few years ago, students complained about the lack of diverse content. "What," I asked, "do you mean? You have different cultures in the course—Nuers, Tikopias, Navahos." "No," the students replied, "we want books by and not just about members of different cultures." Since then I've often left part of the syllabus blank so that students can suggest appropriate works previously unknown to me.

A corollary to this general principle is that new texts read in old ways produce little change. Habits of reading must also change. In the graduate seminar we all discovered that a number of the new texts did not speak in the language of anthropological research. After a couple of false starts we began to read the new texts for their projects, for their fresh questions, perceptions, and definitions of problems. The class then assumed the burden of exploring how fresh ideas can be translated into anthropological research projects.

In teaching a new course that grew out of the Western Culture controversy at Stanford University, the instructors juxtaposed the unexpected. I, for example, juxtaposed Augustine's *Confessions* and a Navaho life history, Left Handed's *Son of Old Man Hat*. Next to a writer relatively uninfluenced by a major world religion, Augustine's inner struggle with his own paganism became less abstract and more vivid. And next to Augustine, in a course where the assigned books were deemed great, *Son of Old Man Hat* became quite unlike the book I had taught in anthropology courses. It became a book of wisdom and, in addition to speaking about uxorilocality and sheep, the class discussed ideas of knowledge, human judgment, and spiritual harmony.

Such accounts risk being celebrated in ways that do not prepare instructors for the intensity and pain they also will likely face. In part the pain derives from having to share authority more than before. Once diversity is valued as an intellectual and human resource, teachers cannot be equally versed in all texts and issues. Instructors will probably find themselves listening to their students with the care and intensity that they once reserved for their own speech. The pain also comes from how closely or distantly students feel connected with the readings. New course readings often tug at their hearts and involve their feelings more deeply and directly than earlier readings did. Classrooms then produce a range of feelings, from intimate to distant, and the feelings have to be addressed. In my experience such classrooms, even at their most uncomfortable, have produced student work of exceptional quality.

In the classroom multiculturalism involves both a civil rights agenda for institutional change and an intellectual agenda for testing ideas and projects against a more demanding and diverse range of perspectives. Sometimes people ask whether multiculturalism will change the reservation, the barrio, or the ghetto. If diversity were fully implemented it doubtless would bring, even as its implementation would require, wider societal changes. Yet institutional change revolves more immediately around self-interest than disinterested altruism. Colleges and universities stand to be the primary beneficiaries of democratizing movements, both in relation to their communitarian existence and in relation to their central agendas of education and critical thought. Can our major institutions continue to include only a narrow spectrum of the population? Can this nation remain a democracy and condone systemic apartheid in the composition of its classrooms and in the content of its curriculum?

Allow me now to turn to the role of anthropologists in the processes of institutional change just outlined. For anthropologists, the stakes are high in the struggles over multiculturalism. Like it or not, the discipline is present in conflicts over educational democracy. Certain humanists, for example, speak of the gulf separating high literary culture (the best of human thought) from culture in the anthropological sense (a phrase uttered with contempt). In fact, a significant number of anthropologists have been involved in and made significant contributions to multiculturalism. An anthropologist, for example, directs the American Cultures Program at the University of California, Berkeley, and the first new course offered after the Western Culture controversy at Stanford University included an anthropologist among its three teachers. I could offer many more such examples. Perhaps a series of straightforward reports on what anthropologists have done to promote institutional change, including achievements and obstacles, would help transform disciplinary consciousness.

Yet, if one can believe a spate of letters in the *Anthropology Newsletter*, a number of cultural anthropologists feel excluded from the movements for educational reform that promote diversity and multiculturalism. The newsletter reactions seem heartfelt yet strangely off the mark. Are anthropologists awaiting a formal invitation, perhaps as paid expert consultants in multiculturalism? A counter-message could be: Do not ask what multiculturalism can do for you. Volunteer, get active, take initiative, and work to make anthropology an integral, indispensable part of multiculturalism. Learn about and follow the examples of anthropologists who already have contributed to institutional change.

It may help to keep in mind that the notion of culture has long been anthropology's master concept and the discipline has an extended history of exploring its intricacies. Thus, some of the newsletter readers lament that interlopers from other fields have added the prefix multi- to the term cultural and, without a word of acknowledgment, stolen valuable disciplinary property from its rightful home, In the finger-pointing moments of the newsletter's epistolary melodramas, humanists have played the villains who maliciously rob and exclude their social scientist colleagues from the multicultural action. Some readers argue that literary critics have gained a near monopoly on multiculturalism. Because of their failure to draw on anthropological expertise, other readers claim, humanists have condemned themselves to reinventing a century of intellectual labor on the concept of culture.

Certain anthropologists claim as well that proponents of multiculturalism could stand to learn about the concept of culture advanced by Franz Boas, a key founder of modern anthropology. Boas argued for the integrity of separate cultures which were equal with respect to their values. Differences between cultures with respect to technological development confered them with neither moral superiority nor moral inferiority. The historical importance of Boasian cultural relativism and related efforts to combat racism cannot be denied.

Yet the notions of Franz Boas seem oddly incomplete and at times beside the point. This is especially the case when one considers that educational democracy involves not only honoring other cultures in their unique integrity, but also working simultaneously with a diversity of human beings— women and men, gays and straights, people of color and Anglos. We are all equal partners in a shared project of renegotiating the sense of belonging, inclusion, and full enfranchisement in our major institutions. Such renegotiations require time, patience, and careful listening. For example, men participate in building diverse communities, not by issuing decrees, but by listening to women's statements about their subordination, their forms of well-being, and their sense of full enfranchisement. How many men worry in middle-class neighborhoods about how they will walk to their cars at night? How many women do not have such concerns? Settings where diversity resides in a single room require a reworking of anthropology at its core, including serious reformulations of the historically significant Boasian doctrine of separate and equal cultures.

Culture and Truth argues that anthropology has undergone a sea change since the late 1960s. This shift has been stimulated by changes in the world, notably decolonization, the civil rights movement, the fuller emergence of a global economy, and the massive interventions of development. The emergent research program for ethnography has placed increased emphasis on history and politics in contexts of inequality and oppression based on such factors as Westernization, media imperialism, invasions of commodity culture, and differences of class, gender, race, ethnicity, and sexual orientation.

Recent experimentation in ethnographic writing arguably derives from the remaking of social analysis rather than from experimentation for its own sake. Modes of composition have changed because the discipline's research agenda has shifted from the search for structures to theories of practice that explore the interplay of both structure *and* agency. In such endeavors, knowledge and power are intertwined because the observer's point of view always influences the observations she makes. Rather than stressing timeless universals and the sameness of human nature, this perspective emphasizes human diversity, historical change, and political struggle.

In this context, classic modes of analysis, which in their pure type rely exclusively on a detached observer using a neutral language to study a unified world of brute facts, no longer hold a monopoly on truth. Instead they now share disciplinary authority with other analytical perspectives. The move from singular to plural forms of analysis implies a need to decenter and reread ethnographic classics, not to dismiss or discard them. In the humanities, social sciences, and legal studies, canonical lists of classics pose problems, not because of what they include (the books are good), but because of what they exclude (other good books). Critics of bad faith all too often conflate an insistence on greater diversity (whether in approaches to social analysis, modes of composition, or socially esteemed texts and authors) with demeaning or throwing out the classics. The vision for change strives for greater inclusion, not an inversion of previous forms of exclusion.

In my view, critical anthropology and interdisciplinary cultural studies attempt to valorize subordinate forms of knowledge. Attempts to blur the boundaries of ethnography create space for historically subordinated perspectives otherwise excluded or marginalized from official discourse. Such perspectives complicate and enrich social analysis, but they do not represent the one and only authentic truth. Human beings always act under conditions they do not fully know and with consequences they neither fully intend nor can fully foresee. Yet subordinate perspectives must be included in social analysis. Our objects of analysis are also analyzing subjects whose best perceptions, not unlike the ethnographer's own, are shaped by distinctive cultures, histories, and relations of inequality. Neither ethnographers nor their subjects hold a monopoly on the truth.

Current conflicts over educational democracy implicate anthropology and interdisciplinary cultural studies. If people take initiatives, they may find themselves at the center of the present-day struggle for institutional enfranchisement. In this struggle, the treasured anthropological concept of culture has already been widely disseminated, used in diverse quarters, and thereby refashioned. Culture and power have become intertwined in a world and in institutional settings where diverse groups, themselves internally diverse, interact and seek full enfranchisement and social justice under conditions of inequality. Ongoing institutional conflicts over diversity and multiculturalism in higher education are localized symptoms of a broader renegotiation of full citizenship in the United States. And such struggles are the context for the explorations in *Culture and Truth*.

Preface

When someone with the authority of a teacher, say, describes the world and you are not in it, there is a moment of psychic disequilibrium, as if you looked into a mirror and saw nothing.
   —Adrienne Rich, "Invisibility in Academe"

THESE DAYS questions of culture seem to touch a nerve because they quite quickly become anguished questions of identity. Academic debates about multicultural education similarly slip effortlessly into the animating ideological conflicts of this multicultural nation. How can the United States both respect diversity and find unity? Does this country need a "melting pot" to homogenize people into a "culturally invisible" mainstream? Or can it now develop alternative doctrines more fully accountable to its cultural diversity? This book deliberately engages dominant national dogma about melting pots and core values by trying to articulate a pluralistic vision of culture and truth consonant with divergent North American identities.

My present understanding of the remaking of social analysis was catalyzed by the "Western Culture Controversy" at Stanford University during 1986–88. Without this academic battle my book would have been finished more quickly, but less well. Required of first-year undergraduates, Stanford's year-long Western Culture course obliged students to read a "core list" of "great books" from the traditional European canon. More often treated as sacred monuments to be worshiped than as fellow humans to be engaged in dialogue, the great authors supposedly represented a grand tradition that stretched in a straight line from Homer through Shakespeare to Voltaire. Students were told that they must learn "our heritage" before going on to study "other" cultural traditions.

Conflict erupted, however, when a significant number of students and faculty questioned the "we" who was defining "our heritage" as a shelf of books written in another time (before World War I) and in another place (ancient Athens and Western Europe). How could a self-appointed academic aristocracy in the United States wrap itself in a cultural heritage that included no authors from the Americas, not to mention any women or persons of non-European origin? Although all citizens of the United States could feel marginalized by the great books list, certain faculty members— because of their field of study, gender, or cultural heritage— felt particularly affronted by the Western Culture course. We suffered the annihilation poet Adrienne Rich depicts so incisively in the epigraph above.

Cultural anthropology in recent years has been reshaping itself in part because of what it has learned from such conflicts about multicultural social reality. At the same time the discipline has discovered that it can make significant contributions to issues that culturally diversifying nations now face. This book has emerged from the double process of being reshaped by wider conflicts and finding new positions from which to voice thoughts and feelings about cultural diversity. For me as a Chicano, questions of culture emerge not only from my discipline, but also from a more personal politics of identity and community.

The shifts in social thought described and reformulated in this book have grown out of a broad movement; they are not the property of any single individual, discipline, or school. I have learned from the writings of numerous predecessors, contemporaries, and successors who have contributed to the remaking of social analysis. This book crystallized during a year at the Stanford Humanities Center (1986–87) when I drafted much of the manuscript. I read widely on issues pertinent to this project during a year at the Center for Advanced Study in the Behavioral Sciences (1980–81) which was financed by the National Science Foundation (#BNS 76 22943) and a postdoctoral fellowship for minorities administered by the National Research Council. Earlier versions of certain chapters in this book were published elsewhere, and I remain thankful for comments by individuals whose names I previously acknowledged but do not repeat here. My earliest formulations of this project benefited from the editorial advice and encouragement of Grant Barnes, Bill Carver, Vikram Seth, and Helen Tartar.

This book has been significantly shaped by interdisciplinary faculty reading groups at Stanford University, particularly the cultural studies research group and the faculty seminar at the Stanford center for Chicano Research, where I am currently director. I am grateful to two Stanford University graduate student reading groups, one in social theory from the history department and the other in the theory of practice from the anthropology department, both of which gave critical comments on a draft of this book. I benefited from similar discussions by members of the cultural studies working group of the Inter-University Program on Latino Issues and by the Latino summer seminar held at Stanford in 1988. I also wish to thank the following individuals who

xxiv | PREFACE

commented on drafts of this manuscript: Eytan Bercovitch, Russell Berman, Bud Bynack, Richard Chabrán, James Clifford, Rosemary Coombe, Ethan Goldings, Smadar Lavie, Rick Maddox, Donald Moore, Kirin Narayan, Kathleen Newman, Víctor Ortiz, Vicente Rafael, José Saldívar, and Cynthia Ward. Joanne Wyckoff at Beacon Press provided valuable editorial advice and Sharon Yamamoto did more than usual as copy editor. As a life partner and intellectual companion, Mary Louise Pratt has inspired much of the thought and feeling that informs this book.

CULTURE AND TRUTH

Introduction · Grief and a Headhunter's Rage

IF YOU ASK an older Ilongot man of northern Luzon, Philippines, why he cuts off human heads, his answer is brief, and one on which no anthropologist can readily elaborate: He says that rage, born of grief, impels him to kill his fellow human beings. He claims that he needs a place "to carry his anger." The act of severing and tossing away the victim's head enables him, he says, to vent and, he hopes, throw away the anger of his bereavement. Although the anthropologist's job is to make other cultures intelligible, more questions fail to reveal any further explanation of this man's pithy statement. To him, grief, rage, and headhunting go together in a self-evident manner. Either you understand

1

it or you don't. And, in fact, for the longest time I simply did not.

In what follows, I want to talk about how to talk about the cultural force of emotions.[1] The *emotional force* of a death, for example, derives less from an abstract brute fact than from a particular intimate relation's permanent rupture. It refers to the kinds of feelings one experiences on learning, for example, that the child just run over by a car is one's own and not a stranger's. Rather than speaking of death in general, one must consider the subject's position within a field of social relations in order to grasp one's emotional experience.[2]

My effort to show the force of a simple statement taken literally goes against anthropology's classic norms, which prefer to explicate culture through the gradual thickening of symbolic webs of meaning. By and large, cultural analysts use not *force* but such terms as *thick description, multivocality, polysemy, richness*, and *texture*. The notion of force, among other things, opens to question the common anthropological assumption that the greatest human import resides in the densest forest of symbols and that analytical detail, or "cultural depth," equals enhanced explanation of a culture, or "cultural elaboration." Do people always in fact describe most thickly what matters most to them?

The Rage in Ilongot Grief

Let me pause a moment to introduce the Ilongots, among whom my wife, Michelle Rosaldo, and I lived and conducted field research for thirty months (1967–69, 1974). They number about 3,500 and reside in an upland area some 90 miles northeast of Manila, Philippines.[3] They subsist by hunting deer and wild pig and by cultivating rain-fed gardens (swiddens) with rice, sweet potatoes, manioc, and vegetables. Their (bilateral) kin relations are reckoned through men and women. After marriage, parents and their married daughters live in the same or adjacent households. The largest unit within the society, a largely territorial descent group called the *bertan*, becomes manifest primarily in the context of feuding. For themselves, their neighbors, and their ethnographers, head-hunting stands out as the Ilongots' most salient cultural practice.

When Ilongots told me, as they often did, how the rage in bereavement could impel men to headhunt, I brushed aside their one-line accounts as too simple, thin, opaque, implausible, stereotypical, or otherwise unsatisfying. Probably I naively equated grief with sadness. Certainly no personal experience allowed me to imagine the powerful rage Ilongots claimed to find in bereavement. My own inability to conceive the force of anger in grief led me to seek out another level of analysis that could provide a deeper explanation for older men's desire to headhunt.

Not until some fourteen years after first recording the terse Ilongot statement about grief and a headhunter's rage did I begin to grasp its overwhelming force. For years I thought that more verbal elaboration (which was not forthcoming) or another analytical level (which remained elusive) could better explain older men's motives for headhunting. Only after being repositioned through a devastating loss of my own could I better grasp that Ilongot older men mean precisely what they say when they describe the anger in bereavement as the source of their desire to cut off human heads. Taken at face value and granted its full weight, their statement reveals much about what compels these older men to headhunt.

In my efforts to find a "deeper" explanation for headhunting, I explored exchange theory, perhaps because it had informed so many classic ethnographies. One day in 1974, I explained the anthropologist's exchange model to an older Ilongot man named Insan. What did he think, I asked, of the idea that headhunting resulted from the way that one death (the beheaded victim's) canceled another (the next of kin). He looked puzzled, so I went on to say that the victim of a beheading was exchanged for the death of one's own kin, thereby balancing the books, so to speak. Insan reflected a moment and replied that he imagined somebody could think such a thing (a safe bet, since I just had), but that he and other Ilongots did not think any such thing. Nor was there any indirect evidence for my exchange theory in ritual, boast, song, or casual conversation.[4]

In retrospect, then, these efforts to impose exchange theory on one aspect of Ilongot behavior appear feeble. Suppose I had discovered what I sought? Although the notion of balancing the ledger does have a certain elegant coherence, one wonders how such bookish dogma could inspire any man to take another man's life at the risk of his own.

My life experience had not as yet provided the means to imagine the rage that can come with devastating loss. Nor could I, therefore, fully appreciate the acute problem of meaning that Ilongots faced in 1974. Shortly after Ferdinand Marcos declared martial law in 1972, rumors that firing squads had become the new punishment for headhunting reached the Ilongot hills. The men therefore decided to call a moratorium on taking heads. In past epochs, when headhunting had become impossible, Ilongots had allowed their rage to dissipate, as best it could, in the course of everyday life. In 1974, they had another option; they began to consider conversion to evangelical Christianity as a means of coping with their grief. Accepting the new religion, people said, implied abandoning their old ways, including headhunting. It also made coping with bereavement less agonizing because they could believe that the deceased had departed for a better world. No longer did they have to confront the awful finality of death.

The force of the dilemma faced by the Ilongots eluded me at the time. Even when I correctly recorded their statements about grieving and the need to throw away their anger, I simply did not grasp the weight of their words. In 1974, for example, while Michelle Rosaldo and I were living among the Ilongots, a six-month-old baby died, probably of pneumonia. That afternoon we visited the father and found him terribly stricken. "He was sobbing and staring through glazed and bloodshot eyes at the cotton blanket covering his baby."[5] The man suffered intensely, for this was the seventh child he had lost. Just a few years before, three of his children had died, one after the other, in a matter of days. At the time, the situation was murky as people present talked both about evangelical Christianity (the possible renunciation of taking heads) and their grudges against lowlanders (the contemplation of headhunting forays into the surrounding valleys).

Through subsequent days and weeks, the man's grief moved him in a way I had not anticipated. Shortly after the baby's death, the father converted to evangelical Christianity. Altogether too quick on the inference, I immediately concluded that the man believed that the new religion could somehow prevent further deaths in his family. When I spoke my mind to an Ilongot friend, he snapped at me, saying that "I had missed the point: what the man in fact sought in the new religion was not the denial of our inevitable deaths but a means of coping with his grief. With the advent of martial law, headhunting was out of the question as a means of venting his wrath and thereby lessening his grief. Were he to remain in his Ilongot way of life, the pain of his sorrow would simply be too much to bear."[6] My description from 1980 now seems so apt that I wonder how I could have written the words and nonetheless failed to appreciate the force of the grieving man's desire to vent his rage.

Another representative anecdote makes my failure to imagine the rage possible in Ilongot bereavement all the more remarkable. On this occasion, Michelle Rosaldo and I were urged by Ilongot friends to play the tape of a headhunting celebration we had witnessed some five years before. No sooner had we turned on the tape and heard the boast of a man who had died in the intervening years than did people abruptly tell us to shut off the recorder. Michelle Rosaldo reported on the tense conversation that ensued:

As Insan braced himself to speak, the room again became almost uncannily electric. Backs straightened and my anger turned to nervousness and something more like fear as I saw that Insan's eyes were red. Tukbaw, Renato's Ilongot "brother," then broke into what was a brittle silence, saying he could make things clear. He told us that it hurt to listen to a head-hunting celebration when people knew that there would never be another. As he put it: "The song pulls at us, drags our hearts, it makes us think of our dead uncle." And again: "It would be better if I had accepted God, but I still am an Ilongot at heart; and when I hear the song, my heart aches as it does when I must look upon unfinished bachelors whom I know that I will never lead to take a head." Then Wagat, Tukbaw's wife, said with her eyes that all my questions gave her pain, and told me: "Leave off now, isn't that enough? Even I, a woman, cannot stand the way it feels inside my heart."[7]

From my present position, it is evident that the tape recording of the dead man's boast evoked powerful feelings of bereavement, particularly rage and the impulse to headhunt. At the time I could only feel apprehensive and diffusely sense the force of the emotions experienced by Insan, Tukbaw, Wagat, and the others present.

The dilemma for the Ilongots grew out of a set of cultural practices that, when blocked, were agonizing to live with. The cessation of headhunting called for painful adjustments to other modes of coping with the rage they found in bereavement. One could compare their dilemma with the notion that the failure to perform rituals can create anxiety.[8] In the Ilongot case, the cultural notion that throwing away a human head also casts away the anger creates a problem of meaning when the headhunting ritual cannot be performed. Indeed, Max Weber's classic problem of meaning in *The Protestant Ethic and the Spirit of Capitalism* is precisely of this kind.[9] On a logical plane, the Calvinist doctrine of predestination seems flawless: God has chosen the elect, but his decision can never be known by mortals. Among those whose ultimate concern is salvation, the doctrine of predestination is as easy to grasp conceptually as it is impossible to endure in everyday life (unless one happens to be a "religious virtuoso"). For Calvinists and Ilongots alike, the problem of meaning resides in practice, not theory. The dilemma for both groups involves the practical matter of how to live with one's beliefs, rather than the logical puzzlement produced by abstruse doctrine.

How I Found the Rage in Grief

One burden of this introduction concerns the claim that it took some fourteen years for me to grasp what Ilongots had told me about grief, rage, and headhunting. During all those years I was not yet in a position to comprehend the force of anger possible in bereavement, and now I am. Introducing myself into this account requires a certain hesitation both because of the discipline's taboo and because of its increasingly frequent violation by essays laced with trendy amalgams of continental philosophy and autobiographical snippets. If classic ethnography's vice was the slippage from the ideal of detachment to actual indifference, that of present-day reflexivity is the tendency for the self-absorbed Self to lose sight altogether of the culturally different Other. Despite the risks involved, as the ethnographer I must enter the discussion at this point to elucidate certain issues of method.

The key concept in what follows is that of the positioned (and repositioned) subject.[10] In routine interpretive procedure, according to the methodology of hermeneutics, one can say that ethnographers reposition themselves as they go about understanding other cultures. Ethnographers begin research with a set of questions, revise them throughout the course of inquiry, and in the end emerge with different questions than they started with. One's surprise at the answer to a question, in other words, requires one to revise the question until lessening surprises or diminishing returns indicate a stopping point. This interpretive approach has been most influentially articulated within anthropology by Clifford Geertz.[11]

Interpretive method usually rests on the axiom that gifted ethnographers learn their trade by preparing themselves as broadly as possible. To follow the meandering course of ethnographic inquiry, field-workers require wide-ranging theoretical capacities and finely tuned sensibilities. After all, one cannot predict beforehand what one will encounter in the field. One influential anthropologist, Clyde Kluckhohn, even went so far as to recommend a double initiation: first, the ordeal of psychoanalysis, and then that of fieldwork. All too often, however, this view is extended until certain prerequisites of field research appear to guarantee an authoritative ethnography. Eclectic book knowledge and a range of life experiences, along with edifying reading and self-awareness, supposedly vanquish the twin vices of ignorance and insensitivity.

Although the doctrine of preparation, knowledge, and sensibility contains much to admire, one should work to undermine the false comfort that it can convey. At what point can people say that they have completed their learning or their life experience? The problem with taking this mode of preparing the ethnographer too much to heart is that it can lend a false air of security, an authoritative claim to certitude and finality that our analyses cannot have. All interpretations are provisional; they are made by positioned subjects who are prepared to know certain things and not others. Even when knowledgeable, sensitive, fluent in the language, and able to move easily in an alien cultural world, good ethnographers still have their limits, and their analyses always are incomplete. Thus, I began to fathom the force of what Ilongots had been telling me about their losses through my own loss, and not through any systematic preparation for field research.

My preparation for understanding serious loss began in 1970 with the death of my brother, shortly after his twenty-seventh birthday. By experiencing this ordeal with my mother and father, I gained a measure of insight into the trauma of a parent's losing a child. This insight informed my account, partially described earlier, of an Ilongot man's reactions to the death of his seventh child. At the same time, my bereavement was so much less than that of my parents that I could not then imagine the overwhelming force of rage possible in such grief. My former position is probably similar to that of many in the discipline. One should recognize that ethnographic knowledge tends to have the strengths and limitations given by the relative youth of field-workers who, for the most part, have not suffered serious losses and could have, for example, no personal knowledge of how devastating the loss of a long-term partner can be for the survivor.

In 1981 Michelle Rosaldo and I began field research among the Ifugaos of northern Luzon, Philippines. On October 11 of that year, she was walking along a trail with two Ifugao companions when she lost her footing and fell to her death some 65 feet down a sheer precipice into a swollen river below. Immediately on finding her body I became enraged. How could she abandon me? How could she have been so stupid as to fall? I tried to cry. I sobbed, but rage blocked the tears. Less than a month later I described this moment in my journal: "I felt like in a nightmare, the whole world around me expanding and contracting, visually and viscerally heaving. Going down I find a group of men, maybe seven or eight, standing still, silent, and I heave and sob, but no tears." An earlier experience, on the fourth anniversary of my brother's death, had taught me to recognize heaving sobs without tears as a form of anger. This anger, in a number of forms, has swept over me on many occasions since then, lasting hours and even days at a time. Such feelings can be aroused by rituals, but more often they emerge from unexpected reminders (not unlike the Ilongots' unnerving encounter with their dead uncle's voice on the tape recorder).

Lest there be any misunderstanding, bereavement should not be reduced to anger, neither for myself nor for anyone else.[12] Powerful visceral emotional states swept over me, at times separately and at other times together. I experienced the deep cutting pain of sorrow almost beyond endurance, the cadaverous cold of realizing the finality of death, the trembling beginning in my abdomen and spreading through my body, the mournful keening that started without my willing, and frequent tearful sobbing. My present purpose of revising earlier understandings of Ilongot headhunting, and not a general view of bereavement, thus focuses on anger rather than on other emotions in grief.

Writings in English especially need to emphasize the rage in grief. Although grief therapists routinely encourage awareness of anger among the bereaved, upper-middle-class Anglo-American culture tends to ignore the rage devastating losses can bring. Paradoxically, this culture's conventional wisdom usually denies the anger in grief at the same time that therapists encourage members of the invisible community of the bereaved to talk in detail about how angry their losses make them feel. My brother's death in combination with what I learned about anger from Ilongots (for them, an emotional state more publicly celebrated than denied) allowed me immediately to recognize the experience of rage.[13]

Ilongot anger and my own overlap, rather like two circles, partially overlaid and partially separate. They are not identical. Alongside striking similarities, significant differences in tone, cultural form, and human consequences distinguish the "anger" animating our respective ways of grieving. My vivid fantasies, for example, about a life insurance agent who refused to recognize Michelle's death as job-related did not lead me to kill him, cut off his head, and celebrate afterward. In so speaking, I am illustrating the discipline's methodological caution against the reckless attribution of one's own categories and experiences to members of another culture. Such warnings against facile notions of universal human nature can, however, be carried too far and harden into the equally pernicious doctrine that, my own group aside, everything human is alien to me. One hopes to achieve a balance between recognizing wide-ranging human differences and the modest truism that any two human groups must have certain things in common.

Only a week before completing the initial draft of an earlier version of this introduction, I rediscovered my journal entry, written some six weeks after Michelle's death, in which I made a vow to myself about how I would return to writing anthropology, if I ever did so, "by writing Grief and a Headhunter's Rage . . ." My journal went on to reflect more broadly on death, rage, and headhunting by speaking of my "wish for the Ilongot solution; they are much more in touch with reality than Christians. So, I need a place to carry my anger—and can we say a solution of the imagination is better than theirs? And can we condemn them when we napalm villages? Is our rationale so much sounder than theirs?" All this was written in despair and rage.

Not until some fifteen months after Michelle's death was I again able to begin writing anthropology. Writing the initial version of "Grief and a Headhunter's Rage" was in fact cathartic, though perhaps not in the way one would imagine. Rather than following after the completed composition, the catharsis occurred beforehand. When the initial version of this introduction was most acutely on my mind, during the month before actually beginning to write, I felt diffusely depressed and ill with a fever. Then one day an almost literal fog lifted and words began to flow. It seemed less as if I were doing the writing than that the words were writing themselves through me.

My use of personal experience serves as a vehicle for making the quality and intensity of the rage in Ilongot grief more readily accessible to readers than certain more detached modes of composition. At the same time, by invoking personal experience as an analytical category one risks easy dismissal. Unsympathetic readers could reduce this introduction to an act of mourning or a mere report on my discovery of the anger possible in bereavement. Frankly, this introduction is both and more. An act of mourning, a personal report, *and* a critical analysis of anthropological method, it simultaneously encompasses a number of distinguishable processes, no one of which cancels out the others. Similarly, I argue in what follows that ritual in general and Ilongot headhunting in particular form the intersection of multiple coexisting social processes. Aside from revising the ethnographic record, the paramount claim made here concerns how my own mourning and consequent reflection on Ilongot bereavement, rage, and headhunting raise methodological issues of general concern in anthropology and the human sciences.

Death in Anthropology

Anthropology favors interpretations that equate analytical "depth" with cultural "elaboration." Many studies focus on visibly bounded arenas where one can observe formal and repetitive events, such as ceremonies, rituals, and games. Similarly, studies of word play are more likely to focus on jokes as programmed monologues than on the less scripted, more free-wheeling improvised interchanges of witty banter. Most ethnographers prefer to study events that have definite locations in space with marked centers and outer edges. Temporally, they have middles and endings. Historically, they appear to repeat identical structures by seemingly doing things today as they were done yesterday. Their qualities of fixed definition liberate such events from the untidiness of everyday life so that they can be "read" like articles, books, or, as we now say, *texts*.

Guided by their emphasis on self-contained entities, ethnographies written in accord with classic norms consider death under the rubric of ritual rather than bereavement. Indeed, the subtitles of even recent ethnographies on death make the emphasis on ritual explicit. William Douglas's *Death in Murelaga* is subtitled *Funerary Ritual in a Spanish Basque Village;* Richard Huntington and Peter Metcalf's *Celebrations of Death* is subtitled *The Anthropology of Mortuary Ritual;* Peter Metcalf's *A Borneo Journey into Death* is subtitled *Berawan Eschatology from Its Rituals.*[14] Ritual itself is defined by its formality and routine; under such descriptions, it more nearly resembles a recipe, a fixed program, or a book of etiquette than an open-ended human process.

Ethnographies that in this manner eliminate intense emotions not only distort their descriptions but also remove potentially key variables from their explanations. When anthropologist William Douglas, for example, announces his project in *Death in Murelaga*, he explains that his objective is to use death and funerary ritual "as a heuristic device with which to approach the study of rural Basque society."[15] In other words, the primary object of study is social structure, not death, and certainly not bereavement. The author begins his analysis by saying, "Death is not always fortuitous or unpredictable."[16] He goes on to describe how an old woman, ailing with the infirmities of her age, welcomed her death. The description largely ignores the perspective of the most bereaved survivors, and instead vacillates between those of the old woman and a detached observer.

Undeniably, certain people do live a full life and suffer so greatly in their decrepitude that they embrace the relief death can bring. Yet the problem with making an ethnography's major case study focus on "a very easy death"[17] (I use Simone de Beauvoir's title with irony, as she did) is not only its lack of representativeness but also that it makes death in general appear as routine for the survivors as this particular one apparently was for the deceased. Were the old woman's sons and daughters untouched by her death? The case study shows less about how people cope with death than about how death can be made to appear routine, thereby fitting neatly into the author's view of funerary ritual as a mechanical programmed unfolding of prescribed acts. "To the Basque," says Douglas, "ritual is order and order is ritual."[18]

Douglas captures only one extreme in the range of possible deaths. Putting the accent on the routine aspects of ritual conveniently conceals the agony of such unexpected early deaths as parents losing a grown child or a mother dying in childbirth. Concealed in such descriptions are the agonies of the survivors who muddle through shifting, powerful emotional states. Although Douglas acknowledges the distinction between the bereaved members of the deceased's domestic group and the more public ritualistic group, he writes his account primarily from the viewpoint of the latter. He masks the emotional force of bereavement by reducing funerary ritual to orderly routine.

Surely, human beings mourn both in ritual settings *and* in

the informal settings of everyday life. Consider the evidence that willy-nilly spills over the edges in Godfrey Wilson's classic anthropological account of "conventions of burial" among the Nyakyusa of South Africa:

That some at least of those who attend a Nyakyusa burial are moved by grief it is easy to establish. I have heard people talking regretfully in ordinary conversation of a man's death; I have seen a man whose sister had just died walk over alone towards her grave and weep quietly by himself without any parade of grief; and I have heard of a man killing himself because of his grief for a dead son.[19]

Note that all the instances Wilson witnesses or hears about happen outside the circumscribed sphere of formal ritual. People converse among themselves, walk alone and silently weep, or more impulsively commit suicide. The work of grieving, probably universally, occurs both within obligatory ritual acts and in more everyday settings where people find themselves alone or with close kin.

In Nyakyusa burial ceremonies, powerful emotional states also become present in the ritual itself, which is more than a series of obligatory acts. Men say they dance the passions of their bereavement, which includes a complex mix of anger, fear, and grief:

"This war dance (ukukina)," said an old man, "is mourning, we are mourning the dead man. We dance because there is war in our hearts. A passion of grief and fear exasperates us (ilyyojo likutusila)." . . . Elyojo means a passion or grief, anger or fear; ukusila means to annoy or exasperate beyond endurance. In explaining ukusila one man put it like this: "If a man continually insults me then he exasperates me (ukusila) so that I want to fight him." Death is a fearful and grievous event that exasperates those men nearly concerned and makes them want to fight.[20]

Descriptions of the dance and subsequent quarrels, even killings, provide ample evidence of the emotional intensity involved. The articulate testimony by Wilson's informants

makes it obvious that even the most intense sentiments can be studied by ethnographers.

Despite such exceptions as Wilson, the general rule seems to be that one should tidy things up as much as possible by wiping away the tears and ignoring the tantrums. Most anthropological studies of death eliminate emotions by assuming the position of the most detached observer.[21] Such studies usually conflate the ritual process with the process of mourning, equate ritual with the obligatory, and ignore the relation between ritual and everyday life. The bias that favors formal ritual risks assuming the answers to questions that most need to be asked. Do rituals, for example, always reveal cultural depth?

Most analysts who equate death with funerary ritual assume that rituals store encapsulated wisdom as if it were a microcosm of its encompassing cultural macrocosm. One recent study of death and mourning, for example, confidently begins by affirming that rituals embody "the collective wisdom of many cultures."[22] Yet this generalization surely requires case-by-case investigation against a broader range of alternative hypotheses.

At the polar extremes, rituals either display cultural depth or brim over with platitudes. In the former case, rituals indeed encapsulate a culture's wisdom; in the latter instance, they act as catalysts that precipitate processes whose unfolding occurs over subsequent months or even years. Many rituals, of course, do both by combining a measure of wisdom with a comparable dose of platitudes.

My own experience of bereavement and ritual fits the platitudes and catalyst model better than that of microcosmic deep culture. Even a careful analysis of the language and symbolic action during the two funerals for which I was a chief mourner would reveal precious little about the experience of bereavement.[23] This statement, of course, should not lead anyone to derive a universal from somebody else's personal knowledge. Instead, it should encourage ethnographers to ask whether a ritual's wisdom is deep or conventional, and

whether its process is immediately transformative or but a single step in a lengthy series of ritual and everyday events.

In attempting to grasp the cultural force of rage and other powerful emotional states, both formal ritual and the informal practices of everyday life provide crucial insight. Thus, cultural descriptions should seek out force as well as thickness, and they should extend from well-defined rituals to myriad less circumscribed practices.

Grief, Rage, and Ilongot Headhunting

When applied to Ilongot headhunting, the view of ritual as a storehouse of collective wisdom aligns headhunting with expiatory sacrifice. The raiders call the spirits of the potential victims, bid their ritual farewells, and seek favorable omens along the trail. Ilongot men vividly recall the hunger and deprivation they endure over the days and even weeks it takes to move cautiously toward the place where they set up an ambush and await the first person who happens along. Once the raiders kill their victim, they toss away the head rather than keep it as a trophy. In tossing away the head, they claim by analogy to cast away their life burdens, including the rage in their grief.

Before a raid, men describe their state of being by saying that the burdens of life have made them heavy and entangled, like a tree with vines clinging to it. They say that a successfully completed raid makes them feel light of step and ruddy in complexion. The collective energy of the celebration with its song, music, and dance reportedly gives the participants a sense of well-being. The expiatory ritual process involves cleansing and catharsis.

The analysis just sketched regards ritual as a timeless, self-contained process. Without denying the insight in this approach, its limits must also be considered. Imagine, for example, exorcism rituals described as if they were complete in themselves, rather than being linked with larger processes unfolding before and after the ritual period. Through what processes does the afflicted person recover or continue

to be afflicted after the ritual? What are the social consequences of recovery or its absence? Failure to consider such questions diminishes the force of such afflictions and therapies for which the formal ritual is but a phase. Still other questions apply to differently positioned subjects, including the person afflicted, the healer, and the audience. In all cases, the problem involves the delineation of processes that occur before and after, as well as during, the ritual moment.

Let us call the notion of a self-contained sphere of deep cultural activity the *microcosmic view,* and an alternative view *ritual as a busy intersection.* In the latter case, ritual appears as a place where a number of distinct social processes intersect. The crossroads simply provides a space for distinct trajectories to traverse, rather than containing them in complete encapsulated form. From this perspective, Ilongot headhunting stands at the confluence of three analytically separable processes.

The first process concerns whether or not it is an opportune time to raid. Historical conditions determine the possibilities of raiding, which range from frequent to likely to unlikely to impossible. These conditions include American colonial efforts at pacification, the Great Depression, World War II, revolutionary movements in the surrounding lowlands, feuding among Ilongot groups, and the declaration of martial law in 1972. Ilongots use the analogy of hunting to speak of such historical vicissitudes. Much as Ilongot huntsmen say they cannot know when game will cross their path or whether their arrows will strike the target, so certain historical forces that condition their existence remain beyond their control. My book *Ilongot Headhunting, 1883–1974* explores the impact of historical factors on Ilongot headhunting.

Second, young men coming of age undergo a protracted period of personal turmoil during which they desire nothing so much as to take a head. During this troubled period, they seek a life partner and contemplate the traumatic dislocation of leaving their families of origin and entering their new wife's household as a stranger. Young men weep, sing, and burst out in anger because of their fierce desire to take a head and wear the coveted red hornbill earrings that adorn the ears of men who already have, as Ilongots say, arrived (*tabi*). Volatile, envious, passionate (at least according to their own cultural stereotype of the young unmarried man [*buintaw*]), they constantly lust to take a head. Michelle and I began fieldwork among the Ilongots only a year after abandoning our unmarried youths; hence our ready empathy with youthful turbulence. Her book on Ilongot notions of self explores the passionate anger of young men as they come of age.

Third, older men are differently positioned than their younger counterparts. Because they have already beheaded somebody, they can wear the red hornbill earrings so coveted by youths. Their desire to headhunt grows less from chronic adolescent turmoil than from more intermittent acute agonies of loss. After the death of somebody to whom they are closely attached, older men often inflict on themselves vows of abstinence, not to be lifted until the day they participate in a successful headhunting raid. These deaths can cover a range of instances from literal death, whether through natural causes or beheading, to social death where, for example, a man's wife runs off with another man. In all cases, the rage born of devastating loss animates the older men's desire to raid. This anger at abandonment is irreducible in that nothing at a deeper level explains it. Although certain analysts argue against the dreaded last analysis, the linkage of grief, rage, and headhunting has no other known explanation.

My earlier understandings of Ilongot headhunting missed the fuller significance of how older men experience loss and rage. Older men prove critical in this context because they, not the youths, set the processes of headhunting in motion. Their rage is intermittent, whereas that of youths is continuous. In the equation of headhunting, older men are the variable and younger men are the constant. Culturally speaking, older men are endowed with knowledge and stamina that their juniors have not yet attained, hence they care for (*saysay*) and lead (*bukur*) the younger men when they raid.

In a preliminary survey of the literature on headhunting, I found that the lifting of mourning prohibitions frequently occurs after taking a head. The notion that youthful anger and older men's rage lead them to take heads is more plausible than such commonly reported "explanations" of head-hunting as the need to acquire mystical "soul stuff" or personal names.[24] Because the discipline correctly rejects stereotypes of the "bloodthirsty savage," it must investigate how headhunters create an intense desire to decapitate their fellow humans. The human sciences must explore the cultural force of emotions with a view to delineating the passions that animate certain forms of human conduct.

Summary

The ethnographer, as a positioned subject, grasps certain human phenomena better than others. He or she occupies a position or structural location and observes with a particular angle of vision. Consider, for example, how age, gender, being an outsider, and association with a neo-colonial regime influence what the ethnographer learns. The notion of position also refers to how life experiences both enable and inhibit particular kinds of insight. In the case at hand, nothing in my own experience equipped me even to imagine the anger possible in bereavement until after Michelle Rosaldo's death in 1981. Only then was I in a position to grasp the force of what Ilongots had repeatedly told me about grief, rage, and headhunting. By the same token, so-called natives are also positioned subjects who have a distinctive mix of insight and blindness. Consider the structural positions of older versus younger Ilongot men, or the differing positions of chief mourners versus those less involved during a funeral. My discussion of anthropological writings on death often achieved its effects simply by shifting from the position of those least involved to that of the chief mourners.

Cultural depth does not always equal cultural elaboration. Think simply of the speaker who is filibustering. The
language used can sound elaborate as it heaps word on
word, but surely it is not deep. Depth should be separated
from the presence or absence of elaboration. By the same
token, one-line explanations can be vacuous or pithy. The
concept of force calls attention to an enduring intensity in
human conduct that can occur with or without the dense
elaboration conventionally associated with cultural depth.
Although relatively without elaboration in speech, song, or
ritual, the rage of older Ilongot men who have suffered devastating losses proves enormously consequential in that,
foremost among other things, it leads them to behead their
fellow humans. Thus, the notion of force involves both
affective intensity and significant consequences that unfold
over a long period of time.

Similarly, rituals do not always encapsulate deep cultural wisdom. At times they instead contain the wisdom of
Polonius. Although certain rituals both reflect and create ultimate values, others simply bring people together and deliver a set of platitudes that enable them to go on with their
lives. Rituals serve as vehicles for processes that occur both
before and after the period of their performance. Funeral rituals, for example, do not "contain" all the complex processes of bereavement. Ritual and bereavement should not
be collapsed into one another because they neither fully encapsulate nor fully explain one another. Instead, rituals are
often but points along a number of longer processual trajectories; hence, my image of ritual as a crossroads where
distinct life processes intersect.[25]

The notion of ritual as a busy intersection anticipates the
critical assessment of the concept of culture developed in the
following chapters. In contrast with the classic view, which
posits culture as a self-contained whole made up of coherent
patterns, culture can arguably be conceived as a more porous
array of intersections where distinct processes crisscross
from within and beyond its borders. Such heterogeneous

processes often derive from differences of age, gender, class, race, and sexual orientation.

This book argues that a sea change in cultural studies has eroded once-dominant conceptions of truth and objectivity. The truth of objectivism—absolute, universal, and time- less—has lost its monopoly status. It now competes, on more nearly equal terms, with the truths of case studies that are embedded in local contexts, shaped by local interests, and colored by local perceptions. The agenda for social analysis has shifted to include not only eternal verities and lawlike generalizations but also political processes, social changes, and human differences. Such terms as *objectivity, neutrality,* and *impartiality* refer to subject positions once endowed with great institutional authority, but they are ar- guably neither more nor less valid than those of more en- gaged, yet equally perceptive, knowledgeable social actors. Social analysis must now grapple with the realization that its objects of analysis are also analyzing subjects who criti- cally interrogate ethnographers—their writings, their eth- ics, and their politics.

Part One · Critique

1 | *The Erosion of Classic Norms*

ANTHROPOLOGY INVITES US to expand our sense of human possibilities through the study of other forms of life. Not unlike learning another language, such inquiry requires time and patience. There are no shortcuts. We cannot, for example, simply use our imaginations to invent other cultural worlds. Even those so-called realms of pure freedom, our fantasy and our "innermost thoughts," are produced and limited by our own local culture. Human imaginations are as culturally formed as distinctive ways of weaving, performing a ritual, raising children, grieving, or healing; they are specific to certain forms of life, whether these be Balinese, Anglo-American, Nyakyusa, or Basque.

25

Culture lends significance to human experience by selecting from and organizing it. It refers broadly to the forms through which people make sense of their lives, rather than more narrowly to the opera or art museums. It does not inhabit a set-aside domain, as does, for example, that of politics or economics. From the pirouettes of classical ballet to the most brute of brute facts, all human conduct is culturally mediated. Culture encompasses the everyday and the esoteric, the mundane and the elevated, the ridiculous and the sublime. Neither high nor low, culture is all-pervasive.

The translation of cultures requires one to try to understand other forms of life in their own terms. We should not impose our categories on other people's lives because they probably do not apply, at least not without serious revision. We can learn about other cultures only by reading, listening, or being there. Although they often appear outlandish, brutish, or worse to outsiders, the informal practices of everyday life make sense in their own context and on their own terms. Human beings cannot help but learn the culture or cultures of the communities within which they grow up. A New Yorker transferred at birth to the Pacific island of Tikopia will become a Tikopian, and vice versa. Cultures are learned, not genetically encoded.

Cultural Patterns and Cultural Borderlands

Let me use a series of illustrative anecdotes about dogs and children to discuss two contrasting conceptions of the task of cultural studies. To begin close to home, most Anglo-Americans regard dogs as household pets, animals to be fed, cared for, and treated with a certain affection. Most families with dogs have one or maybe two. Relations between Anglo-Americans and their dogs are not altogether unlike relations between them and their children. Pet dogs are treated with impatience, indulgence, and affection.

The Ilongots of northern Luzon, Philippines, also have

dogs, but an enormous amount would be lost in translation if we simply said that the Ilongot name for dog is *atu*, and left it at that. Most of what we would assume about dog-human relations would be mistaken. For example, Ilongots find it important to say that, unlike certain of their neighbors, they don't eat their dogs. The very thought of doing so disgusts them. In addition, from eight to fifteen dogs (not zero, one, or two) live alongside the people who reside in one-room, unpartitioned homes. Used in the hunt, Ilongot dogs are skinny but strong; unlike other domestic animals (except pigs), they are fed cooked food, usually sweet potatoes and greens. Ilongots regard dogs as useful animals, not pets. In a hunting accident, for example, an Ilongot man gashed his dog's head. The man returned home in tears of anger and frustration; he fumed about the difficulty of replacing his dog, but showed no affection toward the wounded animal. On another occasion, however, a baby pig's illness moved its caretaker to tears accompanied by cooing, cuddling, and tender baby talk. In this respect, our notion of pets more nearly applies to Ilongot relations with their baby pigs than with their dogs. Yet the Ilongot term *bilek* applies not only to pets (baby pigs, but not puppies), but also to houseplants and an infant's playthings.

My contrast between Anglo-American and Ilongot dogs has been drawn in accord with the classic anthropological style of analysis most influentially exemplified by Ruth Benedict in *Patterns of Culture.*[1] In accord with the classic style, each cultural pattern appears as unique and self-contained as each design in a kaleidoscope. Because the range of human possibilities is so great, one cannot predict cultural patterns from one case to the next, except to say that they will not match. One culture's pet is another's means of production; one group indulges its puppies, another coddles its baby pigs. Where one group sees sentimental value, another finds utilitarian worth.

Although the classic vision of unique cultural patterns has

proven merit, it also has serious limitations. It emphasizes shared patterns at the expense of processes of change and internal inconsistencies, conflicts, and contradictions.[2] By defining culture as a set of shared meanings, classic norms of analysis make it difficult to study zones of difference within and between cultures.[3] From the classic perspective, cultural borderlands appear to be annoying exceptions rather than central areas for inquiry.

Conditioned by a changing world, classic norms of social analysis have been eroded since the late 1960s, leaving the field of anthropology in a creative crisis of reorientation and renewal. The shift in social thought has made questions of conflict, change, and inequality increasingly urgent. Analysts no longer seek out harmony and consensus to the exclusion of difference and inconsistency. For social analysis, cultural borderlands have moved from a marginal to a central place. In certain cases, such borders are literal. Cities throughout the world today increasingly include minorities defined by race, ethnicity, language, class, religion, and sexual orientation. Encounters with "difference" now pervade modern everyday life in urban settings.

In my own life, I grew up speaking Spanish to my father and English to my mother. Consider the cultural pertinence of my father's response, during the late 1950s, to having taken our dog, Chico, to the veterinarian. Born and raised in Mexico, my father arrived home with Chico in a mood midway between pain and amusement. Tears of laughter streamed down his cheeks until, finally, he mumbled something like, "What will these North Americans think of next?" He explained that when he entered the veterinarian's office a nurse in white greeted him at the door, sat him down, pulled out a form, and asked, "What is the patient's name?" In my dad's view, no Mexican would ever come so close to confusing a dog with a person. To him, it was unthinkable that a clinic for dogs could ever resemble one for people with its nurses in white and its forms for the "patient." His encounter across cultures and social classes gave him an acute case of borderlands hysteria. Yet a classic concept of culture seeks out the "Mexican" or the "Anglo-American," and grants little space to the mundane disturbances that so often erupt during border crossings.

Borderlands surface not only at the boundaries of officially recognized cultural units, but also at less formal intersections, such as those of gender, age, status, and distinctive life experiences. After Michelle Rosaldo's death, for example, I suddenly discovered "the invisible community of the bereaved" as opposed to those who had suffered no major losses. Similarly, my son, Manny, came up against an unmarked internal border when he left a playgroup where his daily activities were only loosely organized and entered a nursery school shortly after his third birthday. Crossing this barrier proved so traumatic that he came home day after day in tears. We puzzled over his distress until the evening that he told the story of his day as a succession of "times": group time, snack time, nap time, play time, and lunch time. In other words, he was suffering the consequences of moving across the line from days of relatively free play to a world disciplined far beyond anything he had known before. On yet another occasion, when he reached kindergarten, Manny was carefully instructed to avoid strangers, especially those offering candy, rides, or even friendliness. Shortly thereafter, at a movie theater, he surveyed the audience around him and said, "It's good luck. There are no strangers here." To him, strangers were visibly evil, like robbers with masks, rather than people who were neither friends nor acquaintances. The cultural concept "stranger" evidently undergoes certain changes as it crosses the invisible border separating teachers from their kindergarten students.

We all cross such social boundaries in our daily lives. Even the unity of that so-called building block, the nuclear family, is cross-cut by differences of gender, generation, and age. Consider the disparate worlds one passes through in daily life, a round that includes home, eating out, working hours, adventures in consumerland, and a range of relationships, from intimacy to collegiality and friendship to enmity. Encounters with cultural and related differences belong to all of us in our most mundane experiences, not to a specialized domain of inquiry housed in an anthropology department. Yet the classic norms of anthropology have attended more to the unity of cultural wholes than to their myriad crossroads and borderlands.

What follows is a mythic tale about the birth of the anthropological concept of culture and its embodiment in the classic ethnography. Caricature best makes my point because it characterizes in bold strokes with a view not to preserve but to transform the reality it depicts. This "instant history" depicts present-day perceptions of disciplinary norms that guided graduate training until the late 1960s (and, in certain sectors, continue to do so) more than the actual complexities of past research.[4] These perceptions constitute the point of departure against which current experimental efforts attempt to remake ethnography as a form of social analysis. Without further ado, listen to the story of the Lone Ethnographer.

The Rise of Classic Norms

Once upon a time, the Lone Ethnographer rode off into the sunset in search of "his native." After undergoing a series of trials, he encountered the object of his quest in a distant land. There, he underwent his rite of passage by enduring the ultimate ordeal of "fieldwork." After collecting "the data," the Lone Ethnographer returned home and wrote a "true" account of "the culture."

Whether he hated, tolerated, respected, befriended, or fell in love with "his native," the Lone Ethnographer was willy-nilly complicit with the imperialist domination of his epoch. The Lone Ethnographer's mask of innocence (or, as he put it, his "detached impartiality") barely concealed his ideological role in perpetuating the colonial control of "distant" peoples and places. His writings represented the human objects of the civilizing mission's global enterprise as if they were ideal recipients of the white man's burden.

The Lone Ethnographer depicted the colonized as members of a harmonious, internally homogeneous, unchanging culture. When so described, the culture appeared to "need" progress, or economic and moral uplifting. In addition, the "timeless traditional culture" served as a self-congratulatory reference point against which Western civilization could measure its own progressive historical evolution. The civilizing journey was conceived more as a rise than a fall, a process more of elevation than degradation (a long, arduous journey upward, culminating in "us").

In the mythic past, a strict division of labor separated the Lone Ethnographer from "his native" sidekick. By definition, the Lone Ethnographer was literate, and "his native" was not. In accord with fieldwork norms, "his native" spoke and the Lone Ethnographer recorded "utterances" in his "fieldnotes."[5] In accord with imperialist norms, "his native" provided the raw material ("the data") for processing in the metropolis. After returning to the metropolitan center where he was schooled, the Lone Ethnographer wrote his definitive work.

The sacred bundle the Lone Ethnographer handed to his successors includes a complicity with imperialism, a commitment to objectivism, and a belief in monumentalism. The context of imperialism and colonial rule shaped both the monumentalism of timeless accounts of homogeneous cultures and the objectivism of a strict division of labor between the "detached" ethnographer and "his native." The key practices so bequeathed can be subsumed under the general rubric of *fieldwork*, which is often regarded as an initiation into the mysteries of anthropological knowledge. The product of the Lone Ethnographer's labors, the ethnography, appeared to be a transparent medium. It portrayed a "culture" sufficiently frozen to be an object of "scientific" knowledge. This genre of social description made itself, and the culture so described, into an artifact worthy of being housed in the collection of a major museum.

The myth of the Lone Ethnographer thus depicts the birth of ethnography, a genre of social description. Drawing on models from natural history, such accounts usually moved upward from environment and subsistence through family and kinship to religion and spiritual life. Produced by and for specialists, ethnographies aspired to the holistic representation of other cultures; they portrayed other forms of life as totalities. Ethnographies were storehouses of purportedly incontrovertible information to be mined by armchair theorists engaged in comparative studies. This genre seemingly resembled a mirror that reflected other cultures as they "really" were.

Much as routinization follows charisma and codification comes on the heels of insight, the heroic epoch of the Lone Ethnographer gave way to the classic period (say, not altogether inaccurately, but with mock precision, 1921–1971). During that period, the discipline's dominant objectivist view held that social life was fixed and constraining. In her recent ethnography, for example, anthropologist Sally Falk Moore emphasizes the absolute clarity and certitude of the objectivist research program: "A generation ago society was a system. Culture had a pattern. The postulation of a coherent whole discoverable bit by bit served to expand the significance of each observed particularity."[6] Phenomena that could not be regarded as systems or patterns appeared to be unanalyzable; they were dubbed exceptions, ambiguities, or irregularities. They held no theoretical interest because they could not be subsumed under the ongoing research agenda. By assuming the answers to the questions that should have been asked, the discipline confidently asserted that so-called traditional societies do not change.[7]

Classic ethnographers, particularly in Great Britain, usually invoked the French sociologist Emile Durkheim as their "founding father." In this tradition, culture and society determined individual personalities and consciousness; they enjoyed the objective status of systems. Not unlike a grammar, they stood on their own, independent from the individuals who followed their rules. After all, we did not, as individuals, invent the tools we use or the institutions within which we work. Like the languages we speak, culture and social structure existed before, during, and after any particular individual's lifetime. Although Durkheim's views have undeniable merit, they pass altogether too lightly over processes of conflict and change.

Along with objectivism, the classic period codified a notion of monumentalism. Until quite recently, in fact, I accepted without qualification the monumentalist dogma that the discipline rests on a solid foundation of "classic ethnographies." For example, I recall that on a foggy night a short number of years ago I found myself driving with a physicist along the mountainous stretch of Route 17 between Santa Cruz and San Jose. Both of us felt anxious about the weather and somewhat bored, so we began to discuss our respective fields. My companion opened by asking me, as only a physicist could, what anthropologists had discovered.

"Discovered?" I asked, pretending to be puzzled. I was stalling for time. Perhaps something would come to me.

"Yes, you know, something like the properties or the laws of other cultures."

"Do you mean something like $E = mc^2$?"

"Yes," he said.

Inspiration unexpectedly arrived and I heard myself saying, "There's one thing that we know for sure. We all know a good description when we see one. We haven't discovered any laws of culture, but we do think there are classic ethnographies, really telling descriptions of other cultures."

Classic works long served as models for aspiring ethnographers. At once maps of past investigations and programs for future research, the classics were regarded as exemplary cultural descriptions. They did, indeed, appear to be the one thing we knew for sure, especially when pressed by an inquisitive physicist. Leading anthropologists continue to voice the monumentalist credo that theories rise and fall, but fine ethnographic descriptions represent enduring achievements. T. O. Beidelman, for example, introduced his recent ethnography in this manner: "Theories may change, but ethnography remains at the heart of anthropology; it is the test and measure of all theory."[8] In fact, classic ethnographies have proven durable compared with the relatively short shelf life of such schools of thought as evolutionism, diffusionism, culture and personality, functionalism, ethnoscience, and structuralism.

To anticipate the discussion in subsequent pages, monumentalism conflates a loosely shared, ever-changing analytical project with a canonical list of classic ethnographies. Even if one were to grant that the discipline's core resides in its "classics," it does not follow that, like a solid foundation, these esteemed works remain the "same." Practitioners constantly reinterpret them in light of changing theoretical projects and reanalyze them against newly available evidence. From the point of view of their reception, the cultural artifacts we call ethnographies constantly change, despite the fact that, as verbal texts, they are fixed.

The exploration of theoretical issues that arise from and play themselves out in concrete ethnographic studies is the burden of this book. What follows argues that present-day experiments with ethnographic writing both reflect and contribute to an ongoing interdisciplinary program that has been transforming social thought. This remaking of social analysis derives from the political and intellectual movements that arose during the newly postcolonial, yet intensely imperialistic, period of the late 1960s. In this context, certain social thinkers redirected the agenda of theory from discrete variables and lawlike generalizations to the interplay of different factors as they unfold within specific cases.

The Politics of Remaking Social Analysis

If the classic period more tightly wove together the Lone Ethnographer's legacy—the complicity with imperialism, the doctrine of objectivism, and the credo of monumentalism—the political turbulence of the late 1960s and early 1970s began a process of unraveling and reworking that continues into the present. Not unlike the reorientations in other fields and in other countries, the initial impetus for the conceptual shift in anthropology was the potent historical conjuncture of decolonization and the intensification of American imperialism. This development led to a series of movements from the civil rights struggle to the mobilization against the war in Vietnam. Teach-ins, sit-ins, demonstrations, and strikes set the political tone for this period on American college and university campuses.

During this period, the annual business meetings of the American Anthropological Association became a verbal battleground, where resolutions on certain major issues of the day were fiercely debated. Anthropological research in Chile and Thailand was attacked from within the discipline because of its potential uses in counterinsurgency efforts. Elsewhere, the so-called natives began to charge anthropologists with conducting research in ways that failed to aid local efforts to resist oppression and with writing in ways that perpetuated stereotypes.

The New Left in the United States helped produce a spectrum of political movements responsive to internally imperialized groups that organized around forms of oppression based on gender, sexual preference, and race. Women, for example, began to organize because, among other reasons, the New Left more often placed them in secretarial rather than leadership roles. As emergent feminists immediately realized, sexism permeated the entire society, not simply the New Left in its beginning phases. Racism and homophobia led to similar realizations in other sectors of society. The call for a social analysis that made central the aspirations and demands of groups usually deemed marginal by the dominant national ideology came from the counterculture, environmentalism, feminism, gay and lesbian movements, the Native American movement, and the struggles of blacks, Chicanos, and Puerto Ricans.[9]

My own vision of anthropology's possibilities and failings has been shaped through participation in the campus Chicano movement. Involvement in this struggle has clarified my understanding of the need to attend with care to the per-

ceptions and aspirations of subordinate groups. My resulting concerns include historical change, cultural difference,
and social inequality. Ethnographic history, the translation
of cultures, and social criticism now seem intertwined as
fields of study laden with ethical imperatives.

The transformation of anthropology showed that the received notion of culture as unchanging and homogeneous
was not only mistaken but irrelevant (to use a key word of
the time).[10] Marxist and other discussion groups sprang up.
Questions of political consciousness and ideology came to
the foreground. How people make their own histories and
the interplay of domination and resistance seemed more
compelling than textbook discussions of system mainte-
nance and equilibrium theory. Doing committed anthropology made more sense than trying to maintain the fiction of
the analyst as a detached, impartial observer. What once appeared to be archaic questions of human emancipation now
began to sound an urgent note.

The reorientation of anthropology was itself part of a series of much broader social movements and intellectual reformulations. In *The Restructuring of Social and Political
Theory*, for example, Richard Bernstein attributes the redirection of American social thought after the late 1960s in
large part to the revival of once-rejected intellectual currents. Among these critical currents, he includes linguistic
philosophy, the history and philosophy of science, phenome-
nology, hermeneutics, and Marxism.[11] Bernstein attributes
these changes in the project of social analysis to critical perspectives developed by younger academics who, as former
student leaders, found that their criticism of society also led
them to mount forceful critiques of their disciplines. Although educated in the most advanced formal research
methods of the day, the new generation of students made
their criticisms from within, which proved as effective as
they were distressing to already established professionals
who could otherwise easily fend off assaults from beyond
disciplinary boundaries by calling them ill-informed or
biased.

From within anthropology, Clifford Geertz has spoken eloquently about the "refiguration of social thought" since the late 1960s. Social scientists, he says, have increasingly turned their attention from general explanatory laws to cases and their interpretation. To achieve their new aims, they have blurred the boundaries between the social sciences and the humanities. Their forms of social description even use key words drawn from the humanities, such as text, story, and social drama. After thus characterizing the current ferment in the human sciences, Geertz argues that objectivist assumptions about theory, language, and detachment no longer hold because of how social analysis has shifted its agenda:

A challenge is being mounted to some of the central assumptions of mainstream social science. The strict separation of theory and data, the "brute fact" idea; the effort to create a formal vocabulary of analysis purged of all subjective reference, the "ideal language" idea; and the claim to moral neutrality and the Olympian view, the "God's truth" idea—none of these can prosper when explanation comes to be regarded as a matter of connecting action to its sense rather than behavior to its determinants. The refiguration of social theory represents, or will if it continues, a sea change in our notion not so much of what knowledge is but of what we want to know.[12]

According to Geertz, the social sciences have undergone deep changes in their conceptions of (*a*) the object of analysis, (*b*) the language of analysis, and (*c*) the position of the analyst. The once-dominant ideal of a detached observer using neutral language to explain "raw" data has been displaced by an alternative project that attempts to understand human conduct as it unfolds through time and in relation to its meanings for the actors.

The task ahead is daunting. Both the methods and the subject matter of cultural studies have undergone major changes as their analytical project has taken a new turn. Culture, politics, and history have become intertwined and brought to the foreground as they were not during the classic period. This new turn has transformed the task of theory, which now must attend to conceptual issues raised by the study of particular cases rather than restrict itself to the pursuit of generalizations.

The "refiguration of social thought" has coincided with a critique of classic norms and a period of experimentation in ethnographic writing. Speaking zestfully of an "experimental moment," a number of anthropologists have become self-consciously playful about literary form.[13] Their writings celebrate the creative possibilities released by loosening the strict codes that governed the production of ethnographies during the classic period. Yet, rather than a case of experimentation for experimentation's sake or a matter of being caught between research paradigms, the current "experimental moment" in ethnographic writing has been driven by enduring, not transitory, ethical and analytical issues.[14] Changes in global relations of domination have conditioned both social thought and the experimental ethnography.

Decolonization and the intensification of imperialism have led social analysis since the late 1960s to shift its research program, and this shift has in turn produced a crisis in ethnographic writing. The difficulties of attempting to use classic ethnographic forms for new research programs raise conceptual issues, which in turn call for a widening of ethnography's modes of composition. The "experimental moment" in ethnographic writing and the remaking of social analysis are inextricably linked. Social analysis has sought new forms of writing because it has changed its central topics and what it has to say about them.

Remaking Ethnography as a Form of Social Analysis

Arguably, ethnography has been cultural anthropology's most significant contribution to knowledge. Social description outside the field of anthropology has both drawn on and reshaped ethnographic technique in its forms of documentary representation. James Clifford, for example, has argued persuasively that ethnography has become central to "an emergent interdisciplinary phenomenon" of descriptive and critical cultural studies that includes fields from historical ethnography to cultural criticism and from the study of everyday life to the semiotics of the fantastic.[15] In my view, even Clifford's expansive list of cultural studies should be extended beyond the academy to areas informed by an ethnographic sensibility, such as documentary film and photo essays, the new journalism, television docudramas, and certain historical novels. As a form of cross-cultural understanding, ethnography now plays a significant role for an array of academics, artists, and media people.

Whether speaking about shopping in a supermarket, the aftermath of a nuclear war, Elizabethan self-fashioning, academic communities of physicists, tripping through Las Vegas, Algerian marriage practices, or ritual among the Ndembu of central Africa, work in cultural studies sees human worlds as constructed through historical and political processes, and not as brute timeless facts of nature. It is marvelously easy to confuse "our local culture" with "universal human nature." If ideology often makes cultural facts appear natural, social analysis attempts to reverse the process. It dismantles the ideological in order to reveal the cultural, a peculiar blend of objective arbitrariness (things human could be, and indeed elsewhere are, otherwise) and subjective taken-for-grantedness (it's only common sense—how could things be otherwise?).

In presenting culture as a subject for analysis and critique, the ethnographic perspective develops an interplay between making the familiar strange and the strange familiar. Home cultures can appear so normal to their members that their common sense seems to be based in universal human nature. Social descriptions by, of, and for members of a particular culture require a relative emphasis on defamiliarization, so they will appear—as they in fact are—humanly made, and not given in nature. Alien cultures, however, can appear so exotic to outsiders that everyday life seems to be floating in a bizarre primitive mentality. Social descriptions about cultures distant from both the writer and the reader require a relative emphasis on familiarization, so they will appear—as they also in fact are—sharply distinct in their differences, yet recognizably human in their resemblances.

Paradoxically, ethnography's success as an informing perspective for a wide range of cultural studies coincides with a crisis in its home discipline. Readers of classic ethnographies have increasingly become afflicted with "emperor's new clothes syndrome." Works that once looked fully clothed, even regal, now appear naked, even laughable. Words that once read like the "real truth" now appear parodic, or as only one among a number of perspectives. The shift in social thought—its object, its language, and the moral position of its analysts—has been profound enough to make the tedium of once-revered forms of ethnographic writing breathtakingly apparent.

The literary theorist Mary Louise Pratt, for example, has observed, "There are strong reasons why field ethnographers so often lament that their ethnographic writings leave out or hopelessly impoverish some of the most important knowledge they have achieved, including the self-knowledge. For the lay person, such as myself, the main evidence of a problem is the simple fact that ethnographic writing tends to be surprisingly boring. How, one asks constantly, could such interesting people doing such interesting things produce such dull books? What did they have to do to themselves?"[16] Although they never did make the blood run faster, ethnographies written for a captive professional audience once appeared so authoritative that few dared say out loud that they were boring. Nor did it occur to readers to wonder about the kind of knowledge being suppressed by the discipline's relatively narrow norms of composition.

Critique from the outside has been more than matched by insiders. An eminent ethnographer, the late Victor Turner, for example, spoke forcefully against received ethnographic form, saying, "It is becoming increasingly recognized that the anthropological monograph is itself a rather rigid literary genre which grew out of the notion that in the human sciences reports must be modeled rather abjectly on those of the natural sciences."[17] For Turner, classic ethnographies have proven dreadfully poor vehicles for apprehending how reason, feeling, and will come together in people's daily lives. In a more political vein, he goes on to say that older-style ethnographies split subject from object and present other lives as visual spectacles for metropolitan consumption. "Cartesian dualism," he says, "has insisted on separating subject from object, us from them. It has, indeed, made voyeurs of Western man, exaggerating sight by macro- and micro-instrumentation, the better to learn the structures of the world with an 'eye' to its exploitation."[18] Turner thus connects the "eye" of ethnography with the "I" of imperialism.

Similarly, the psychologist Jerome Bruner has argued that the social descriptions of certain respected ethnographies initially appear persuasive, but then, on closer examination, crumble into implausibility. He begins by musing, "Perhaps there have been societies, at least for certain periods of time, that were 'classically' traditional and in which one 'derived' one's actions from a set of more or less fixed rules."[19] He remembers how his pleasure at reading about the classic Chinese family reminded him of watching a formal ballet where rules and roles were meticulously followed. Later, however, he learned about how Chinese warlords used brute force to gain people's allegiance and alter their lives, as legitimate rule rapidly passed from one party to the next. "I found myself concluding," he says, "that 'equilibrium' accounts of cultures are useful principally to guide the writing of older style ethnographies or as political instruments for use by those in power to subjugate psychologically those who must be ruled."[20] Although depictions of traditional societies where people slavishly follow strict rules have a certain charming formality, alternative accounts of the same societies lead Bruner to a harsh conclusion, not unlike my own. He regards the once-dominant ethnographic portrait of the timeless traditional society as a fiction used to aid in composition and to legitimate the subjugation of human populations.

Classic norms of ethnographic composition had a significant role in reinforcing the slippage from working hypotheses to self-fulfilling prophecies about unchanging social worlds where people are caught in a web of eternal recurrence. Anthropological theory of the day was dominated by the concepts of structure, codes, and norms; it correspondingly developed largely implicit descriptive practices that prescribed composition in the present tense. Anthropologists have in fact proudly used the phrase "the ethnographic present" to designate a distanced mode of writing that normalized life by describing social activities as if they were always repeated in the same manner by everyone in the group.

The societies so described appeared uncomfortably close to Edward Said's notion of "orientalism."[21] Said underscored the links between power and knowledge, between imperialism and orientalism, by showing how seemingly neutral, or innocent, forms of social description both reinforced and produced ideologies that justified the imperialist project. In Said's view, the orientalist records observations about a transaction in the corner of the marketplace, or child care under a thatched roof, or a rite of passage, in order to generalize to a larger cultural entity, the Orient, which by definition is homogeneous in space and unchanging through time. Under such descriptions, the Orient appears to be both a benchmark against which to measure Western European "progress" and an inert terrain on which to impose imperialist schemes of "development."

The classic notion that stability, orderliness, and equilibrium characterized so-called traditional societies thus derived in part from the illusion of timelessness created by the rhetoric of ethnography. The following passage, from E. E. Evans-Pritchard's classic ethnography on the Nuer, a pastoralist group from the Sudan, illustrates the tendencies just depicted: "Seasonal and lunar changes repeat themselves year after year, so that a Nuer standing at any point of time has conceptual knowledge of what lies before him and can predict and organize his life accordingly. A man's structural future is likewise already fixed and ordered into different periods, so that the total changes in status a boy will undergo in his ordained passage through the social system, if he lives long enough, can be foreseen."[22] The ethnographer speaks interchangeably of the Nuer or of a Nuer man because, differences of age aside (questions of gender barely enter Evans-Pritchard's androcentric work), the culture is conceived as uniform and static. Yet, at the very time the ethnographer was conducting his research, the Nuer were being subjected to enforced changes by the British colonial regime's efforts at so-called pacification.

The Museum and the Garage Sale

Consider the art museum as an image of classic ethnographies and the cultures they describe. Cultures stand as sacred images; they have an integrity and coherence that enables them to be studied, as they say, on their own terms, from within, from the "native" point of view. Not unlike the grand art of museums, each culture stands alone as an aesthetic object worthy of contemplation. Once canonized, all cultures appear to be equally great. Questions of relative merit will only wind up with imponderables, incomparables, and incommensurables. Just as the professional literary critic does not argue about whether Shakespeare is greater than Dante, the ethnographer does not debate the relative merits of the Kwakiutl of the northwest coast versus the Trobriand Islanders of the Pacific. Both cultures exist and both can sustain extensive cultural analysis.

Ethnographic monumentalism, however, should not be confused with that of high-culture humanism. Despite its problems, the ethnographic impulse to regard cultures as so many great works of art has a deeply democratic and egalitarian side. All cultures are separate and equal. If one culture lords it over another, it is not because of its cultural superiority. The high-culture monumentalists, in contrast, envision a sacred heritage extending directly from Homer through Shakespeare to the present. They find nothing of comparable value either in so-called popular culture or outside the "West." Anthropologists of any political persuasion appear subversive (and indeed, during the 1980s, have received relatively little institutional support) simply because their work valorizes other cultural traditions.

In his pithy discussion of the current ferment in anthropology, Louis A. Sass cites an eminent anthropologist who worried that recent experimentation with ethnographic form could subvert the discipline's authority, leading to its fragmentation and eventual disappearance: "At a conference in 1980 on the crisis in anthropology, Cora Du Bois, a retired Harvard professor, spoke of the distance she felt from the 'complexity and disarray of what I once found a justifiable and challenging discipline. . . . It has been like moving from a distinguished art museum into a garage sale.'"[23] The images of the museum, for the classic period, and the garage sale, for the present, strike me as being quite apt, but I evaluate them rather differently than Du Bois. She feels nostalgia for the distinguished art museum with everything in its place, and I see it as a relic from the colonial past. She detests the chaos of the garage sale, and I find it provides a precise image for the postcolonial situation where cultural artifacts flow between unlikely places, and nothing is sacred, permanent, or sealed off.

The image of anthropology as a garage sale depicts our present global situation.[24] Analytical postures developed during the colonial era can no longer be sustained. Ours is definitively a postcolonial epoch. Despite the intensification of North American imperialism, the "Third World" has imploded into the metropolis. Even the conservative national politics of containment, designed to shield "us" from "them," betray the impossibility of maintaining hermetically sealed cultures. Consider a series of efforts: police fight cocaine dealers, border guards detain undocumented workers, tariffs try to keep out Japanese imports, and celestial canopies promise to fend off Soviet missiles. Such efforts to police and barricade reveal, more than anything else, how porous "our" borders have become.

The Lone Ethnographer's guiding fiction of cultural compartments has crumbled. So-called natives do not "inhabit" a world fully separate from the one ethnographers "live in." Few people simply remain in their place these days. When people play "ethnographers and natives," it is ever more difficult to predict who will put on the loincloth and who will pick up the pencil and paper. More people are doing both, and more so-called natives are among the ethnographer's readers, at times appreciative and at times vocally critical. One increasingly finds that Native American Tewas, South Asian Sinhalese, and Chicanos are among those who read and write ethnographies.

If ethnography once imagined it could describe discrete cultures, it now contends with boundaries that crisscross over a field at once fluid and saturated with power. In a world where "open borders" appear more salient than "closed communities," one wonders how to define a project for cultural studies. Neither "getting on with the job" and pretending nothing has changed nor "moaning about meaning" and producing more discourse on the impossibility of anthropology will result in the needed remaking of social analysis. Such at any rate is the position from which I develop a critique of classic norms for doing ethnography.

2 | *After Objectivism*

AFTER FALLING HEAD OVER HEELS in love, I paid a ceremonial visit, during the summer of 1983, to the "family cottage" on the shores of Lake Huron in western Ontario. Much as one would expect (unless one was, as I was, too much in the thick of things), my prospective parents-in-law treated me, their prospective son-in-law, with reserve and suspicion. Such occasions are rarely easy, and this one was no exception. Not unlike other rites of passage, my mid-life courtship was a blend of conventional form and unique personal experience.

My peculiar position, literally surrounded by potential in-laws, nourished a project that unfolded over a two-week period in barely conscious daydreams. The daily family breakfast started turning in my mind into a ritual described in the distanced normalizing mode of a classic ethnography. On the morning of my departure, while we were eating breakfast, I revealed my feelings of tender malice by telling my potential in-laws the "true" ethnography of their family breakfast: "Every morning the reigning patriarch, as if just in from the hunt, shouts from the kitchen, 'How many people would like a poached egg?' Women and children take turns saying yes or no.

"In the meantime, the women talk among themselves and designate one among them the toast maker. As the eggs near readiness, the reigning patriarch calls out to the designated toast maker, 'The eggs are about ready. Is there enough toast?'

"'Yes,' comes the deferential reply. 'The last two pieces are about to pop up.' The reigning patriarch then proudly enters bearing a plate of poached eggs before him.

"Throughout the course of the meal, the women and children, including the designated toast maker, perform the obligatory ritual praise song, saying, 'These sure are great eggs, Dad.'"

My rendition of a family breakfast in the ethnographic present transformed a relatively spontaneous event into a generic cultural form. It became a caricatured analysis of rituals of dominance and deference organized along lines of gender and generation.

This microethnography shifted jaggedly between words ordinarily used by the family (mainly in such direct quotes as "These sure are great eggs, Dad") and those never used by them (such as "reigning patriarch," "designated toast maker," and "obligatory ritual praise song"). The jargon displayed a degree of hostility toward my potential father-in-law (the reigning patriarch) and hesitant sympathy with my potential sisters-in-law (the designated toast maker and the singers of the praise song). Far from being a definitive objective statement, my microethnography turned out to be a timely intervention that altered mealtime practices without destroying them. The father approaching retirement and his daughters already established in their careers were in the process of remolding their relations with one another. For all its deliberate caricature, my description contained an analysis that offered my potential in-laws a measure of insight into how their family breakfast routines, by then approaching empty ritual, embodied increasingly archaic familial relations of gender and hierarchy. Indeed, subsequent observations have confirmed that the ritual praise songs honoring the poached eggs and their maker have continued to be sung, but with tongue in cheek. To defamiliarize the family breakfast was to transform its taken-for-granted routines.

The reader will probably not be surprised to hear that my potential in-laws laughed and laughed as they listened to the microethnography about (and with which I had interrupted) their family breakfast. Without taking my narrative literally, they said they learned from it because its objectifications made certain patterns of behavior stand out in stark relief—the better to change them. The reception of my tale, as became evident in retrospect, was conditioned by their family practice of taking pleasure in witty teasing banter laced with loving malice.

The experience of having gales of laughter greet my microethnography made me wonder why a manner of speaking that sounds like the literal "truth" when describing distant cultures seems terribly funny as a description of "us." Why does a mode of composition flip between being parodic or serious depending in large measure on whether it is applied to "ourselves" or to "others"? Why does the highly serious classic ethnographic idiom almost inevitably become parodic when used as self-description?

In the previous chapter I argued that during the classic period (roughly 1921–1971), norms of distanced normalizing description gained a monopoly on objectivity. Their authority appeared so self-evident that they became the one and only legitimate form for telling the literal truth about other cultures. Proudly called the ethnographic present, these norms prescribed, among other things, the use of the present tense to depict social life as a set of shared routines and the assumption of a certain distance that purportedly conferred objectivity. All other modes of composition were marginalized or suppressed altogether.

In my view, no mode of composition is a neutral medium, and none should be granted exclusive rights to scientifically legitimate social description. Consider, for a moment longer, my mini-ethnography of the family breakfast. Although classic norms only rarely allowed for variants, mine was not the only possible version of the family meal. One could have told the tale of how this breakfast differed from all others. Such a telling could include specific conversations, the intrusive potential son-in-law, and the moods and rhythms with which the event unfolded. In addition, the narrator could have assumed the father's point of view and described how the "family provider" distributed his gifts to the "starving horde." Or the tone of this account could have been droll, or sincere, or whimsical, or earnest, or angry, or detached, rather than mockingly parodic.

One plausible criterion for assessing the adequacy of social descriptions could be a thought experiment: How valid would we find ethnographic discourse about others if it were used to describe ourselves? The available literature, not to mention the family breakfast episode, indicates that a division between serious conception and laughing reception can separate the author's intentions from the reader's responses. Human subjects have often reacted with bemused puzzlement over the ways they have been depicted in anthropological writings.

The problem of validity in ethnographic discourse has reached crisis proportions in a number of areas over the past fifteen years. In Chicano responses to anthropological depictions of themselves, the most balanced yet most devastating assessment has been put forth by Américo Paredes. He begins rather gently by saying, "I find the Mexicans and Chicanos pictured in the usual ethnographies somewhat unreal."[1] He goes on to suggest that the people studied find ethnographic accounts written about them more parodic than telling: "It is not so much a sense of outrage, that would betray wounded egos, as a feeling of puzzlement, that *this* is given as a picture of the communities they have grown up in. Many of them are more likely to laugh at it all than feel indignant."[2] His critique of the somewhat unreal picture put forth in ethnographies about Chicanos continues with a stunning item-by-item enumeration of such errors as mistranslations, taking jokes seriously, missing double meanings, and accepting an apocryphal story as the literal truth about brutal initiation rites in youth gangs.[3]

Paredes's diagnosis is that most ethnographic writing on Mexicans and Chicanos has failed to grasp significant variations in the tone of cultural events. In an ethnography he sees as representative, Paredes observes that the Chicanos portrayed "are not only literal-minded, they never crack a joke."[4] He argues that ethnographers who attempt to interpret Chicano culture should recognize "whether a gathering is a wake, a beer bust, or a street-corner confabulation."[5] Knowledge about the cultural framing of events would aid the ethnographer in distinguishing an earnest speech from a joking speech. Even when using technical concepts, the analysis should not lose sight of whether the event was serious (to be taken literally) or deadpan (to be read as farce).

Lest there be any confusion, I am saying neither that the native is always right nor that Paredes as native ethnographer could never be wrong. Instead, my claim is that we should take the criticisms of our subjects in much the same way that we take those of our colleagues.[6] Not unlike other ethnographers, so-called natives can be insightful, sociologically correct, axe-grinding, self-interested, or mistaken. They do know their own cultures, and rather than being ruled out of court, their criticisms should be listened to and taken into account, to be accepted, rejected, or modified, as we reformulate our analyses. At issue is not the real truth versus the ethnographic lie. After all, the pragmatic concerns of everyday life can diverge from those of disciplined inquiry. A person "falling in love" speaks with quite different desires and purposes than the psychiatrist who describes the "same" phenomenon as "object cathexis." Technical and everyday vocabularies differ in large measure because their respective projects are oriented to different goals. In this case, Paredes has called attention to how the "objects" of study can find an earnest ethnography about themselves as parodic as did the participants in the Canadian family breakfast. His incisive critique calls for ethnographers to reassess their rhetorical habits.

The difficulties of using ethnographic discourse for self-description should have long been apparent to anthropologists, most of whom have read Horace Miner's classic (if heavy-handed) paper, "Body Ritual among the Nacirema." (Nacirema spelled backwards, of course, is American.) In that paper, an ethnographic sketch of Nacirema "mouth-rites," written in accord with classic norms, was parodic in its application to Americans:

The daily body ritual performed by everyone includes a mouth-rite. Despite the fact that these people are so punctilious about care of the mouth, this rite involves a practice which strikes the uninitiated stranger as revolting. It was reported to me that the ritual consists of inserting a small bundle of hog hairs into the mouth, along with certain magical powders, and then moving the bundle in a highly formalized series of gestures.[7]

His essay thus defamiliarizes both through the narrator's position as uninitiated stranger and through the distanced idiom that transforms everyday life practices into more elevated ritual and magical acts.

Clearly there is a gap between the technical idiom of ethnography and the language of everyday life.[8] Miner's description employs terms used by a certain group of professionals rather than the words most of "us" Americans usually use in talking about brushing "our" teeth. The article becomes parodic precisely because of the discrepancy between what we all know about brushing our teeth and the ethnographer's elevated, distanced, normalizing discourse. Unlike my account of the family breakfast, jarring discordance here does not become fully explicit in the text (despite what text positivists may think). Instead, it resides in the disjunction between Miner's technical jargon and the North American reader's knowledge that the mouth-rites refer to brushing one's teeth in the morning.

In retrospect, one wonders why Miner's article was taken simply as a good-natured joke rather than as a scathing critique of ethnographic discourse. Who could continue to feel comfortable describing other people in terms that sound ludicrous when applied to ourselves? What if the detached observer's authoritative objectivity resides more in a manner of speaking than in apt characterizations of other forms of life?

Lest it appear that no ethnography has ever been written in the manner of Miner's Nacirema mouth-rites, one should probably cite an actual case. Otherwise, the reader could regard the classic norms as a figment of my imagination rather than as the discipline's until recently (and, in many quarters, still) dominant mode of representing other cultures.

Consider, for example, the description of "weeping rites" in A. R. Radcliffe-Brown's classic ethnography about the Andaman Islanders, a hunter-gatherer group residing southeast of India:

When two friends or relatives meet after having been separated, the social relation between them that has been interrupted is about to be renewed. This social relation implies or depends upon the existence of a specific bond of solidarity between them. The weeping rite (together with the subsequent exchange of presents) is the affirmation of this bond. The rite, which, it must be remembered, is obligatory, compels the two participants to act as though they felt certain emotions, and thereby does, to some extent, produce these emotions in them.[9]

The reader should keep in mind that this passage describes tears of greeting between long-separated old friends. Nonetheless, the ethnographer manifests skepticism about whether or not the weepers actually feel anything. Evidently, he regards their tears as mere playacting. To the limited extent that emotions are present, the ethnographer explains them as the consequence of having performed the obligatory weeping rites.

Yet the status of Radcliffe-Brown's term "obligatory" remains obscure. Does it mean that when he witnessed weeping greeters, they always turned out to be long-lost intimates? How could he have observed greetings without tears between long-lost intimates? Or did people simply tell the ethnographer that when long-lost intimates greet one another, they weep? Despite its analytical import, the reader is left to wonder what Radcliffe-Brown means by the term *obligatory*.

Nonetheless, most anthropological readers of Radcliffe-Brown probably take his account at face value. When, for example, I told a colleague about my dissatisfaction with Radcliffe-Brown's depiction of Andaman weeping rites, she correctly followed the code for ethnographic readers and replied, "Yes, but for them, unlike for us, the rites are obligatory." Such are the costs of following rarely examined habits of reading.

The problem resides less in the use of such descriptions than in an uncritical attachment to them as the sole vehicle for literal objective truth. Radcliffe-Brown so detached himself from his human subjects that his account lends itself to being read as unwittingly parodic, and even absurd. When tearful greetings between long-lost intimates are described as obligatory weeping rites, they become so defamiliarized as to appear simply bizarre.

The idiom of classic ethnography characteristically describes specific events as if they were programmed cultural routines and places the observer at a great distance from the observed. The systematic effects of classic modes of composition were rarely explored because they purportedly held a monopoly on objectivity. The point, however, is not to discard classic norms but to displace them so that they become only one among a number of viable forms of social description rather than the one and only mode of writing about other cultures. Radcliffe-Brown's detached, dehumanizing descriptive idiom potentially offers analytical insight not available through concepts more frequently used in everyday life. The Canadian breakfast episode, as I said, suggests that distanced normalizing descriptions can be used with a deliberately satirical intent to jolt people into thinking afresh about their everyday lives.[10]

Although my description of the family breakfast formally resembles Radcliffe-Brown's, the objectifications differ markedly in their impact. When read in accord with classic norms, Radcliffe-Brown's account appears to be the only objective way of describing social reality. It is the literal truth. My more parodic account stands as one among a number of possible descriptions. Its accuracy matters, but it objectifies more with a view to speeding a process of change than with producing a timeless truth. How social descriptions are read depends not only on their formal linguistic properties but also on their content and their context. Who is speaking to whom, about what, for what purposes, and under what circumstances? The differences between distinct forms of objectification reside in the analyst's position within a field of social interaction rather than in the text regarded as a document with intrinsic meaning.

What follows deliberately objectifies classic canons of objectivity with a view to moving not beyond conventions (which, in any case, is impossible) but toward the use of a wider range of rhetorical forms in social description. As a corrective to the literal-mindedness with which classic social descriptions are habitually read, this chapter deliberately defamiliarizes the rhetoric of objectivism (which, arguably, unwittingly defamiliarizes the everyday world) in order to indicate how short the gap is between objective characterization and objectifying caricature. My goal in thus objectifying objectivism is to speed a process of change already underway in the modes of composition for ethnography as a form of social analysis.

Death in North American Culture

In what follows I will discuss anthropological writings on death and mourning, with a view toward exploring the limits of classic norms for social description. In a manner peculiarly at odds with the intense emotions it arouses, the topic of death has proven a particularly fertile area in the production of distanced normalizing accounts. The analytical problems that emerge so clearly with reference to mourning and bereavement also are present in a number of other areas, including passionate love, social improvisations, and spontaneous fun. Death, however, has the virtue of being relatively well represented in the anthropological literature.

The fact that death has proven so vexing for ethnographic analysis probably does not surprise most North American readers. The majority of intensive ethnographic studies have been conducted by relatively young people who have no personal experience of devastating personal losses. Furthermore, such researchers usually come from upper-middle-class Anglo-American professional backgrounds, where (unlike those with higher mortality rates, such as policemen and crop dusters) people often shield themselves by not talking about death and other people's bereavement. Such ethnographers probably have grown up with the notion that it is rude and intrusive to ask the chief mourners about their experience of grieving.

My characterization of bereavement in upper-middle-class Anglo-American culture represents a central tendency, more a statistical probability than a monolithic certainty. Since readers can usually judge the representativeness of anecdotes about their own culture, a brief example from my local newspaper, a familiar source rarely used in academic writing, probably will suffice as an illustration. This story, about how parents react to their children's deaths, claimed that most upper-middle-class people strive to live out the illusion of being in control of their lives. Death, however, threatens their fiction of being in control. Listen to Pamela Mang, whose daughter Jessica died of cancer: "One of the most profound insights I got out of Jessica's illness was that most of us try to protect ourselves from disasters and difficulties, and that we miss a lot of life because of that. . . . Oh, God, you just want to get it out, to talk about it, because somehow getting it out into the air makes it something of a size that is manageable, that you can handle."[11] Yet most North Americans, especially those without personal experience of loss, find death a subject best avoided. In trying to shield themselves from their own mortality, North Americans often claim that the bereaved don't want to speak about their losses (despite what Pamela Mang says). Although other cultures focus lavish attention on death,[12] most ethnographers would find it extremely difficult to interview chief mourners because, for "us," grief is a private and personal matter. Hence the ethnography of death's striking adherence to classic norms that verbally transform particular losses into general descriptions of what all funeral rituals share.

Classic norms especially shaped Jack Goody's ethnography of death among the West African LoDagaa. The chapter called "The Day of Death: Mourning the Dead," for example, begins with a composite account of patterns of mourning among the close kin of the deceased ("the immediate mourners"):

While the xylophones are playing, the lineage "wives" and "sisters" of the dead man walk and run about the area in front of the house, crying lamentations and holding their hands behind the nape of the neck in the accepted attitude of grief. . . . From time to time, one of the immediate mourners breaks into a trot, even a run, and a bystander either intercepts or chases after the bereaved and quietens him by seizing his wrist.[13]

The analyst positions himself as a spectator who looks on from the outside. Are the lamentations of the dead man's wives and sisters little more than conventional gestures, as the description suggests? What about the intensely bereaved person who is being restrained?

Goody goes on to discuss, not bereavement, but how people's relations of kinship to the deceased determine the means—tying by hide, tying by fiber, and tying with string around the ankle—by which bystanders restrain them when, in their grief, they attempt to injure or kill themselves. He presents the following table:

MAN'S FUNERAL

Father . . . . Tied by hide
Mother . . . . Tied by hide
Wife . . . . Tied by hide
Brother . . . . Tied by fibre
Sister . . . . Tied by fibre
Son . . . . String tied around the ankle
Daughter . . . . String tied around the ankle [14]

Put into words, the table simply says that when the bereaved attempt to injure or kill themselves, bystanders use ties of hide to restrain a dead man's parents and wife, ties of fiber to restrain his siblings, and ties of string around the ankle to restrain his children. (One can only wonder at the objectifying impulse to present such a readily verbalized statement in tabular form.) The ethnographer's position as uninvolved spectator becomes yet more evident when he says, "Before analyzing these categories of bereaved in greater detail, note should be taken of some other ways in which mourners are visually differentiated." [15] The spectacle itself, seen from the outside, is largely visual. The violent upheaval of grief, its wailing and attempts at self-injury and suicide, appear under this description as normal routines.

Most ethnographic descriptions of death stand at a peculiar distance from the obviously intense emotions expressed, and they turn what for the bereaved are unique and devastating losses into routine happenings. In following classic norms, Goody consistently links intense expressions of bereavement to conventional expectations:

A man *will be expected* to display great grief at the death of a young son.[16]

Another indication of the same imbalance in the parent-child relationship is to be seen in the occurrence of suicide attempts, which are a *standardized method* of demonstrating grief at the loss of a relative.[17]

The passages cited above substitute the term *conventional* for Radcliffe-Brown's key term, *obligatory*. Why do ethnographers so often write as if a father losing a son or a bereaved person attempting suicide were doing little more than following convention? Unreflective talk about culturally expected expressions of grief easily slips into skepticism about the reality of the emotions expressed. It is all too easy to elide the force of conventional forms of life with the merely conventional, as if forceful emotions were mere motions.

Neither one's ability to anticipate appropriately other people's reactions nor the fact that people express their grief in culturally specific ways should be conflated with the notion that the devastatingly bereaved are merely conforming to conventional expectations. Even eyewitness reports cast in the normalizing ethnographic idiom trivialize the events they describe by reducing the force of intense emotions to spectacle. Such accounts visualize people's actions from the outside and fail to provide the participants' reflections on their own experiences. They normalize by presenting generalized recipes for ritual action rather than attempting to grasp the particular content of bereavement.[18]

Classic norms of ethnographic discourse make it difficult to show how social forms can be both imposed by convention *and* used spontaneously and expressively. In relying exclusively on such an idiom, ethnographies can represent other lives *as if* they doubted even the most visible agonies of the bereaved, including, for instance, a father mourning a son or a husband grieving for his wife who died in childbirth.

Theory as the Reification of Classic Norms

Most prominently, Claude Lévi-Strauss has taken the classic norms and dressed them in their most general theoretical garb:

Men do not act, as members of a group, in accordance with what each feels as an individual; each man feels as a function of the way in which he is permitted or obliged to act. Customs are given as external norms before giving rise to internal sentiments, and these non-sentient norms determine the sentiments of individuals as well as the circumstances in which they may, or must, be displayed.[19]

Lévi-Strauss dismisses not only the explanatory import but the very reality of emotions:

Moreover, if institutions and customs drew their vitality from being continually refreshed and invigorated by individual sentiments, like those in which they originated, they ought to conceal an affective richness, continually replenished, which would be their positive content. We know that this is not the case, and that the constancy which they exhibit usually results from a conventional attitude.[20]

In his view, institutions and customs appear so emotionally barren that he claims that human beings experience affect only in the violation, not in the performance, of conventional acts: "Emotion is indeed aroused, but when the custom, in itself indifferent, is violated."[21] If people suffer through their bereavement, it hardly appears objective to represent their experiences as if they were merely conforming with conventions by going through the expected motions. Yet, evidence presented in accord with the classic norms of social description appears to support abstract theoretical statements that are neither humane nor accurate. In attempting to apprehend the complexities of other cultures, disciplined inquiry can ill afford to build its theories on such a questionable foundation.

When classic norms gain exclusive rights to objective

truth, ethnography becomes as likely to reveal where objectivity lies as where it tells the truth. What, then, can supplement normalizing distanced discourse in ethnographic writing? Myriad modes of composition, of course, are possible—moral indignation, satire, critique, and others. Several have been used, even in this chapter. For present illustrative purposes, however, I shall consider how personal narratives offer an alternative mode of representing other forms of life.

Although personal narratives often appear in ethnographies written in the classic mode, they usually have been relegated quite literally to the margins: prefaces, introductions, afterwords, footnotes, and italicized or small-print case histories. In fact, the classic norms usually achieved their authority at the expense of personal narratives and case histories. Yet the latter forms often facilitate the analysis of social processes that have proven difficult even to perceive through distanced normalizing discourse.

Anthropologist Clifford Geertz, for example, has described the dilemmas that surfaced during an Indonesian funeral on the island of Java. After opening his account with a brief normalizing description ("the men begin to cut wooden grave markers and to dig a grave"),[22] he shifts to the past tense and describes a particular boy's funeral where one thing after another went wrong. The cutting of wooden grave markers, just cited as recipe, becomes transformed: "After a half hour or so, a few of the abangans began to chip half-heartedly away at pieces of wood to make grave markers and a few women began to construct small flower offerings for want of anything better to do; but it was clear that the ritual was arrested and that no one quite knew what to do next. Tension slowly rose."[23] Always at risk in living through the anguish of loss, routine funerary rites broke down as conflicts erupted between Moslem and Hindu-Buddhist participants. Delving into the particulars of this agonizing event rather than the generalities of a composite construction revealed the severe limits of collapsing mourning with ritual and ritual with routine.

In yet another instance, anthropologist Loring Danforth provides an account that moves from spectacle to rather more intimate biographical portraits of mourners. His account begins in a vivid, though external manner:

Soon the graveyard was alive with activity, and a forest of candles burned at the foot of each grave. About ten women, all dressed in shades of black, brown, or blue, busied themselves lighting lamps and sweeping around the graves. Several women began hauling water in large buckets from the faucet in the church courtyard nearby.[24]

Danforth depicts a visual spectacle the mood of which is one of bucolic calm and routine. Yet as the account proceeds, the analysis shifts so that the reader soon learns the particular histories of the mourners:

The death of Irini's twenty-year-old daughter Eleni was generally acknowledged to have been the most tragic the village of Potamia had experienced in many years. Eleni died almost five years earlier, in August 1974. She had been a very attractive young woman, tall, with long black hair. . . . One month before she was to begin her first teaching job, Eleni was struck by a car and killed in a hit-and-run accident in the city of Thessaloniki.[25]

The reader then hears verbatim laments, learns how Irini did not leave her house for a full year following her daughter's death, discovers how a friendship developed between Irini and another bereaved mother, and witnesses the daughter's exhumation as the participants, by then known in certain biographical particulars, find themselves overcome with emotion. The ethnographer provides a sense of the emotions experienced by the actors through their words, their gestures, and their biographies.

There is no single recipe for representing other cultures. Indeed, my observations on the Canadian family breakfast suggest that the classic norms, used in a deliberately parodic or distorting manner, can at times yield forceful accounts. Normalizing descriptions can both reveal *and* conceal aspects of social reality. Ethnographies written in accord with classic norms need to be reread, not banished from anthropology. Rather than discarding distanced normalizing accounts, the discipline should recover them, but with a difference. They must be cut down to size and relocated, not replaced. No longer enshrined as ethnographic realism, the sole vehicle for speaking the literal truth about other cultures, the classic norms should become one mode of representation among others. Thus, for example, their satirical potential could be explored in cross-cultural studies as well as in reflections on North American society. They could be used alongside other modes of composition in exploring the interplay between routine and improvisation in everyday life.

Certainly, standing current fashion on its head by substituting tales of specific cases for distanced normalizing discourse will not yield a solution to the vexed problem of representing other lives. Instead, an increased disciplinary tolerance for diverse legitimate rhetorical forms will allow for any particular text to be read against other possible versions. Allowing forms of writing that have been marginalized or banned altogether to gain legitimacy could enable the discipline to approximate people's lives from a number of angles of vision. Such a tactic could enable us better to advance the ethnographic project of apprehending the range of human possibilities in their fullest complexity.

An Oblique Account of Warfare

All anthropologists surely have been moved, if not shaken, by the astute ethnographic observations that their subjects of research have made about North American or European culture. The most dramatic experience of this kind in my fieldwork suggests a dialogic potential, one of critical reflection and reciprocal perceptions, as yet rarely realized in the official rhetoric of anthropology.

When I was residing in the late 1960s as an ethnographer among the Ilongots of northern Luzon, Philippines, I was struggling against a diffusely overwhelming reaction to one of their central cultural practices: headhunting. Despite my indoctrination in cultural relativism, headhunting seemed utterly alien and morally reprehensible. At the time, I wanted simply to bracket my moral perception in order to carry out the ethnographic project of understanding the practice in its own terms.

Early questioning made it appear that headhunting had ended with the last Japanese soldier beheaded in June 1945. These beheadings, Ilongots said, aided the American army. When I asked about more recent headhunting episodes, they indignantly replied, "How could you think such a thing of us? I helped carry you across a stream. I fed you. I've cared for you. How could you think such a thing?" I could not but agree.

After about a year of fieldwork, my Ilongot brother Tukbaw and I were flying in a small plane when he pointed down below and said, "That's where we raided." He went on to tell me that he had gone headhunting there more recently than I had dared imagine. Soon everyone began to tell me their headhunting stories. Within a few weeks I realized that every man in the settlement had taken a head. I was shocked and disoriented because my companions had indeed been kind and generous. How could such caring hosts also be brutal killers?

Some months later I was classified 1-A for the draft. My companions immediately told me not to fight in Vietnam, and they offered to conceal me in their homes. Though it corresponded to my sentiments, their offer could not have surprised me more. Unthinkingly, I had supposed that headhunters would see my reluctance to serve in the armed forces as a form of cowardice. Instead, they told me that soldiers are men who sell their bodies. Pointedly they interrogated me, "How can a man do as soldiers do and command his brothers to move into the line of fire?"

This act of ordering one's own men (one's "brothers") to risk their lives was utterly beyond their moral comprehension. That their telling question ignored state authority and hierarchical chains of command mattered little. My own cultural world suddenly appeared grotesque. Yet their earnest incomprehension significantly narrowed the moral chasm between us, for their ethnographic observation about modern war was both aggressive and caring. They condemned my society's soldiering at the same time that they urged me not to sell my body.

Through such encounters the possibility for reciprocal critical perceptions opened between the Ilongots and me. This encounter suggests that we ethnographers should be open to asking not only how our descriptions of others would read if applied to ourselves but how we can learn from other people's descriptions of ourselves. In this case I was repositioned through an Ilongot account of one of my culture's central institutions. I could no longer speak about headhunting as one of the clean addressing the dirty. My loss of innocence enabled me and the Ilongots to face each other on more nearly equal ground, as members of flawed societies. We both lost positions of purity from which to condemn the other, without at the same time having to condone what we found morally reprehensible in ourselves and in the other. Neither war nor headhunting, in deeply serious ways, has been the same for me since.

I have deliberately cast my story of conflicting perceptions of legitimate social violence as a dialogue between me and the Ilongots. The anecdote's very narrative form better fits a notion of the cultural borderlands than of cultural patterning. If cultural borderlands explicitly provoke and reflect intense ideological debate, cultural patterning does so tacitly. Whether found in the museum or at the garage sale, culture is always already laced with the politics of conflicting ideologies.

Although most interpretations of culture enter the fields of political conflict that occasion them, I did not expect my anecdote about Ilongot perceptions of modern warfare to make a cameo appearance in the national media's arena of ideological debate. It all began with an article some years later that included a version of the preceding anecdote. It appeared in the October 10, 1984, issue of *Campus Report*, Stanford University's weekly news magazine for faculty and staff. The story was then transmitted on national wire services.

Eleven days later, a brief news item appeared under the headline "Headhunting Tribe Provides a Lesson," in the *Chicago Tribune:*

Members of the Ilongot tribe in the Philippines are headhunters because the act of beheading strangers is their way of venting anger and grief when loved ones die, an anthropologist has found. Renato Rosaldo of Stanford University's anthropology department discovered a markedly different view of violence and life among the Ilongots than is commonly held in the West. While they view headhunting as a ritual that frees a bereaved person of his burden, the Ilongots are shocked at the concept of soldiers and armies fighting wars. The idea of ordering one's comrades to place their lives in danger was repugnant to the headhunters and they referred to being a soldier as selling one's body.[26]

This item subsequently appeared in other newspapers under other headlines, such as "War Is Shocking to Headhunters," from the *Indianapolis Star* of November 4, 1984. The story succeeded in concisely conveying the jarring shock Ilongot perceptions had given me.

The story about the Ilongot moral conviction that no man has the right to tell another to "sell" his body initially caught my attention during the period of draft resistance against the Vietnam War. Ilongot perceptions of modern warfare partially coincided with those held by members of the antiwar movement. At the same time, they grew out of a significantly different form of life. In their everyday lives, Ilongots were relatively "anarchistic"; they often said that no person has the right to tell another what to do. Transported to the modern nation-state, Ilongot "anarchism" becomes subversive because it threatens "our" notion that certain people can command others, and even order them to risk their lives.

My retelling of the story about Ilongot perceptions of modern warfare took place on the eve of Reagan's 1984 reelection. In the name of individualism and free enterprise, the North American regime had dramatically increased state power and promoted the greatest peacetime military buildup in the nation's history. During this era of intense militarization, the radical right felt an enormous sense of empowerment. It eagerly rushed to intimidate and suppress the opposition. In this context, the threat posed by Ilongot perceptions of modern warfare was not lost on editorial writer John Lofton of the *Washington Times*. He phoned to "interview" me in the late afternoon of New Year's Day 1985. After explaining his interest in following up on the *Campus Report* story, he began screaming at me. It did not take too long to realize that this was no interview. It was a verbal mugging designed to intimidate me. My New Year's gift left me quite shaken.

After telling colleagues about this incident, I learned that Reverend Moon's Unification Church owned the *Washington Times*. A few weeks later, I received a clipping of "John Lofton's Journal" with the headline "And This Is How Profs Get Ahead." Lofton retold my story with citations from the *Campus Report* article liberally seasoned with parenthetical remarks about his readers' upset stomachs: "Ponder please, if your stomach lining can take it, the sad plight of one Renato Rosaldo, an associate professor of anthropology at Stanford University . . . (and for this you should be lying down flat or, better yet, be sitting in a tub full of Pepto Bismol)." He went on to tell of our phone conversation, but neglected to mention that he was screaming at me. No doubt about it, he was my enemy.

On May 14, 1985, the story surfaced again in the *National Enquirer*, but this time Ilongot perceptions of modern warfare were omitted. Instead the article stressed the connection Ilongots perceive between the anger in bereavement and headhunting. As often happens, the story's headline— "Headhunter Horror: Just 90 Miles from Big City, Bizarre Tribe Still Beheads Innocent People"—had little to do with its content. In fact, it was not an altogether bad rendition of Ilongot cultural practices. This story, as it happened, signaled the conclusion of Ilongot contributions to a national media debate.

Cultural studies has entered a world where its critical readership, as well as the societies it depicts, no longer can be narrowly circumscribed. Much as Ilongots can comment on modern North American warfare, John Lofton and the *National Enquirer* can listen in on my professional talk, and I on theirs. This does not make our lives more comfortable than before, or writing a book for such diverse potential audiences easier than in the classic period, but it does help make apparent how cultural interpretations are both occasioned by and enter arenas of ideological conflict. Under such circumstances, neither the notion of a neutral language nor that of brute facts can prosper. The next chapter attempts to unmask further the "innocence" of the detached observer.

3 | *Imperialist Nostalgia*

MY ANGER AT RECENT FILMS that portray imperialism with nostalgia informs this chapter. Consider the enthusiastic reception of *Heat and Dust, A Passage to India, Out of Africa,* and *The Gods Must Be Crazy.* The white colonial societies portrayed in these films appear decorous and orderly, as if constructed in accord with the norms of classic ethnography. Hints of these societies' coming collapse only appear at the margins where they create not moral indignation but an elegiac mode of perception. Even politically progressive North American audiences have enjoyed the elegance of manners governing relations of dominance and subordination between the "races." Evidently, a mood of nostalgia makes racial domination appear innocent and pure.

68

Much as the previous chapter showed that the language of social analysis is not a neutral medium, this one argues that the observer is neither innocent nor omniscient. In my view, it is a mistake to urge social analysts to strive for a position of innocence designated by such adjectives as detached, neutral, or impartial. Under imperialism, metropolitan observers are no more likely to avoid a certain complicity with domination than they are to avoid having strong feelings toward the people they study. Such recognitions need not lead either to confessional breast-beating or to galloping bias. If social analysts realize that they cannot be perfectly "clean," they no more should become as "dirty" as possible than airline pilots, invoking the limitations of human fallibility, should blind their eyes. The usual notions of evidence, accuracy, and argumentation continue to apply for their studies. Because researchers are necessarily both somewhat impartial and somewhat partisan, somewhat innocent and somewhat complicit, their readers should be as informed as possible about what the observer was in a position to know and not know. To return to this book's introduction, has the writer of an ethnography on death suffered a serious personal loss?

Mourning for What One Has Destroyed

Curiously enough, agents of colonialism—officials, constabulary officers, missionaries, and other figures from whom anthropologists ritually dissociate themselves—often display nostalgia for the colonized culture as it was "traditionally" (that is, when they first encountered it). The peculiarity of their yearning, of course, is that agents of colonialism long for the very forms of life they intentionally altered or destroyed. Therefore, my concern resides with a particular kind of nostalgia, often found under imperialism, where people mourn the passing of what they themselves have transformed.

Imperialist nostalgia revolves around a paradox: A person kills somebody, and then mourns the victim. In more attenuated form, someone deliberately alters a form of life, and then regrets that things have not remained as they were prior to the intervention. At one more remove, people destroy their environment, and then they worship nature. In any of its versions, imperialist nostalgia uses a pose of "innocent yearning" both to capture people's imaginations and to conceal its complicity with often brutal domination.

Imperialist nostalgia occurs alongside a peculiar sense of mission, "the white man's burden," where civilized nations stand duty-bound to uplift so-called savage ones. In this ideologically constructed world of ongoing progressive change, putatively static savage societies become a stable reference point for defining (the felicitous progress of) civilized identity. "We" (who believe in progress) valorize innovation, and then yearn for more stable worlds, whether these reside in our own past, in other cultures, or in the conflation of the two. Such forms of longing thus appear closely related to secular notions of progress. When the so-called civilizing process destabilizes forms of life, the agents of change experience transformations of other cultures as if they were personal losses.

Nostalgia is a particularly appropriate emotion to invoke in attempting to establish one's innocence and at the same time talk about what one has destroyed. Don't most people feel nostalgic about childhood memories? Aren't these memories genuinely innocent? Indeed, much of imperialist nostalgia's force resides in its association with (indeed, its disguise as) more genuinely innocent tender recollections of what is at once an earlier epoch and a previous phase of life. For my generation, one can, for example, evoke nostalgia by imitating radio voices saying "Call for Philip Morris," "The Shadow knows," or "Who was that masked man?" The relatively benign character of most nostalgia facilitates imperialist nostalgia's capacity to transform the responsible colonial agent into an innocent bystander. If most such recollections were not fairly harmless, the imperialist variety would not be nearly as effective as it is.

To "us," feelings of nostalgia seem almost as "natural" as

motor reflexes. How can one help but feel nostalgic about childhood memories? Don't all people in all times and in all places feel nostalgia? Yet even the history of the concept in Western Europe reveals the historical and cultural specificity of our notion of nostalgia. Far from being eternal, the term *nostalgia* dates from the late seventeenth century, when, according to sociologist Fred Davis, a Swiss physician coined the term (from the Greek *nostos*, a return home, and *algos*, a painful condition) to refer to pathological conditions of homesickness among his nation's mercenaries who were fighting far from their homeland. (Even in its origins, the term appears to have been associated with processes of domination.) Davis explains that the symptoms of "nostalgia" among the Swiss mercenaries included "despondency, melancholia, lability of emotion, including profound bouts of weeping, anorexia, a generalized 'wasting away,' and, not infrequently, attempts at suicide."[1] Evidently, nostalgia in the late seventeenth century was a weightier matter than the more innocent mood "we" at times experience in recalling our youths. In any case, the changing meanings of "nostalgia" in Western Europe (not to mention that many cultures have no such concept at all) indicate that "our" feelings of tender yearning are neither as natural nor as panhuman, and therefore not necessarily as innocent, as one might imagine.

Imperialist nostalgia has recently been analyzed by a number of scholars who regard the process of yearning for what one has destroyed as a form of mystification, although they do not use the term *imperialist nostalgia*. In a manuscript on the invention of Appalachia as a cultural category, anthropologist Allen Batteau, for example, studies the phenomenon in historical perspective.[2] He argues that during the last decade of the nineteenth century, as the frontier was closing, racism was codified and people began to deify nature and its Native American inhabitants. This attitude of reverence toward the natural developed at the same time that North Americans intensified the destruction of their human and natural environment. In showing how cultural notions about Appalachia were part of a larger dynamic, Batteau likens this process of idealization to forms of sacrifice where people draw a line between the profane (their civilization) and the sacred (nature), and then worship the very thing their civilizing process is destroying.

In a related analysis, North American historian Richard Slotkin suggests that frontier mythology in part revolves around a hunter hero who lives out his dreams in spiritual sympathy with the creatures of the wilderness who teach him their secret lore. "But his intention," Slotkin says, "is always to use the acquired skill against the teachers, to kill or assert his dominance over them. The consummation of his hunting quest in the killing of the quarry confirms him in his new and higher character and gives him full possession of the powers of the wilderness."[3] In this analysis, the disciple turns on his spiritual masters and achieves redemption by killing them. This frontier myth, which Slotkin calls regeneration through violence, shaped American experience from the westward expansion through the imperialist venture in the Philippines to the early official rhetoric of the Vietnam War.

Yet other scholars attempt to demystify imperialist nostalgia through a more frontal assault: They vigorously assert that the past was no better, and most probably worse, than the present. Rather than claim that nostalgia conceals guilt, they try to eliminate altogether the validity of elegiac postures toward small towns and rural communities. In a recent stimulating book on modernity, for example, social critic Marshall Berman attacks reverential postures toward traditional society by claiming that they are "idealized fantasies" designed to gloss over violence and brutality. The devastating portrait of such a society in Goethe's Gretchen tragedy in *Faust*, he says, "should etch in our minds forever the cruelty and brutality of so many of the forms of life that modernization has wiped out. So long as we remember Gretchen's fate, we will be immune to nostalgic yearning for the worlds we have lost."[4] Although Berman and I both aspire to "immunize" readers from such nostalgia, he apparently misses the paradox in his claim that modernization has "wiped out" brutal forms of life. His vigorous denial appears peculiar when one considers that the author, who condemns past "cruelty and brutality" (does he mean barbarism?), lives in a modern world noted for napalm, concentration camps, atomic bombs, torture, and systematic genocide. In my view, Berman combats overly romantic visions of bygone harmonious societies by simply standing them on their head. Instead of inflating the value of small-scale communities, he comes uncomfortably close to reproducing an ideology of progress that celebrates modernity at the expense of other forms of life.

The preceding analysts share a classic perspective that asserts that ideologies are fictions (in the sense of falsehoods) designed to conceal feelings of guilt. In more general terms, this mode of analysis argues that the work of ideology is either deliberately to disguise real class interests or unintentionally to express underlying social strains. The former posits a conspiracy to deceive subordinate groups and the latter assumes an unthinking connection rather like that between a disease and its symptom. Thus, an analysis will reveal that the ruling class, for example, ideologically beats the drums about tax simplification in order to conceal that it has stood Robin Hood on his head by taking from the poor and the middle-class in order to give to the very rich. Such demystifying approaches have proven their value. However, they all too often short-circuit their analyses by rushing to reveal the "real" interests involved and failing to show how ideology convinces those caught in its thrall. If the cultural forms involved never convince and never prove compelling, why not study more directly the "interests" they conceal or the "social strains" they express? In the extreme cases, why bother to speak of ideology at all?

What follows attempts to dismantle rather than demystify ideology. Presented more in the manner of a montage than a linear narrative, my heterogeneous examples attempt to show how ideology can be at once compelling, contradictory, and pernicious.[5] The dismantling occurs by giving voice to the ideologies, even at their most persuasive, and allowing them, as the analysis proceeds, to fall under their own weight as the inconsistencies within and between voices become apparent. Just as no ideology is as coherent as it tries to appear, no single voice remains without its inconsistencies and contradictions. My dismantling analytical strategy attempts to infect the reader, so to speak, with a minor case of the ideology's persuasiveness in order to provide immunity against more pathological episodes.

The Civilizing Mission

Let me now turn to North America's imperial venture in the Philippines by working with materials related to my field research among the Ilongots. I shall discuss in turn a series of voices, ranging from certain writings by an early twentieth-century lieutenant in the Philippine Constabulary, to more recent evangelical Christian missionaries, to a turn-of-the-century anthropologist, to present-day anthropologists Michelle Rosaldo and myself. The writers discussed move from a man who enforced law and order under imperialism, to people who imposed their religion on a non-Christian group, to three individuals who tried not to change the culture they studied. Despite the differences that divide them, I shall argue that all are complicit in reproducing the ideology of imperialist nostalgia.

My discussion begins with the writings of Wilfrid Turnbull, a lieutenant in the Philippine Constabulary during the first decade of this century. Turnbull spent time among the Ilongots, especially in 1909 and 1910, when he was in pursuit of the men who murdered an American ethnographer named William Jones (who in turn is discussed later in this chapter).

The *Philippine Magazine* of 1929 carried a story by Turnbull entitled "Among the Ilongots Twenty Years Ago." His story, for the most part, turns out to be a dry, unsentimental piece written in the ethnographic present and laced with native terms. Turnbull's ethnographic observations on subsistence, material culture, and customary practices on the whole are reasonably accurate, despite his modest disclaimer: "The writer of the present article wishes it to be considered as an assembly of reminiscences of the people and conditions as found by him, a layman with no pretense to a knowledge of anthropology, twenty years ago."[6] Turnbull's disarming denial of expertise did not inhibit him from using the classic norms of ethnographic description, however.

In the article as a whole, lapses from conventional form are more occasional than representative. Excesses usually surface during attributions of character, an especially fertile site for the cultivation of ideology. After describing the so-called Ilongot man—a fictional construct, if there ever was one—as "wonderfully active" and "effeminate in appearance," he goes on to describe the Ilongot man's warrior vices of sloth, male dominance, vanity, and surliness: "Taught from childhood to regard himself as a fighting man and nothing else, that it is below his dignity to perform any but the prescribed manual labor which is hazardous, that he is of superior mould to the female who is given him as a slave and admirer, all tend to make him somewhat arrogant and vain, and with advancing years he is apt to become overbearing and finally crabbed, some of the old men reminding one of old bad-tempered canines."[7] The canine simile in this American colonial condemnation of the "Ilongot man" appears particularly striking because, as the article draws to a close, Turnbull simultaneously reintroduces his simile and adopts a more sympathetic stance toward the Ilongots: "Formerly it was customary to kill the Ilongots on sight; they were hunted like mad dogs."[8]

In a more striking instance, Turnbull abruptly interrupts his detached, distanced description with a personal narrative that begins as follows:

The presentation of the seventeen *cabezas* [heads] not having produced the pleasure and enthusiasm anticipated, the Ilongots gave the writer two live children, a boy and a girl of about ten years of age, from different rancherias and unrelated. The youngsters were quite agreeable to the transfer, were accepted, given soap with directions necessary for its use, were deloused and sterilized as nearly as possible with materials at hand, were furnished with new wardrobes, and became the source of great usefulness and much entertainment.[9]

This story begins very much in the middle. The seventeen human heads appear without antecedent or explanation; the narrative makes it appear that they were given against the lieutenant's wishes. On the other hand, the two children appear to be a more welcome gift (at least after their induction to civilization via ritual cleansing).

Turnbull's willingness to assume adoptive paternity gives an air of innocence to the whole exchange. The author goes on to tell a version of the wild child story. When, for example, the two Ilongot children enter their first Christian settlement, they yell in excitement, according to Turnbull, "'Look, sir, there are carabao, shoot them'—not being able to understand why it was not done. To them the keeping of a live animal was just a waste of food."[10] As a guardian, Turnbull enjoyed a somewhat indulgent paternal relation toward his two wards. When the Ilongot boy sharpens his long knife and tells a Christian Filipino that he wants to behead him, Turnbull stands back and notes that the boy's fun "caused several undesirable situations."[11] If the wild child mixes naive innocence with violent impulses, Turnbull combines fond indulgence with patronizing understanding. The narrative embodies an attitude of humanitarian imperialism.

Turnbull makes his adoption of the children appear humane and intelligible. Yet the reader still wonders about the mysterious appearance of the seventeen human heads. For further illumination one must consult an earlier text, which Turnbull wrote as an official constabulary report at the time the episode actually occurred in 1909. There the lieutenant explains that he instigated the decapitations and personally received the heads as he pursued the murderers of the ethnographer William Jones. Written to a senior officer, Turnbull's 1909 report describes how Ilongots were in his camp to hunt down Jones's murderers:

As the people of Alicad and Tamsi were in camp in compliance with an order of the governor to hunt these people, an expedition was organized next day and rationed (2 chupas of corn per man per day) by me with instructions to surround and capture all these people. . . . On the 8th the cabecilla [headman] of Tamsi and the people from Panipigan returned with two heads, claiming that they were unable to find any but these, who showed fight and could not be captured. . . . The head-taking ceremony was celebrated and lasted two days, men, women, and children participating.[12]

Turnbull did not literally order the Ilongots to deliver human heads. But this episode repeats itself often enough in the report to suggest that the lieutenant must have known that his orders were more likely to result in decapitations than in the taking of prisoners. The mystery and lack of pleasure he shows at the gift of human heads, as depicted in the *Philippine Magazine*, appears quite at odds with his 1909 report. Indeed, one suspects that in 1909 the gift of heads must have been less surprising to Turnbull than the presentation of the two children he received as wards and hostages.

In a later piece, published in a 1937 issue of the *Philippine Magazine* and appropriately entitled "Return to Old Haunts," Turnbull describes his return, as a prospector, to Ilongot territory he first knew in 1909 and 1910. His essay revolves around a series of before and after contrasts, as seen in the following: "I noted several significant divergences from former local Ilongot custom at old Panippagan. The present day house has its floor only about four instead of ten or more feet from the ground and the ordinary native *hagdan* or ladder has replaced the notched pole. . . . Stinking clothing was also in evidence."[13] Turnbull's efforts to comprehend change tacitly use items of material culture to represent larger processes: houses close to the ground indicate the end of headhunting (earlier houses on high stilts served as protection against raiders); the disappearance of the notched pole signals deculturation (the loss of a "typical" item of material culture); stinking clothes stand for debasement (Christian garb as opposed to Ilongot bark cloth). Turnbull's portrait presents the culture as a tableau frozen in two slices in time, before and after. It remakes the culture in miniature, not unlike the minidrama of foster-parenting the two Ilongot children. Relations that once were paternalistic have soured and become beggarly.

Turnbull explicitly remarks on the civilizing process in these terms:

The present condition of the people and houses at Pongo was a shock! If such condition is a necessary stage to the less than semi-civilization of the nearby Christian settlements, it were better to segregate the Ilongots and allow them to follow their own mode of life. If there is a real desire to improve these people—and they are well worth it, especially the women—suitable teachers should be sent into the interior who by precept and example will show them the advantages of real civilization. For the right kind of teacher, the protection of soldiers is neither necessary nor desirable.[14]

These humanitarian sentiments—moral uplift, the value of education, and the white man's burden—appear curiously at odds with Turnbull's own role as a constabulary officer. Rather than the stark dichotomy of savage and civilized, this passage plays more complexly on semicivilization, defined primarily in economic terms, versus real civilization, known through moral values imparted by education.

Yet in his essay, the former lieutenant, as if speaking in another voice, recalls his punitive expedition after the Jones murder: "The people of Dickni visited us frequently, attracted to a certain extent by our winning ways, I should like to say, but fear it was only by the rice the cargadors [carriers] fed them and the crackers I dealt out to the children. I did not grudge them anything they got, for in 1910 I destroyed the settlement to the very last camote [sweet potato] plant and in self-defence had to kill one man, all of which I now know was more my fault than theirs, due to my ignorance of local customs."[15] Once he was harsh and ignorant, now he is older and wiser. Not unlike his seemingly self-effacing denial of ethnographic competence, his apparently humble posture authorizes him to go on, by now forgiven his youthful excesses, and describe his warrior feats. His textual field of inconsistent discourses ranges from innocence (his soldiering had nothing to do with the Ilongots' degradation) to valor (but he completely destroyed a settlement and killed a man).

Moreover, the changes that Turnbull encountered on his return as a prospector to his old haunts were, in part, produced by (or at any rate, happened in accord with) his design, as his 1909 report indicates. There, he suggests that Ilongots be given help "to adopt better methods of cultivation, seeds, one or more carabao, ploughs, cultivators, harrows, etc. be provided; and that trails be built *within* this section during the coming year. . . . Later trails can be made to connect with the outside, and gradually all will become friendly." [16]

Agricultural development, the end of headhunting, and contact with the outside appear to have been the primary changes that Turnbull witnessed in his 1937 article. His vision of 1909 had come true, but apparently he didn't like what he saw. He felt nostalgia for things as they had been when he first encountered the Ilongots, and this attitude absolved him of guilt and responsibility.

To bring the "civilizing mission" up to date, one must at least speak briefly about the major role evangelical missionaries have played in transforming Ilongot culture from the mid-1950s onward. The most active group in the area has been the largely Baptist organization called the New Tribes Mission, which operates throughout the world among remote tribal groups. These missionaries quite often spoke with joy at how Ilongots had, as they put it, accepted Christ as their personal savior. Perhaps this jubilant discourse can best be seen in an article called "Old Things Are Passed Away," which appeared in the New Tribes Mission magazine, *Island Challenge*. The article by Sarabelle Graves, the wife of one of the region's first New Tribes missionaries, describes the initial phase of converting the Ilongots:

How I wish you could hear the children of Taang when they get together! Marvin [her husband] told me of the great difference between them and those in savage villages where he and Florentino [his Tagalog-speaking companion] have been. Children just big enough to walk can be seen smoking, chewing betel nut, singing the head-hunting song and doing the dance; but the children of Taang love to gather around many times a day to sing "Isn't it Grand to be a Christian," "Thank You Lord for Saving My Soul," and many, many other songs they have learned in Tagalog. Yes, the POWER of God, the Gospel, has transformed these precious lives.[17]

It's clear that, for Sarabelle Graves, there are two types of Ilongots, the savage and the Christian. This passage displays a reverential mood, not of nostalgia for the old form of life but of a similar tenderness toward the transformed precious lives of new converts. Can one speak of nostalgia for the new?

My first personal encounter with the discourse of imperialist nostalgia in fact came while doing field research among the Ilongots in 1969. Although the incident was not inscribed in my field notes, I vividly recall a conversation with a Tagalog-speaking evangelical New Tribes missionary. She began to reminisce, perhaps because she thought it would interest an anthropologist, about how things were when she first arrived about a decade earlier. She spoke with nostalgia about threats on their lives from men she called "headhunters," about how people always sang their indigenous songs, and about the absence of store-bought shirts. These remarks puzzled me; they seemed ill-fitting to a missionary. Ilongot baptized believers, as the New Tribes missionaries called them, purposely abandoned their songs, saying they tugged at their hearts and awakened their old ways. The end of headhunting, for the missionary, marked the success of her evangelical efforts. Many of the shirts were donations that she herself had distributed. She had played a major role in producing, and evidently desired, the changes that took place. At the time I puzzled that she could yearn for the

Ilongots to be as they had been before she transformed their lives. The notion of imperialist nostalgia had not yet occurred to me.

Mourning the Passing of Traditional Society

By now most anthropologists probably find such notions as the "vanishing primitive" or "mourning the passing of traditional society" more conventional than insightful. Like most clichés, they once were good metaphors, and they have enjoyed a venerable history in the discipline. Bronislaw Malinowski, for example, anticipated a theme played throughout Claude Lévi-Strauss's *Tristes Tropiques*, when he said, "Ethnology is in the sadly ludicrous, not to say tragic position, that at the very moment when it begins to put its workshop in order, to forge its proper tools, to start ready for work on its appointed task, the material of its study melts away with hopeless rapidity."[18] Malinowski himself, of course, was articulating the doctrine of salvage ethnography—record the precious culture before it disappears forever—that helped authorize the funding and institutional support of field research. One should probably add that the vision of the vanishing primitive has proven sometimes false and sometimes true. Confronted with the assaults of imperialism and capitalism, cultures can show remarkable resilience (as among the Native American Pueblos), and they can also disappear (as have many Negrito groups in the Philippines).

The notion of the "vanishing savage" forms an ideological pattern recently explored, for example, by James Clifford, who points out that the pattern extends beyond ethnography.[19] He notes that, in *Middlemarch*, George Eliot uses a broadly ethnographic mode to describe a society placed about thirty years into the less industrialized past.[20] Clifford locates this ideological pattern primarily in the act of writing, the inscription of oral culture into textual modes. He argues that bringing a culture into writing, rather like sacrifice, simultaneously creates the culture as book and destroys it as oral life. Where I diverge from Clifford's view is when he asserts that ethnographic writing is primarily an allegory about writing, much in the modernist sense that the subject of much poetry is poetry itself. Surely such allegories are also related to the imperialist project.

What follows further explores imperialist nostalgia with a view to reaching the uncomfortable recognition that missionaries, constabulary officers, and ethnographers inhabit partially overlapping ideological spaces, as can be seen in the writings of William Jones, Michelle Rosaldo, and myself. Lest there be any confusion, I recognize that anthropologists have often used the notion of the "vanishing savage" to criticize the destructive intrusions of imperialism and its colonial regimes. Similarly, somewhat idealized versions of the "primitive" have served as foils against which to judge modern industrial society. In her film *To Keep the Balance*, for example, anthropologist Laura Nader uses a sympathetic portrait of Mexican Zapotec Indian legal practices to satirize "our" own more dehumanized system of law. Nonetheless, my discussion in what follows underscores the ideological similarities between anthropologists and the agents of change from which "we" so often attempt to separate ourselves.

While doing field research among the Ilongots, anthropologist William Jones wrote a letter home, dated February 25, 1909. Letters home, of course, are the exemplary genre for nostalgic discourse, and this one, as can be seen from the following, in which he laments what his own home—the Oklahoma territory—has become, was no exception:

I wish the plains could have remained as they were when I was a "kid." . . . I cannot put into words the feeling of remorse that rose within me at the things I saw. The whole region was disfigured with a most repelling ugliness—windmills, oil wells, wire fences. Go to so and so for drugs, go to another for groceries, and so on. The cowboy and the frontiersman were gone. The Indians were in overalls and looked like "bums." The picturesque costumes, the wigwams, horsemen, were things of the past. The virgin prairies were no more. And now they say that the place is a state! Nevertheless you saw the stars that I used to see. Did you ever behold clearer moonlight nights anywhere else? Did you hear the lone cry of the wolf and the yelp of the coyote? I wish you could have seen the longhorn and the old time punchers. The present would-be punchers are of a different build.[21]

Jones's longing for an irretrievably lost time, at once his childhood and a period of history, can appear almost natural, as if it were only human nature to be nostalgic for lost youth and bygone eras. His letter surely manifests authentic and deeply felt sentiments, yet even such pure subjectivity does not remain untouched by ideology.

About a decade before, Jones, then a Harvard student, an Indian, and a former cowboy, had been asked to serve in the Rough Riders as they prepared for the Spanish-American War, the invasion of Cuba, and the taking of the Philippines as an American colony. Written from the interior of America's colony, the letter home uses not a panhuman spontaneous sentiment but a discourse already appropriated by Teddy Roosevelt. Roosevelt, of course, attempted to mask the harsh realities of industrialization and immigration by invoking rugged individualism, especially as personified in the cowboy and the frontiersman.[22] His actual frontier was an imperialist venture in the Philippines, not the Wild West. Jones's feelings were at once genuine and shaped by North American nationalist ideology of the time. Even in Jones's heartfelt letter home, it becomes apparent that most cultural phenomena contain tacit ideologies, and most ideologies are culturally shaped. In other words, the terms *culture* and *ideology* refer more to distinct analytical perspectives than to separate realities.

In his field journal, written over the same period as the letters home, Jones strikes quite a different note. He describes, for example, hunting wild carabao or feral water buffalo with a group of Ilongots:

Mangurn ran crouching low; D. made it by standing erect. I could have clubbed him. The carabao then began to move away. I urged the two men to hurry; when we got to the ridge the herd had gone around it and were just entering the thick wood of the mountain. It was bitter disappointment, for from the ridge I could have had a fine shot. These people cannot come upon game like an Indian.[23]

Jones finds that the Ilongots, in contrast with American Indians, are miserable hunters. Hunting, the very activity around which James Fenimore Cooper could so readily construct a romance in the forest primeval, appears as a shabby field for disappointment. Possible nostalgia has been interrupted by nationalism, the sense that Philippine savages are inferior to the American variety.

Another representative passage from Jones's field journal shows a side of his activities, his material relations with the Ilongots, that a published ethnography would most probably have concealed. He often tells of the strain and distress created, on all sides, by the "gifts" he gave, both spontaneously and in compensation for specific services. Once, when he was going through his mail, an Ilongot woman and her boy came to ask him for brass wire, a scarce good much valued by Ilongots for making belts and jewelry:

While going through my mail in came Anan and her boy. She took her seat on the box near me. She was hardly through panting when she began begging for the wire. I asked her to wait, told her that I was busy and that we would see about it later. She almost broke into tears, her eyes watered; she told me it was hard work coming up the mountain, that it was painful to her legs. And this evening she and her husband took me aside and told me to give them the wire secretly at night, and that they would go home with it tomorrow without anyone seeing it! I was surprised to find that my remarks on such a course, that it was not a right thing to do, met with no heed.[24]

Jones's "gifts" of brass wire, cloth, combs, and beads to the Ilongots doubtless produced only small changes in their lives, but they were part of a larger economy that was penetrating the region. Although the ethnographer was not a central agent in transforming the Ilongot form of life, he did participate in and bear witness to the changes taking place under the colonial regime. Yet ethnographic discourse of

the time saw its mission as the textual preservation of traditional society. It would not have seen fit, as if it were
a breach of etiquette, to describe the exchanges of goods
and services between the ethnographer and the people under study.

Let me continue with a brief consideration of the research
that Michelle Rosaldo and I conducted among the Ilongots.
Like William Jones, letters home were no doubt the most
nostalgic texts I wrote about the Ilongots. In late December
1968, a group of Ilongots and I walked to the nearest lowland municipal center, where we witnessed the mayor's
inauguration on January 1. During that walk, my Ilongot
companions appeared in my imagination as if they were
Hollywood Apaches (at other times, incidentally, I imagined
them as pirates), and the towns we visited appeared (to me)
to be straight out of the Wild West. All of this entered letters
home in some detail, yet my field journal, with perhaps a
greater sense of decorum than Malinowski's indiscretions
would suggest, contains only the laconic phrase, "All very
frontier town," referring no doubt to my vivid fantasies of
cowboys and Indians. In my ethnography this nostalgia enters, but by then in an ironic mode: "Like William Jones, I
felt that I was bearing witness to the end of an era. Yet no
one would have been more surprised than Jones to learn
that nearly 60 years after his death I would be meeting
Ilongot young men who still walked about in G-strings
and red hornbill earrings (a sign of having taken a human
head)."[25] This, as I now see it, was an effort to undermine yet
acknowledge the force of an ideology, the quest to experience "real" fieldwork, that led me to the Ilongots in the first
place. Because there seemed to be no other available trope, I
recast nostalgia for the "vanishing savage" in the ironic
mode rather than as sincere romance. Had classic norms
still been in full force, I could have simply ignored what
Jones saw and did before me as well as the present-day social forces—loggers, settlers, missionaries, schools, and hy-
droelectric projects—that, under such a description, appear
alien to Ilongot traditional culture. At the time I could only

acknowledge (but not as fully as I now would) that the very processes that aided my presence among the Ilongots were bringing devastating changes on them.

In September 1981, Michelle Rosaldo and I returned for a brief visit among the Ilongots, and she wrote in her field journal: "Much of me wanted to write an article, a sort of nostalgia for a time when my nostalgia seemed to make more sense, reflections on the reason that if one were to start NOW one couldn't do as much blocking out of 'the outside' as we had previously." She goes on to speak of the changes she notices: people feel vulnerable to their future; they see hope in evangelical Christianity; they are more caught up in a cash economy; young men are smoking cigarettes instead of chewing betel nut; items of dress and material culture from less than a decade before have been discarded. Her observations redeploy the discourse used by the missionary Sarabelle Graves, who spoke with such passion about the smoking betel chewers versus the transformed converts, and the constabulary officer Wilfrid Turnbull, who took such sad note of the changes he witnessed on returning to his old haunts.

It seems that times had changed. Yet when Michelle's field journal described our initial trip to a projected field site, she said, "I was pained to find myself in quest of something everyone said was dying: where are their priests? do any young men learn this? which hamlets have most betel chewers, G-strings." When asked, people told her that item by item—priests, betel chewers, G-strings—the "traditional culture" was dying. Although she once embraced the romantic quest for the "vanishing savage," she now found it painful. No doubt it is easier, if perhaps more painful, to discern an ideological pattern as it begins to lose its grip. This chapter is part of a larger effort to speed the pattern's demise, all the while reminding "us" of our complicity with imperialism. Mourning the passing of traditional society and imperialist nostalgia cannot neatly be separated from one another. Both attempt to use a mask of innocence to cover their involvement with processes of domination.

This chapter began with the notion of imperialist nostalgia, the curious phenomenon of people's longing for what they themselves have destroyed. Rather than attempting an explanation in terms of a coherent self, a person who worships or reveres what he or she has killed, I have tried to show the place of this discourse within a heterogeneous field, where writers, such as Wilfrid Turnbull, can at once yearn for the old ways and acknowledge their warrior role in destroying them. Nostalgia at play with domination, as in Turnbull's relation with his Ilongot foster children, uses compelling tenderness to draw attention away from the relation's fundamental inequality. In my view, ideological discourses work more through selective attention than outright suppression.

Ethnography has participated in much the same ideological discourse as that of Sarabelle Graves and Wilfrid Turnbull. In Jones's case, official discourse suppresses painful observations: disappointment in Ilongot hunting prowess, excruciating material transactions, and the brutal changes he witnessed. Processes of drastic change often are the enabling condition of ethnographic field research, and herein resides the complicity of missionary, constabulary officer, and ethnographer. Just as Jones received visits from American constabulary officers during his field research, Michelle Rosaldo and I often used the missionary airplane for transportation in the Ilongot region. Jones did not police and we did not evangelize, but we all bore witness, and we participated, as relatively minor players, in the transformations taking place before our eyes.

Part Two · Reorientation

4 | *Putting Culture in Motion*

AFTER BEING WIDOWED in the autumn of 1981, I heard about a man who, shortly after his wife's death, put a sign on his refrigerator saying, "Life is what happens while you're making other plans."[1] Transported into the human sciences, the widower's sign cries out against theories of cultural interpretation that give too much primacy to explicit norms and static structures. What follows urges that social analysis recognize how much of life happens in ways that one neither plans nor expects. Plans and expectations themselves can also change in ways that are usually passed over in silence.

Perhaps a wise word from Ann Landers can clarify the practical grounds of this critique. In January 1984, her

91

column carried a letter from an adamantly heterosexual "middle-aged woman" who had "struck up a lovely friendship with Miss X":

We go to lunch together twice a week. After the second lunch she started to kiss me "hello" and "goodbye." I don't like it. I have a strange feeling that she might be one of those funny ones. If this kissing continues, our friendship must come to an end. But how does one find out for certain if she is—uh—different? I can't come right out and ask her. I would feel terrible if I ended our friendship on a hunch and later learned I was wrong. Please tell me what to do.

Ann Landers replied, "The 'evidence' you have cited is far from conclusive. Many straight women kiss hello and goodbye. Time is your best ally. Until you have something more specific to go on, don't jump to any hasty conclusions."

For all its fortune-cookie diction, this reply persuasively suggests that in everyday life the wise guide themselves as often by waiting to see how events unfold as by plans and predictions. When in doubt, people find out about their worlds by living with ambiguity, uncertainty, or simple lack of knowledge until the day, if and when it arrives, that their life experiences clarify matters. In other words, we often improvise, learn by doing, and make things up as we go along.

Ann Landers's reply indicates that people often live with ambiguity, spontaneity, and improvisation. Human relations can be negotiated, in dispute, or up for grabs. In such cases, fixed cultural expectations and social norms do not suffice as a guide to behavior. Classic ethnographies, on the other hand, often read as if they were a concerted effort to refute Ann Landers's reply. Under such descriptions, social life appears to be regulated by clear-cut, uniformly shared programs for behavior. In this view, human beings simply follow the rules, rather than waiting to see what time will tell.

The wisdom contained in Ann Landers's reply resembles a position developed within anthropology under the name *processual analysis*. This view stresses the case history method; it shows how ideas, events, and institutions interact and change through time. Such studies more nearly resemble the medical diagnosis of a particular patient than lawlike generalizations about a certain disease. Rather than asking, for example, about the causes of heart disease in general, such studies use a combination of generalizations and knowledge of specifics to make complex judgments about how to treat a patient who, say, exercises little, is of a certain age, and has angina, high blood pressure, a history of allergies, and a tendency toward obesity. One thus tries to understand particular cases by showing how a number of factors come together, rather than by separating them out, one by one, and showing their independent effects.

Dilemmas of Processual Analysis

Processual analysis resists frameworks that claim a monopoly on truth. It emphasizes that culture requires study from a number of perspectives, and that these perspectives cannot necessarily be added together into a unified summation. This position, of course, remains controversial. In a recent review essay on the concepts of "system" and "process," anthropologist Joan Vincent concludes that the capacity of systems thinking to generalize makes it more scientific than the ability of processual analysis to diagnose particular cases. "Systems metaphors" she says, "have tended to be hegemonic in professional anthropological discourse; a propensity to systematize is ever present. Processual metaphors have been historically subordinate because of their 'nonscientific' character."[2] Vincent thus interprets the conflict between systems thought and processual analysis as a political battle in which the former occupies a hegemonic position and the latter a subordinate one. In this conflict, however, the (in)subordinate position has gained urgency, momentum, and coherence since the late 1960s.

Anthropologists Clifford Geertz and the late Victor Turner have played leading roles in developing methodologies of processual analysis that practitioners have used in navigating seas made heavy by the barrages of systems thinking. They have spoken of informal practices and cultural performances, and they have given a central place to the study of case histories.[3] Under the rubric of the "social drama," Turner has made the case history the cornerstone of his methodology. Alongside his focus on cultural systems, Geertz has similarly emphasized "thick description," "documentary method," and "deep play."[4]

Although Geertz and Turner have hastened the erosion of classic norms of social description, their early work shows particularly well how a paradigm in decline often loses its grip slowly and unevenly, more quickly or completely here than there. Like an archaic cultural pattern at odds with its present context, certain central tenets of classic norms have persisted even in the work of those who have labored most to hasten their demise. The conceptual dilemma of past norms working against present projects is manifest in the peculiar disparity between thick descriptions and thin conclusions displayed in their use of case histories. In my view, this gap separating description and conclusion derives from an unresolved tension about whether to describe cultures as loosely tied bundles of informal practices, or as well-formed systems regulated by control mechanisms, or as the interplay of both.

In an influential essay on interpretive theory, for example, Geertz presents a case history from Morocco in about 1912.[5] The French had just arrived on the scene as colonial enforcers of peace when a group of Berbers robbed a Jewish merchant named Cohen and killed two of his companions. Cohen then asked the French to collect indemnity due him under traditional rules of the trade pact. The officials told him that this matter did not come under their law, but he could go ahead and try to collect. "If you get killed," they added, "it's your problem." Amazingly enough, Cohen recruited his allies from another Berber group and collected his payment: some five hundred sheep in all. When the French officials saw Cohen's success, they concluded that he must be a Berber spy (for how otherwise could he have done the impossible?), and threw him in prison. After his release from prison, Cohen complained to the local French colonel, who told him, "I can't do anything about the matter. It's not my problem."

After presenting his case history, Geertz provides a summarizing conclusion in which he describes his analytical task as

sorting out the structures of signification . . . and determining their social ground and import. Here, in our text, such sorting would begin with distinguishing the three unlike frames of interpretation ingredient in the situation, Jewish, Berber, and French, and would then move on to show how (and why) at that time, in that place, their copresence produced a situation in which systematic misunderstanding reduced traditional form to social farce. What tripped Cohen up, and with him the whole, ancient pattern of social and economic relationships within which he functioned, was a confusion of tongues.[6]

According to Geertz, the whole episode involved a series of misunderstandings, which most insightfully can be sorted out along cultural vectors separating Jews, Berbers, and French.

Yet an analysis in terms of social farce and a confusion of tongues stresses free-floating cultural idioms in a manner that seems inadequate to the violence done by the robbery of Cohen, the murder of his two companions, the startling indemnity payment, and the subsequent imprisonment of Cohen. What if one redescribed the three frames of cultural misunderstanding as the colonial culture of brutal disagreements? The latter description, for example, highlights the newborn colonial regime's predictable uncertainties about when to use force and when to compel people to help themselves ("it's your problem") rather than receive official help. Even an analysis in terms of the confusion of tongues, however, should note the unequal, shifting, and often ambiguous power relations among the parties to the conversation. Geertz's actual case history reveals much more about the conflict than he indicates in his conclusion about failures of communication resulting from cultural incomprehension.

A similar disparity between dense case histories and slender conclusions appears in Turner's social dramas. In his classic ethnography on the Ndembu of east Africa, Turner presents a series of cases that involve witchcraft, slander, death, and power struggles, all placed within a field of social contention.[7] Nonetheless, his conclusions usually reduce complex human dramas to mere illustrations of supposedly explanatory structural principles. "This book," he says, "is dominantly a study of social conflict and of the social mechanisms brought into play to reduce, exclude or resolve that conflict. Beneath all other conflicts in Ndembu society is the concealed opposition between men and women over descent and in the economic system."[8] Yet the social dramas make it apparent, first, that structural principles cause as much conflict as they contain and, second, that they fail to explain many things about why the dramas unfolded as they did. Turner says, for example, that a woman was accused of witchcraft because she was an outsider to the group, prodigiously hard-working, and sexually promiscuous. Yet from the accused woman's viewpoint, structural principles concerning descent and labor produced more disturbance than they resolved. Nor did any structural principle determine either her diligence or her adultery. His concluding analysis fails to convey the understanding embodied in his case materials about how and why things happened as they did. Put otherwise, Turner's conclusions emphasize principles of social structure more than the human processes he so thickly dramatizes.

Culture, Control, and the Nightmare of Chaos

The divide separating thick case histories from thin conclusions in the early work of Geertz and Turner arguably derives from their shared conviction that culture and society must be regarded as mechanisms of control. For Geertz, distinct Jewish, Berber, and French "cultural systems" determine divergent ways of understanding human relations;

for Turner, a number of "social structural" mechanisms regulate endemic Ndembu conflicts of gender, descent, and economics. Paradoxically, their concluding focus on issues of social control tends to exclude precisely the informal cultural practices whose study they elsewhere advocate and whose workings their case studies so effectively illuminate.

In characterizing his case history methodology, Victor Turner explicitly equates culture and society with control mechanisms. He asserts that "individual and group structures, carried in people's heads and nervous systems, have a steering function, a 'cybernetic' function, in the endless succession of social events, imposing on them the degree of order they possess."[9] Turner's exploration of social order uses an up-to-date cybernetic image to express a classic view of the need for social mechanisms to control violent human nature. Culture and society thus have the function of regulating human behavior.

Similarly, an early essay by Clifford Geertz broadly equates the concept of culture with a cybernetic control mechanism:

I want to propose two ideas. The first of these is that culture is best seen not as complexes of concrete behavior patterns—customs, usages, traditions, habit clusters—as has, by and large, been the case up to now, but as a set of control mechanisms—plans, recipes, rules, instructions (what computer engineers call "programs")—for the governing of behavior. The second idea is that man is precisely the animal most desperately dependent upon such extragenetic, outside-the-skin control mechanisms, such cultural programs, for ordering his behavior.[10]

Because human beings have been given "incomplete" genetic programs, our species cannot get its bearings in daily life until we acquire cultural gyroscopes. Culture of necessity becomes analogous to genetic instructions that tell us how to do the things we do in our workaday lives.

Geertz goes on to invoke the nightmare that would result if human beings were suddenly shorn of their cultural control mechanisms. In a vivid passage, rather reminiscent of literature of the fantastic, he explains:

There is no such thing as a human nature independent of culture. Men without culture would not be the clever savages of Golding's *Lord of the Flies* thrown back upon the cruel wisdom of their animal instincts; nor would they be the nature's noblemen of Enlightenment primitivism or even, as classical anthropological theory would imply, intrinsically talented apes who had somehow failed to find themselves. They would be unworkable monstrosities with very few useful instincts, fewer recognizable sentiments, and no intellect: mental basket cases.[11]

Must one agree that without cultural plans humans become grotesque creatures disoriented beyond any capacity for desire, feeling, or thought? Do our options really come down to the vexed choice between supporting cultural order or yielding to the chaos of brute idiocy?

This stark Manichaean choice between order and chaos has more than accidental affinities with its nineteenth-century antecedents, most notably Matthew Arnold's opposition between culture and anarchy. Ultimately, it refers to an earlier position, usually attributed to Hobbes, that without regulative norms people become pathologically violent. In characterizing this view, as I am, only to disagree, Harry Stack Sullivan has said, "One of the great social theories is, you know, that society is the only thing that prevents everybody from tearing everybody to bits."[12] Although often implicit, this view has so profoundly informed social analysis that one often equates culture with order (as against chaos) and social norms with regulation (as against anarchic violence). By and large, the phrases "cultural order" and "normative regulation" are more redundant than informative.

In their conceptions of society and culture as control mechanisms, Geertz and Turner reveal the lingering influence of the Hobbesian vision of violence inherited by classic ethnography from turn-of-the-century French sociologist

Emile Durkheim. In his early writings, Durkheim equated the social, his field of study, with constraint and the law. This theoretical view linking—indeed, usually conflating— society, constraint, and the law was developed in opposition to the utilitarian notion that maximizing the greatest number of individual interests simultaneously maximizes the social good. In this context, Durkheim waxes Hobbesian as he argues for the need to impose social order. "Where interest," he says, "is the only ruling force each individual finds himself in a state of war with every other since nothing comes to mollify the egos, and any truce in this eternal antagonism would not be of long duration. There is nothing less constant than interest. Today, it unites me to you; tomorrow, it will make me your enemy."[13] In alluding to the "war of one against all," Durkheim attempts by fiat to demonstrate the basic violence of human nature and the consequent need for social regulation. Elsewhere he reiterates his vision of the social violence that prevails in a "state of nature" devoid of social regulation. "Human passions," he explains, "stop only before a moral power they respect. If all authority of this kind is wanting, the law of the strongest prevails, and latent or active, the state of war is necessarily chronic. That such anarchy is an unhealthy phenomenon is quite evident, since it runs counter to the aim of society which is to suppress, or at least to moderate, war among men, subordinating the law of the strongest to a higher law."[14] That few could desire such open warfare is clear enough. What remains less clear is why social violence should be "natural," and why the imposition of moral authority should be the paramount task of "culture." Why does Durkheim leave so little space between the rule of order and the eruption of chaos? Built on the twin imperatives of integration and regulation, Durkheim's theory of social order goes hand in hand with an only barely articulated what-would-happen-if vision of chaos. Although his theory rests on the threat of mayhem following a collapse of social norms, he rarely gives serious study to the dark side of his vision.

Arguably, social analysis has clung to its diffuse anxiety about impending chaos precisely because, following in Durkheim's footsteps, its nightmare qualities have been left so vague. The vision of chaos following the collapse of the sociocultural order induces a feeling of panic. One cannot help but feel threatened at the prospect of random violence and wholesale destruction. The television film *The Day After,* for example, played out this view in much the manner that "survivalism," defending oneself against rapacious others after nuclear attack, does so in its own settings.[15] In social thought this dreamlike vision of chaos appears more in oblique allusions than in the explicit conceptual treatments granted to such terms as the cultural order and normative regulation. One rarely finds any serious effort to specify the conditions under which such a sociocultural collapse could occur. Nor do many analysts, in this theoretical context, inquire into the causes of such actual human catastrophes as those in Indonesia, Bangladesh, Uganda, Cambodia, and El Salvador (to mention only recent instances).

Social analysis succeeds in using suggestive innuendo to invoke the nightmare vision because of its resonance with current political rhetoric. In such contexts, the vision of chaos appears more as a trope for use in debate (an only half-revealed threat of "what would happen if . . .") than as a subject for analysis. In January 1984, for example, a local newspaper carried a story on a military coup in Nigeria that reported that the country's new ruler, Major Gen. Mohammed Buhari, defended the need for his intervention, saying that, had he not acted, "the whole country would have suffered economic collapse and political chaos."[16] Whether or not they thought the coup was justified, most commentators asserted that the threat of chaos invoked by Buhari was exaggerated at best. The nightmare of chaos invoked by such politicians appears to be more an attempt to persuade by innuendo than a convincing assessment of their situation.

In a more amusing case of social thought's nightmare vision as it appears in everyday life, the same local newspaper in April 1984 reported that a controversy over the "threat" posed by vagrants had erupted in the town of Santa Cruz on the California coast.[17] Conservative critics of the town's liberal officeholders saw violence and chaos as the certain result of allowing itinerants to walk the streets and frequent the local boardwalk. One critic, for example, said, "There's an air of violence in this town which no one's addressing. . . . There's too loose an atmosphere. There's no control over what goes on down there." A liberal councilwoman countered by admitting that certain vagrants on the boardwalk indeed do things that "make people uncomfortable and in some cases downright scared." But, she added, "Some of the things people do there, like muttering to the sun, just are not illegal." Despite the inflated rhetoric of conservative critics, one can safely say that the visions of violent chaos on the streets of Santa Cruz have probably not yet reached the point of justifying a local military dictatorship.

Let me add a brief anecdote, again on visions of the collapse of norms, from my own field research in the Philippines. Ilongots found it difficult to discuss the statistically rare cases of adultery in their society. One day an old woman named Baket, by then in her nineties, was telling me the few adultery stories she had heard over her long lifetime. She acted uneasy in part because her memory was failing and in part because she felt embarrassed to say that such things happened among the Ilongots. At one point she stopped short in mid-tale and asked, "Does this kind of thing happen in your country?" I laughed. Hoping to reassure her, I said that Americans committed adultery much more often than Ilongots. Instead of the relief I expected, a look of shock spread over her face as she asked, "You mean it's spread?"

Baket's anxious vision of contagious adultery rather uncomfortably resembles the domino theory of norms held by social thinkers in a persisting tradition that extends from Hobbes through Durkheim to the classic norms of ethnography. Curiously enough, social analysts who focus on the imposition of order rarely investigate actual eruptions of violence and chaos. Evidently, Durkheim's anxiety about chaos and being out of control cannot easily be laid to rest.

The Space between Order and Chaos

Much as chapter 2 tries to displace classic norms without discarding them, this one attempts to decenter, not eliminate, the study of control mechanisms. The point is to break objectivism's monopoly on truth claims, not throw out the baby with the bathwater. In certain respects, after all, cultural practices do conform to codes and norms. People make plans, and sometimes their plans do work out. Not all expectations remain unmet. Conventional wisdom does not always fail. Yet there is more to human culture than the image of cybernetic steering functions suggests.

When the workings of culture are reduced to those of a control mechanism, such phenomena as passions, spontaneous fun, and improvised activities tend to drop out of sight. An exclusive focus on Durkheim's "problem of order" rules out of bounds all the things that can happen while you're making other plans. It reduces to undifferentiated chaos everything that falls outside the normative order. In my view, social analysis should look beyond the dichotomy of order versus chaos toward the less explored realm of "nonorder."

Surely, as Ann Landers suggests, we often live with uncertainty, giving further life experiences a chance to sort themselves out. Human conduct often results from improvisation. People can even plan to improvise by saying that they'll take things as they come, go one step at a time, or play it by ear. Without intending to do so ahead of time, they can respond to unforeseen contingencies by making it up as they go along. Their improvisations can be earnest, playful, or both; their unexpected life events can be joyous, neutral, or catastrophic.

A focus on nonorder directs attention to how people's actions alter the conditions of their existence, often in ways they neither intend nor foresee. Insofar as it is concerned with how people's actions alter their forms of life, social analysis must attend to improvisation, muddling through, and contingent events. In this context, the study of consciousness becomes central because people always act (however imperfectly) relative to their desires, plans, whims, strategies, moods, goals, fantasies, intentions, impulses, purposes, visions, or gut feelings. No analysis of human action is complete unless it attends to people's own notions of what they are doing. Even when they appear most subjective, thought and feeling are always culturally shaped and influenced by one's biography, social situation, and historical context.

Furthermore, from a processual perspective, change rather than structure becomes society's enduring state, and time rather than space becomes its most encompassing medium. Even on the terrain of natural history, such supposed ecological final states as "the succession to grassland climax" are subject to long-term transformation, as the geographer Carl Sauer has noted:

Systems of classification arose that identified plant and animal complexes with climate. Thus there arose the concept of the "ecologic climax," currently defined as "the final or stable type of plant community reached in a particular climate." A postulate tends to displace reality. Climatic regions are cartographic abstractions, useful as elementary teaching devices to give some first notions of weather contrasts over the earth. "Final or stable" communities are quite exceptional in nature: weather, soils, and surfaces are continually changing; new organisms are immigrating or forming, old ones may be giving way. Change is the order of nature: climax assumes the end of change.[18]

For Sauer, change follows no regular sequence, no lawlike succession, no cultural stages. Changes occur through historical time in a continuous, ongoing fashion, without cessation. Sauer's analysis decenters structures because, with the passage of sufficient time, they either change into other structures or decay and collapse.

In this context, it is worth noting that Durkheim's memorable saying about the enduring character of society—that, like the languages we speak, it exists before, during, and after our lifetimes—was long ago appropriated and reworked, in a more processual vein, by the literary theorist Kenneth Burke. In illustrating his dramatistic mode of analysis, Burke uses the parable of a conversation that goes on before, during, and after any talker's lifetime:

Imagine that you enter a parlor. You come late. When you arrive, others have long preceded you, and they are engaged in a heated discussion, a discussion too heated for them to pause and tell you exactly what it is about. In fact, the discussion had already begun before any of them got there, so that no one present is qualified to retrace for you all the steps that had gone on before. You listen for a while, until you decide that you have caught the tenor of the argument; then you put in your oar. Someone answers; you answer him; another comes to your defence; another aligns himself against you, to either the embarrassment or gratification of your opponent, depending upon the quality of your ally's assistance. However, the discussion is interminable. The hour grows late, you must depart. And you do depart, with the conversation still in progress.[19]

Burke's parable of the endless conversation with no known beginning or ending departs from the monumentalist's preoccupation with permanence and puts the unchanging foundation of classic norms into perpetual motion. You arrive, and the conversation is already in progress; you depart, and it continues without you. More an argument than a cozy chat, the conversation embodies conflict and change. Taking the form of challenge and response, this eternal debate outlives the structures that shape any of its particular phases.

Recent social thinkers have updated Burke's style of analysis by identifying the interplay of "structure" and "agency" as a central issue in social theory.[20] Most central for them, in other words, is the question of how received structures shape human conduct, and how, in turn, human conduct alters received structures. Most disciplines, they say, fail to combine an actor's perspective with a more sociocentric one. Certain fields, such as ethnomethodology, focus on actors' intentions, and others, such as classic ethnography, concentrate on objective determinants of human action. This intellectual division of labor proves debilitating because it obscures the perception that social life is both inherited *and* always being changed.

Most social theorists who invoke the structure/agency dialectic cite a passage from the beginning of Karl Marx's *18th Brumaire of Louis Bonaparte*. Having just stated, with heavy irony, that history repeats itself, appearing first as tragedy and then as farce, Marx says, "Men make their own history, but they do not make it just as they please; they do not make it under circumstances chosen by themselves, but under circumstances directly encountered, given and transmitted from the past."[21] In other words, people make their own histories, but under conditions not of their own choosing, and (the theorists often add) with consequences they did not intend. Marx's dictum stresses the interplay of structure and agency, rather than granting primacy to one or the other.

Topics that thus become central include, among others, consciousness, collective mobilization, and improvisation in everyday life practices. This redirection of cultural studies makes social inequalities and processes of social transformation particularly critical for study. In asking such questions, social analysis redefines its goals and its subject matter by attempting to focus on the unfolding interplay of political struggles, social inequalities, and cultural differences.

Politics, Feelings, and Tempo

Processual analysis concerns itself with a certain "something more" that can neither be reduced to nor derived from structure. In what follows I sketch three related yet distinct versions of a certain "something more" that transcends structure. Raymond Williams, Pierre Bourdieu, and E. P. Thompson assert that feelings, the tempo of everyday life, and the making of class formations cannot simply be deduced from structural factors.

The social historian E. P. Thompson begins his major work on the formation of the English working class by insisting that time is the primary medium of his analysis. For him, class is an active process of making rather than a thinglike structure. Class formations make themselves through an ongoing historical process where "we," who stand united in struggle against "them," forge an identity that can be discerned only as it unfolds over an extended period of time. "The notion of class," Thompson says, "entails the notion of historical relationship. Like any other relationship, it is a fluency which evades analysis if we attempt to stop it dead at any given moment and anatomise its structure."[22] Class formation is an active process rather than a static product; it becomes evident only over the course of extended struggle, and it cannot be frozen for analytical inspection. When preserved as a static object within a slice in time, the phenomenon of class crumbles into so many discrete individuals. It becomes visible only when its members make it so by establishing patterned relationships, institutions, and ideas. Class consciousness cannot, in any simple sense, be derived from class position, or from knowledge of another level of analysis.

Cultural theorist Raymond Williams similarly argues that objectivist social analysis conflates society with already completed processes. When society is reduced to fixed forms, social processes elude analysis. Williams argues that the processes he calls structures of feeling (a deliberate paradox) both shape and reflect the quality of social relations. Structures of feeling differ from such concepts as "worldview" and "ideology" because they are just emerging, still implicit, and not yet fully articulate. Instead, they so tightly interweave feeling and thought as to make them indistinguishable. "We are talking," he says, "about characteristic elements of impulse, restraint, and tone; specifically affective elements of consciousness and relationships: not feeling against thought, but thought as felt and feeling as thought: practical consciousness of a present kind, in a living and inter-relating community."[23] Thought and feeling are inseparable, rather than being opposed as cognition and affect, or reason and the irrational. Ideas are felt, and feelings are conceived. Related parts held in tension, these forms are in transition between being experienced as private and becoming recognized as social.

In *Outline of a Theory of Practice*, French sociologist Pierre Bourdieu argues from roughly the same point of departure as Williams and Thompson. He asserts that objectivism describes completed human events, which therefore can be depicted as totalities, complete with synoptic diagrams and governing rules. What already did happen (and no longer cannot happen) becomes conflated with what necessarily had to happen. Operating in a timeless realm, objectivist social analysis blinds itself to the ways cultural practices are fundamentally defined by their tempo.

Human subjects perceive their practices differently than objectivist social analysts because they are differently positioned. The latter see things from on high, after the fact, with the wisdom of hindsight. They view the past all at once, in its timeless entirety. For the former, on the other hand, timing is of the essence. They orient to their lives as if from midstream because precisely what will happen next, and when it will happen, cannot be predicted. The future, by its very nature, is uncertain.

Working with the minutiae of everyday life, Bourdieu shows how tempo constitutes, rather than being "added onto," cultural practices; to abolish the interval is also to abolish strategy. The period interposed, which must neither be too short (as is clearly seen in gift exchange) nor too long (especially in the exchange of revenge-murders), is quite the opposite of the inert gap of time, the time lag that the objectivist model makes of it. Until they have given in return, receivers are *"obliged,"* expected to show their gratitude toward their benefactors, or, at least, to have regard for them, to refrain from using against them all the weapons they otherwise might, to pull their punches, lest they be accused of ingratitude and stand condemned by "what people say," which is what gives their actions their social meaning.[24] The tempo of cultural practices is laden with consequences and meanings. Atemporal accounts rob such practices of their politics and their cultural significance.

Bourdieu's analysis can be brought home by considering the role of timing in dinner party invitations. In the objectivist view, reciprocity seems to be the golden rule of the dinner party circuit. It organizes and perpetuates social solidarity. I invite you. You invite me in return. The gift demands a countergift, the countergift demands another, and so it goes, back and forth forever.

Most dinner party circuits, however, turn out to function less smoothly than the proverbial well-oiled pendulum. The tempo of the dinner party itself can vary significantly. When hosts provide drinks, dinner, dessert, and then usher their guests out the door in fifty-seven minutes flat, they most probably will—and, in the one case I witnessed, they certainly did—provoke disgruntled gossip. Or think of how I felt when a dinner guest, who was a friend of a friend, appeared, as planned, at a lecture later the same evening, and then introduced himself to me as if we had never met. Or suppose that your dinner guests say farewell by inviting you to dine at their house the very next evening. Or imagine how you would feel if somebody you regard as a close friend waits several years to return your invitation. The timing of reciprocal dinner party invitations reflects and creates relations of differing qualities, from intimate friendship to formal collegiality. In such cases, timing is indeed of the essence.

Thompson, Williams, and Bourdieu have so influenced a certain strand of recent anthropological thought that they are often cited these days as if they were ancestral figures. Their critical dialogue with ethnography and cultural studies has significantly shaped the shift from classic norms to the current remaking of social analysis. Their writings have inspired work on relations of inequality, forms of domination, political mobilization, resistance movements, the critique of ideology, and the practices of everyday life.

5 | *Ilongot Improvisations*

WHEN ANTHROPOLOGISTS SPEAK informally about the pleasures and hardships of fieldwork, they often reflect on the liberation and bafflement of abandoning clock time for quite different tempos of life. In some versions, the so-called natives are habitually late. In others, they have a different sense of time. In yet others, they have no sense of time at all. Yet, for all the work on the cultural construction of time, little has been written on the tempo of everyday life in other cultures. Evidently, a paramount reality of other people's daily lives has eluded the ethnographer's grasp.

Ethnographers' sentiments about abandoning clock time probably echo feelings learned closer to home. The English labor historian E. P. Thompson, for example, has analyzed

109

the protracted struggle that eventually resulted in the "time-discipline" that appears so natural in Anglo-American society: "In all these ways—by the division of labour; the supervision of labour; fines; bells and clocks; money incentives; preachings and schoolings; the suppression of fairs and sports—new labour habits were formed, and a new time-discipline was imposed."[1] Those in our society who fail to conform to the painfully imposed "time-discipline" are commonly described as living by C.P.T. (colored people's time), Indian Time, or Mexican Time. To make my own position clear, I should hasten to say that my having known Mexican Time from the inside has not kept me from having experienced the ethnographer's dilemma of being just plain perplexed about when ceremonial events in other cultures were about to begin.

The tempo of social being I shall attempt to characterize in this chapter usually has been described by its absences, or more precisely, by contrast with its supposed opposite. "We" have "time-discipline," and "they" have, well, something else (or, as we say these days, Otherness). The former quality of time can be described in relation to cultural artifacts, such as clocks, calendars, appointment books, and the like. More significantly, it can be understood in connection with capitalists' desire to discipline and synchronize the labor force, rationalizing production and maximizing profits, but probably not enhancing the quality of life. Certainly this is the drift of the persuasive analyses put forth by E. P. Thompson, and before him, Max Weber.

Weber made the very qualities he studied, discipline and rationalization, appear strange by contrasting them with what he called traditionalism. He illustrated his argument with a hypothetical case in which the employer, who pays piece rates, tries to speed up the labor process by increasing wages, but to no avail. The workers, who have no notion of "work-discipline," respond by slowing the pace of their labor. Rather than trying to maximize their daily earnings by working as hard as possible, they follow "tradition" by keeping their "needs" constant and earning today the same amount they earned in the past. Reflecting on his anecdote, Weber says, "This is an example of what is here meant by traditionalism. A man does not 'by nature' wish to earn more and more money, but simply to live as he is accustomed to live and to earn as much as is necessary for that purpose."[2] Although "we" assume that people will earn as much as possible in a day, Weber argues that in fact such behavior is historically and culturally peculiar, and requires further investigation. In accord with his project, he makes capitalism appear strange, and thus need explanation. At the same time, he follows the technique of negative characterization, by saying what tradition is *not* rather than what it is, and turns it into a residual category. To follow customary practice, in his view, appears to be a matter of human nature that requires no explanation.

The Indeterminacy of "Indian Time"

Although ethnographers have made their project the comprehension of traditionalisms, they have not escaped the problem of characterizing the tempo of social life in "traditional" societies more through absences than in positive terms. The anthropological linguist Susan Philips, for example, has called attention to the quality of time I should like to explore. In a suggestive paper, called "Warm Springs 'Indian Time,'" Philips correctly criticizes ethnographic writings for reducing time to the concepts of segmentation and sequencing.[3] Her analytical goal is to broaden the range of temporal phenomena under study. Her point of departure is that Indian Time appears primarily when non-Indians attend or participate in Indian events, as in the following vivid typification: "They [non-Indians] try to learn from Indians at what time the event will begin. Often the person questioned will say he doesn't know, but if pressed, he may give a specific time—e.g., 8 P.M. or 'some time after 9.' The non-Indians will arrive at that time, only to find that 'nothing is happening' yet, and no one seems to know when something will happen. They may wait anywhere from twenty minutes to several hours before the event 'begins.'"[4] Philips's analysis of Indian Time concentrates on a series of social factors that produce variability and indeterminacy in the timing of ceremonial events. Her factors include whether or not individuals commit themselves to participate, the degree of interdependence among actors, the number of participants needed or possible for an event to take place, and whether the number of repetitions of particular actions is preset or open-ended. Indian Time thus reaches its maximum with absence of commitment to participate, high interdependence among actors, an indeterminate number of actors needed or possible, and open-ended repetitions of particular actions.

By identifying the sources of indeterminacy, Philips has gone part way along the path I wish to follow. My analysis begins where hers leaves off. Instead of concluding with the identification of sources of indeterminacy, I shall start by suggesting that they constitute a social space within which creativity can flourish.

In my view, optionality, variability, and unpredictability produce positive qualities of social being rather than negative zones of analytically empty randomness. Far from being devoid of positive content (presumably because of not being rule-governed), indeterminacy allows the emergence of a culturally valued quality of human relations where one can follow impulses, change directions, and coordinate with other people. In other words, social unpredictability has its distinctive tempo, and it permits people to develop timing, coordination, and a knack for responding to contingencies. These qualities constitute social grace, which in turn enables an attentive person to be effective in the interpersonal politics of everyday life.

Tempo, Social Grace, and Ilongot Visiting

I shall argue that among the Ilongots zones of indeterminacy, particularly in social visits, promote a human capacity for improvisation in response to the unexpccted, and this very capacity can be celebrated as a cultural value. For the moment, however, let me follow Ilongot decorum by approaching gradually the topic of visiting. As a first step, the Ilongots and their notion of visiting now require more extended introduction.

Visiting defines and displays the qualities of Ilongot social relations even more centrally than the kinship system. It would be difficult to exaggerate its import. My field journal assiduously reported who arrived at and who departed from each house in the settlement. During some six months of 1969 I also recorded the number of people who slept overnight in the home where Michelle Rosaldo and I resided. (Almost all overnight guests are "visitors" from other settlements because people from the same settlement virtually always return to their own home for the night.) In that period our household of fourteen permanent members had a low of six and a high of 36 people sleeping overnight. The totals for a representative sequence of days ran as follows: 14, 17, 8, 25, 16. In addition to their brute frequency, visits are a staple of ordinary conversation. They are frequently talked about, both as noteworthy events in themselves and because they bring guests who provide news about other people and places. Here the key term is *beita*, referring at once to a kind of speech, small talk (as opposed, for example, to oratory or storytelling), and to its content, a noteworthy item or news.

Visits, the practices Ilongots call *ba-at*, occur between households of different settlements rather than within a single settlement. People *ba-at* simply to visit, trade, borrow, court, or plan a raid. Visitors can be invited to lend their labor for house building, pollarding, planting, or harvesting; or to support family members afflicted by serious illness; or to participate in meetings about bride-wealth or local conflicts. Visits can, of course, have multiple purposes, carried out simultaneously, in sequence, or both. A visit can also begin as one thing and turn into something quite different. The casual visitor, for example, can be enlisted to hunt, or the young man who came to help pollard can initiate a courtship or be obliged to stay on during an uncle's illness.

Marked by open-endedness, visiting often serves as a metonym for social life. In describing their past lives, for example, Ilongots speak of walking on paths that meander, like the courses of streams they follow, in ways that cannot be foreseen. In depicting residential moves, they talk about a coordinated unfolding among agents at once autonomous and accountable to one another. Ilongot visiting, in such contexts, comprises a concrete exemplar of forms of social life marked by mutually adjusted action and an openness to uncertain futures. Visits are improvised, made up as people go along. Social grace, a culturally valued quality of human intelligence, consists of one's responsiveness to whims, desires, and contingencies, whether these emanate from one's own heart or from those of one's partners in action.

When asked to describe a visit from beginning to end, Ilongots invariably started with the host's account of the guest's arrival rather than with the latter's departure from home. Ilongots say that, when a visitor approaches the house, hosts and guests alike neither speak nor make any other noise. Silence is the only form of greeting.

A man named Tukbaw said, "If you talk, the others will think you're talking about them. The host [pan-abung, 'house owner'] should speak first. That person can say a number of things, such as 'Are you people from there well?' If we just talk abruptly, people take it badly."

Tukbaw's sister-in-law, Sawad, said that visitors do not speak first because they wait "for their sweat to sink in, for their heart [rinawa] to stretch out in happiness [ruyuk]. The host then asks, 'Are you people from there well?'" Visitors speak first only if there is urgent news, like the incipient arrival of soldiers or enemy Ilongot raiders. Otherwise, Sawad elaborated, the visitor "simply waits to be fed."

Another man, named Talikaw, said, "We hush up the kids because they are too noisy for our visitors." When visitors arrive, he said, "We give them betel nut to chew. We go to pound rice because they are hungry. When they finish eating we ask for their news [beita]. We ask, 'Are you people from there well?'"

A cognitive anthropologist could readily rewrite Ilongot typifications of arrival scenes in the form of culturally appropriate expectations. These expectations have formed the evidentiary basis of cultural description for ethnoscientists, such as Charles Frake (author of the pertinent classic essays, "How to Ask for a Drink in Subanun" and "How to Enter a Yakan House"), who has depicted his project as follows:

This conception of a cultural description implies that an ethnography should be a theory of cultural behavior in a particular society, the adequacy of which is to be evaluated by the ability of a stranger to the culture (who may be the ethnographer) to use the ethnography's statements as instructions for appropriately anticipating the scenes of the society. I say "appropriately anticipate" rather than "predict" because a failure of an ethnographic statement to predict correctly does not necessarily imply descriptive inadequacy as long as the members of the described society are as surprised by the failure as is the ethnographer. The test of descriptive adequacy must always refer to informants' interpretations of events, not simply to the occurrence of events.[5]

Cultural typifications thus are understood as distillations of past experience that allow natives and ethnographers to anticipate (but not predict) what will happen during future arrival scenes.

Viewed in this manner, Ilongot arrival scenes could be segmented into the following phases: (1) the proper greeting of silence; (2) the hosts giving their guests betel quids and food; (3) the hosts asking the guests for their news, saying "Are you people from there well?"

Such typifications better enable ethnographers and natives alike to understand how variations in the actual enactment of these scenes can be interpreted (in relation to a standard code) as perfunctory, clumsy, angry, formal, proper, or graceful.[6] Yet the inclination of cognitive anthropology has been to delineate the code and ignore the actual performances, whether perfunctory, graceful, or somewhere in between.

In due time I shall return to these arrival scenes with a

view to exploring the insight yielded by moving from the code of cultural typifications to the social qualities at play in actual practices. In my view, the analysis of typifications is but a point of departure. By itself, it says little about the qualities of social relations displayed and created in the context of arrivals. For the time being, let us move one step at a time in this presentation and continue to mimic the meandering path of Ilongot visitors.

My field journals are laced with reports on (and accounts of discussions of) the comings and goings of visitors and the news brought by them. Visits were intricately woven into the fabric of daily life. Indeed *ba-at* soon became a distinct ethnographic category entered on four-by-six cards. A typical early entry runs as follows: "Lapur stayed with his brother-in-law. He spent three nights."

When I wrote my entries on visits it did not occur to me that I was following a conventional form often found in small-town newspapers. *The Listowel Banner* from western Ontario, for example, carries a regular "Personals" section with about thirty weekly entries on such transitions as deaths, births, weddings, illnesses, and visits. The vast majority of these entries, however, concern visits. The following are representative examples of such entries (all from the issue of September 26, 1984, p. 16):

—Mrs. Goldie Thompson and Mrs. Cathy Cahill of Toronto spent a few days with Mr. and Mrs. George Greer of Holland Centre.
—Mr. and Mrs. Lane Vogan, RR 2, Wroxeter, have returned home following a nine-day holiday trip to Cape Cod. The local couple travelled by bus, crossing into the United States at Niagara Falls. Mr. Vogan notes that it was raining as they left Listowel and raining as they returned, but the sun shone every day while they were away on their trip. They also found the leaves were in vivid colors as they made the return journey.
—Recent visitors with Mrs. Margaret Hawksbee included Mr. and Mrs. Adam Hackett of Vancouver, B.C., Miss Lillian Hackett of Mitchell, Canon and Mrs. C. F. Heathcote of Burlington, and Mr. and Mrs. Harvey Bride of Don Mills.

My entries and *The Listowel Banner's* resemble one another in being cultural forms that register visits as bits of news. Like Ilongot typifications, these news items are more often marked by arrivals than departures. Mr. and Mrs. Lane Vogan, for example, become newsworthy not as they depart but after they return from their sunny vacation in Cape Cod.

My detour to Listowel has been made in the spirit of attending to the range of conventional forms that do (or potentially could) shape field notes. Anthropologists have long attended to matters of method in data collection, data manipulation, and more recently ethnographic writing. However, we have by and large ignored questions about the modes of composition that shape note taking as well as the relations between field notes and ethnographic texts.

When my field journal entries on "visits" were juxtaposed in a string, however, they began to tell a different story. Compiled over a period of days, visits (both actual arrivals and news brought from elsewhere) revealed the fluid intricacies of changing plans. Such shifts of trajectory involved complex judgments about myriad contingencies and unfolding patterns of coordination among individuals. Coordination among autonomous individuals requires a particularly high degree of flexibility and responsiveness because of cultural notions that make it difficult to predict another's conduct. Ilongots can try to persuade their fellow humans to do as they wish, but they cannot simply tell them what to do. Culturally speaking, they simply do not know what is inside another's heart *(rinawa)* unless that person speaks and reveals it.

Once, for example, a man named Insan visited another group to swear a peacekeeping oath by salt (sanctioned by the notion that, like salt in water, violators will dissolve in death). Yet a young man in their party deliberately did not hold the salt because he had treachery in his heart. Years later Insan told me that he had no inkling of the young man's designs because, "When we left that time, he [the young man] did not tell us what was in his heart." If the young man did not speak, his companions could not guess his motives because, culturally speaking, the inner workings of one's heart can be revealed only by explicit speech. Only in retrospect was Insan able to surmise that the young man's heart must have said (to himself): "I'm surveying the way I'm going to walk when I go on a headhunting raid against these Butag people." In fact, Insan did not learn what was in his companion's heart until it was too late. The consequences of not knowing were devastating for him because, as he saw it, his paternal grandfather's subsequent death by accidental gunshot was an act of supernatural retribution brought upon the group whose member violated the oath.[7]

Michelle Rosaldo paraphrased Ilongot talk on knowing what lies in the heart of another person as follows: "We cannot see the hearts of others; we hear words spoken by strangers but fear that these come only from the surface, not from the inner motions of their hearts."[8] She then elaborated:

Ilongots speak of "hearts," then, not to explain behavior by reference to character, motives, or a well-imaged personality, but to indicate those aspects of the self that can be alienated—or engaged—in social interaction. Through talk of hearts, Ilongots characterize the relation between the self and its situation, in terms of whether hearts are closed or open, light or heavy, itching or at ease. What matters in such talk is not "psychology" as we understand it, but the "passions" generated in a self that can always be in conflict with its environment.[9]

Ilongots understand human conduct more as a disconnected series of discrete (and therefore unpredictable) acts than as the unified pattern of an encompassing entity, such as "our" notion of a person's character or personality.

To illustrate the meandering pattern of coordination in Ilongot visiting, I have summarized and pieced together the following series of entries from my four-by-six cards of 1974 on the topic:

—Nov. 3: Two young boys arrived at night from Pengegyaben. Their host, Tepeg, immediately (without a period of silence) asked, "Is something wrong? Is somebody sick?" Tepeg explained that he blurted his questions because the young boys' nocturnal arrival appeared to mean that something was wrong. His eldest son, Keran, was in Pengegyaben at the time.

—Nov. 4: A visitor arrived and told his first cousin Dilap that his wife's return from Keradengan would be delayed because their children were ill. The two cousins said they would hunt together, and then go on to meet the wife and ailing children.

—Nov. 4: Kangat sneezed (a bad omen) as he was about to go and carry home his brother-in-law (who was incapacitated from snakebite). He did not go that day.

—Nov. 5: News arrived that a green viper bit Tepeg's son, Keran, as he started on the trail home.

—Nov. 9: The two cousins set off to hunt, but Dilap returned without seeing his wife and ailing children because his housemates and neighbors had gone to distant evangelical services, leaving nobody else home to feed the pigs.

—Nov. 12: Dilap's wife and children arrived, along with others, including Keran. The boy's mother had worried because news had come that her son was going to arrive two days sooner than he did.

Better for this purpose than the notecards, my field journal conveys the mood surrounding the group's arrival:

Then, close to dusk, people got all excited; the people from Pengegyaben are here; they saw them walking by Asibenglan— we've been eager for their arrival. They came across the river looking all dressed up and pretty, Ilongot fashion. Keran was walking with a cane [because of his snakebite]; his uncle, who was drinking on the other side of the river, would come later; his cousin wasn't clear on when we were going to Pengegyaben.

A young woman who arrived with the group said she would stay one day and then guide me and Michelle Rosaldo to Pengegyaben, near her place. People in our household asked the young woman to stay overnight and help in the garden.

—Nov. 14: The young woman spent the night at a house downstream, but she still did not return home because it was raining too hard today.

—Nov. 15: We walked to Pengegyaben with the young woman.

Strung together, the entries tell about how plans changed in coordination with other people. Ever flexible and shifting, the visitors have developed a fluid responsiveness to the contingencies of everyday life. By their very nature, of course, contingencies cannot be listed as a finite complete set because as-yet-unlisted items will always come up as life goes on. In the two-week period reviewed above, the contingencies included sickness, snakebite, rain, gardening, hunting, evangelical services, pig feeding, and sneezing.

Comparable forms of responsiveness have been vividly depicted for Athabascan hunters in northwestern Canada. Hugh Brody has described how their decision making takes account of multiple factors in this manner:

To make a good, wise, sensible hunting choice is to accept the interconnection of all possible factors, and avoids the mistake of seeking rationally to focus on any one consideration that is held as primary. What is more, the decision is taken in the doing; there is no step or pause between theory and practice. As a consequence, the decision—like the action from which it is inseparable—is always alterable (and therefore may not properly even be termed a decision). The hunter moves in a chosen direction; but, highly sensitive to so many shifting considerations, he is always ready to change his direction.[10]

Not unlike Ilongots, these hunters make synoptic judgments informed by sensitivity, responsiveness, and flexibility. Planning, schedules, and time-discipline indeed are at odds with such an open-ended quality of action.

Ilongot visiting shares this quality of open-endedness. Open-endedness has positive content in that it encourages a social capacity to improvise and respond creatively to life's contingencies. It is precisely this capacity—social grace and a sense of timing—that Ilongots so esteem as a cultural value.[11]

Lest it appear that social grace has no ragged edges, the case of Kama from Butag becomes especially pertinent. Kama was from a distant Ilongot group that had just celebrated the first of two covenants in which he and his companions received indemnity payments for past beheadings from the people of Kakidugen, where Michelle Rosaldo and I resided. During the second covenant, final amends were to be made through payments to the Kakidugen people.

Much to everybody's surprise, however, Kama appeared as a visitor in our house very shortly after the preliminary settlement.

He arrived, looking fresh, bold in his carriage, and dressed in his finest garb. As Ilongots usually do on formal visits, he had stopped near the house at a stream, where he rested, washed, groomed, and put on his body adornment. My companions admired both his elegant dress and his remarkable courage. His arrival was as follows: "In the early afternoon of February 17, Kama and his companion entered the house in silence and sat down. Without a word Tukbaw prepared a betel quid and, as he placed it in my hand, whispered that I should enhance the formality of the occasion. Following my 'brother's' wishes, I walked in measured steps across the room and with my left arm bent horizontally before me I squatted and, moving in slow motion, handed Kama the quid [of betel nut to chew] with my right hand."[12] The silence and slow decorum marked an occasion of high formality. The hosts and guests talked through the afternoon and on into the evening. They told stories of settlers and began to discuss arrangements for the return covenant in which Kama and his group would pay indemnities to the Kakidugen people.

After Kama left the next morning, his hosts began to talk in awed tones about their visitor. They spoke of his bodily elegance, of how he carried himself and his fine adornment. His decorations had cowrie shells, thin brass wire, white horsehair, boar's fangs, and a tall black feather. They adorned his waist, calves, upper arm, and head. He stood erect and moved in a deliberate manner.

Kama's visit had surprised Tukbaw, who admired the man's boldness. Tukbaw said he would never dare visit after celebrating only the initial covenant and not yet the return covenant. Disa, an older woman in the household, chuckled because she had slept near him. He was not, she said, as fearless as he appeared. She knew that he had not slept during the night out of fear that, if he did so, his hosts would behead him.

Ilongot social grace at times spills out at the seams. Even Kama's virtuoso performance both inspired awe and made Disa and her companions chuckle. Kama's vigilance was a condition of his exceptional performance, for had he not been watchful *(taikut)* he would not have dared visit Kakidugen before the celebration of the return covenant. In this case, an exceptional enactment of human qualities that Ilongots value dearly could be realized in daily life only with a measure of ambiguity. In the night, Disa caught a glimpse of the apprehensive actor shaping an awesome performance, and her respect for the man was not so much diminished as tempered by mirth.

Let me return for a moment to Brody's analysis of the Athabascan hunters. He characterizes the ways that hunting decisions (probably not the right word for such a fluid process) unfold through easygoing talk of this and that, and with a mood of waiting to see how things turn out. They speak in detail of different places they could go, and talk about fishing for trout and hunting for moose. "A number of individuals," Brody says, "agree that they will go. But come morning, nothing is ready. No one has made any practical, formal plans. As often as not—indeed, more often than not—something quite new has drifted into conversations, other predictions have been tentatively reached, a new consensus appears to be forming. As it often seems, everyone has changed his mind."[13] Perhaps a meander best describes the trajectory of such action. Yet the notion of a meander fails to characterize how purposive agents take account of multiple human and natural factors. The improvisational ways they chart their courses involve complex judgments and intricate forms of human responsiveness and cooperation.

In a case in point from my own fieldwork, Tagu, a man long afflicted with tuberculosis, became acutely ill. A group of Ilongots and I hastened to see him, as the following extract from my field journal records:

About 10:00 A.M. I went with Bayaw and Lakay to see Tagu. While I was there he got really, really sick: he was talking about who he would give his things to; he said he was dying; he said he had no bad feelings about anybody there [in other words, after death his spirit would not return to afflict the living]. Lots and lots of people came. His brothers were in tears. They sent for another brother and sister because they were afraid he would die. Shelly came by and gave him a shot with shaking, trembling hands. It seemed to make him a little better. I was moved by the concern, the way they cared for him.

People told me that an Ifugao shaman who resided nearby was coming to perform a curing ritual. They spoke, at least to my ears, as if the ritual were going to start that day or the next.

It was not, however, until eleven days later that a young man came to tell me that the Ifugao shaman, in response to our request, had said that we could take notes but no pictures. Three days later, a full two weeks after I thought the shaman was on his way, the ceremony seemed close to beginning, and I wrote the following in my field journal:

About 5:15 P.M. people began to arrive for the ceremony. . . . The expectation was that the ceremony would take place here, but then it turned out otherwise. . . . Shortly after we ate, Ingal arrived and said the shaman was doing a ceremony downstream, so we had best go to sleep because he wouldn't be here until late. . . . We chatted a while and, very uncomfortable with the early hour, we went to bed about 7:30 P.M.—as we were going to sleep, the house was a virtual hospital, with a skeletal Tagu, his brother with rheumatism, lots of people with colds. As we went to sleep, then, we felt pretty depressed: low; itchy; uncomfortable with the early hour; sad at the pervasive sense of illness. At 1:00 A.M. we were awakened. People arrived from downstream. The shaman had awakened them as he passed by; Tagu's brother had come by here to say that the shaman just passed by one house and went to another across the stream [where he would hold the ceremony]—the idea is that you treat a person at the place where he got sick.

My clock-bound frustration permeates the journal entry. Besides noting the time repeatedly (5:15 P.M., 7:30 P.M., 1:00 A.M.), I felt discomfort with going to bed earlier than usual, and my depression was brought on by the creeping, to me befuddling, pace of things. The Ilongots themselves, of course, were mildly puzzled because the Ifugao practices were not fully known and because a shaman's performance, as part of its charisma, cultivates uncertainty and ambiguity. Yet the sense of frustration was much more mine than theirs because I was unable to free myself from the tempo of "work-discipline." Only in retrospect can I readily perceive and appreciate the virtues that inform the pace at which their lives so often unfold, constrained more by human attentiveness than an appointed hour.

The gradual unfolding, the multiple messages, the piece-by-piece revelation of when and where the ceremony would happen, gave the key participants an opportunity to prepare themselves for the shaman's intervention in a life-threatening crisis. Tagu did appear close to death. The shaman was expensive. The social support mobilized was extensive. The dangerous afflicting spirit of Tagu's dead brother was invoked and felt to be present during the ceremony. In retrospect it is little wonder that the event gathered itself together in bits and pieces, moving now forward, now backward. People needed time to collect themselves, both literally in one house and by becoming oriented to a critical event where the stakes were high and the prognosis was uncertain.

In the end, the shaman did arrive, the ritual was performed throughout the night and into the next morning, and Tagu did survive the crisis. His crisis was quite real indeed, yet he lived, frail and tubercular, for more than twelve years after this episode.

A Brother-in-Law's Arrival

The anthropological literature could lead one to infer that the distinctive tempo of Ilongot visiting ends when the formal ritual begins. From this perspective it would seem that local versions of Indian Time fall by the wayside as formal procedures begin to regulate the tempo of programmed ritual time. To contest this widespread anthropological view, it is worth returning to an actual arrival scene marking the formal opening of a visit.

Recall that indigenous typifications made such arrivals appear formal, with a normal sequence of (1) silence, (2) betel quids and food, (3) a request for news ("Are you people from there well?"). Contrast the typifications with an actual arrival scene that took place when a group of visitors reached our household at about 4:30 P.M.

After about five minutes of relative silence, Bayaw, the male host who was still lying down, said, "Give them a betel quid. I have no piper leaf."[14]

The host's nephew began to prepare a quid, and then told a young male visitor, "Your areca nut now."

Tepeg, another male visitor, told Sawad, his sister and the female hostess, "Give me my pouch; give me the stuff for making a betel quid."

Sawad in turn told a child, "Give it to him, Lemmik."

A young male visitor told the host's nephew, "That tobacco of yours now."

The host's nephew told his aunt Sawad, "Give me your tobacco, aunt."

Two more minutes went by and Sawad told a young girl, "Ulling, go and fetch some water."

Then two people begin to talk.

The visitor Tepeg cursed in the general direction of his sister Sawad, the hostess, saying, "Sawad, its beheaded spirit [amet tu]."

As soon as Tepeg cursed, about ten minutes after the visitors' arrival, Sawad began to prepare a meal.

Although cultural typifications can make such arrivals appear routinized, they emerge in practice as a flow of tugs and pulls, requests and counterrequests, where tempo and grace are of the essence. The casually reclining host was telling his brother-in-law not to stand on formality, indicating closeness verging on disrespect. The brother-in-law was making claims on his sister, the hostess, by being blunt and eventually cursing because he'd not been given a visitor's due: a betel quid and a meal.

The precise tempo and mode of unfolding reveal, both as reflection and ongoing negotiation, the quality of social relations among participants. This arrival scene's interpersonal content was manifest in such matters as timing and the directness or obliqueness of requests. Rather than being an end point for analysis, the formal sequence—silence, betel quid and meal, and request for news—served more as a background for understanding actual practices.

Pierre Bourdieu has described the tempo and the politics of so-called reciprocity among Algerian peasants in terms so apt as to serve as a conclusion to this chapter:

When the unfolding of the action is heavily ritualized, as in the dialectic of offence and vengeance, there is still room for strategies which consist of playing on the time, or rather the *tempo*, of the action, by delaying revenge so as to prolong the threat of revenge. And this is true, *a fortiori*, of all the less strictly regulated occasions which offer unlimited scope for strategies exploiting the possibilities offered by manipulation of the tempo of the action—holding back or putting off, maintaining suspense or expectation, or on the other hand, hurrying, hustling, surprising, and stealing a march, not to mention the art of ostentatiously giving time ("devoting one's time to someone") or withholding it ("no time to spare").[15]

Where Bourdieu and I, or most probably Algerian peasants and Philippine tribal people, diverge is in our descriptive aesthetics. His paradigm of challenge and response suggests the aesthetic of the martial arts. The Ilongots and I would choose instead to emphasize social grace, the tempo and rhythms that shape the dance of life. My project has been to describe the differing aesthetics that shape the tempo of everyday life where clock time is not the paramount reality.

6 | *Narrative Analysis*

ALTHOUGH OFTEN DISCUSSED as an apt vehicle for processual analysis, narrative in the human sciences has been restricted to case histories and the discipline of historical studies. What follows will critically explore two broad strengths of narrative analysis with a view to enhancing its use for cultural studies. First, I assess its affinities with the "historical understanding" and with questions of "human agency." The former refers to the interaction of ideas, events, and institutions as they change through time. The latter designates the study of the feelings and intentions of social actors. Second, I discuss issues of analytical perspective, particularly the "double vision" that oscillates between the viewpoint of a social analyst and that of his or her subjects

127

of study. Each viewpoint is arguably incomplete—a mix of insight and blindness, reach and limitations, impartiality and bias—and taken together they achieve neither omniscience nor a unified master narrative but complex understandings of ever-changing, multifaceted social realities.

Yet narrative, as discussed in Part One of this book, has long been suppressed by classic norms of ethnography. In their zeal to become members of a "science," classic writers submitted themselves to the discipline of linguistic asceticism. By their aesthetic standards, "truth" was a manly, serious business; it was earnest, plain, and unadorned, not witty, oblique, and humanly engaging. The followers of classic norms paraded the banner of objectivism and marched against such rhetorical modes as moral indignation, chastisement, exhortation, simile, metaphor, and storytelling. Most classic ethnographies quite literally marginalized narrative, making it into a second-class citizen, by relegating it to prefaces, footnotes, and case histories presented in small print.[1]

Consider how hunting differs when described in a classic mode as opposed to a narrative one. In his fine ethnography on the !Kung San (popularly known as Bushmen) of southern Africa, Richard Borshay Lee, for example, describes "the hunting process" in accord with classic norms: "The man in the lead, if two or more are hunting, follows the spoor and stops only when the track divides or seems to disappear; then the hunters fan out to search for the correct spoor and resume tracking. This can be a laborious process, and if the fresher spoor crosses the one they are following, the hunters may instantly switch to the more promising lead."[2] Lee's composite account derives from careful repeated observations and multiple indigenous reports. Generalizing within !Kung San culture, Lee underscores the common features of all hunts, including their shared parameters of variation. His analysis is accurate, but incomplete.

In my studies of Ilongot hunting, however, I have found that particular case studies combined with indigenous narratives reveal aspects of hunting hidden by classic norms.[3]

Ilongot hunting stories relegate the subject matter of composite accounts (what all hunts have in common) to silence or, more precisely, to tacit background knowledge. Ilongot storytellers and their interlocutors no more need repeat what "everybody" already knows about hunting than a group of avid sports fans need to bore each other by reciting the basic rules of the game. Worse yet, composite accounts usually exclude the very qualities that huntsmen most value.

Indigenous hunting stories concentrate on a quality culturally regarded as crucial in foraging: the huntsmen's capacity to respond to the unexpected. Because deer and wild pigs do not appear on demand, hunters say that they must be prepared to spring into action at any moment. This quality of responsiveness is so culturally valued by Ilongots, as seen in the preceding discussion of visiting, that men tell well-formed "hunting stories" about their ability to improvise while being dragged over thorns by a python, being sent up a tree by a wild pig, or working to dislodge a dog from a crevice. Huntsmen in fact seek out experiences that can be told as stories. In other words, stories often shape, rather than simply reflect, human conduct.

Psychologist Jerome Bruner has similarly argued that stories shape action because they embody compelling motives, strong feelings, vague aspirations, clear intentions, or well-defined goals. In this context, Bruner tells an anecdote about economist Robert Heilbroner, who said that when their theories fail to predict, economists try to explain what actually happened by telling one another stories about the motives or goals of corporate executives in Japan, Zurich, or England. "Businessmen and bankers today," Bruner says, "(like men of affairs of all ages) guide their decisions by just such stories—even when a workable theory is available. These narratives, once acted out, 'make' events and 'make' history. They contribute to the reality of their participants. For an economist (or an economic historian) to ignore them, even on grounds that 'general economic forces' shape the world of economics, would be to don blinders."[4] Not only men and women of affairs but also ordinary people tell themselves stories about who they are, what they care about, and how they hope to realize their aspirations. Such stories significantly shape human conduct. Thus they cannot be ignored by social analysis.

Narrative as a Form of Social Analysis

Let me now turn to an extended debate on the "historical understanding," in which a number of people have advocated the use of narrative in social analysis. History has been the site of this argument because narrative long occupied a canonical status in that discipline comparable to the position of distanced normalizing discourse in anthropology. During the reign of narrative history, practitioners tended to use their favored mode of composition as if it were a transparent medium for telling the "real truth" about the past. Not surprisingly, the hegemony of narrative was countered during the late 1950s by a resistance movement, which, in turn, led to a creative rethinking of the virtues of "narrative as a cognitive instrument."

The initial assault on the hegemony of narrative was led by philosophers of science Carl Hempel and Ernest Nagel. The two philosophers told historians, in no uncertain terms, to get their analytical house in order. As a cure for the discipline's ills, they prescribed the "hypothetico-deductive method." Make a series of deductions from a general law, they said, until you reach a proposition that specifies the kind and amount of data needed to falsify it. Hempel and Nagel imperiously promoted their favored method by calling alternative methodologies nonscience (a code word, it seems, for nonsense).

The challenge of Hempel and Nagel provoked responses from a number of thinkers who decided to explore narrative as a form of knowledge. Rather than telling historians what they ought to do, these thinkers asked what they in fact do. How, they asked, has existing historical knowledge been acquired? Historian and social critic Hayden White, for example, made modes of composition central by arguing that the moment one chooses a particular form of discourse (and not another), it shapes historical knowledge both by what it includes and by what it excludes. "The historian," he says, "performs an essentially *poetic* act, in which he *pre*figures the historical field and constitutes it as a domain upon which to bring to bear the specific theories he will use to explain 'what was *really* happening' in it."[5] When two historians disagree, in other words, they often have conceived "the same" historical reality under such different descriptions that, in effect, they are talking about different realities.

Philosopher of history Louis Mink took a related, yet distinctive tack by arguing for the virtues of narrative as a form of what I have called processual analysis. He affirms that narrative analysis enables historians to transform an episodic sequence ("one damned thing after another") into an unfolding concatenation of ideas, institutions, and contingencies (or, in the idiom of chapter 4, agency, structure, and events). To refer to this distinctive ability to see things together, Mink uses the term "synoptic judgment." "Even supposing," he says, "that all of the facts of the case are established, there is still the problem of comprehending them in an act of judgment which manages to hold them together rather than reviewing them *seriatum*. This is something like, in fact, the sense in which one can *think* of a family as a group of related persons rather than as a set of persons plus their individual relations of kinship."[6] Emphasizing relatedness and context, Mink argues that narrative analysis places potentially discrete factors within larger sets of relationships, rather than isolating them as separate variables.

In Mink's view, social analysis should attempt to reveal not historical laws but an understanding of what happened in a specific place, at a particular time, and under certain circumstances. Unlike those who follow classic ethnographic norms and read case histories for their "detachable conclusions," historians read whole books because they seek synoptic judgment, rather than definitive proofs, findings, or discoveries. Mink's version of the historical understanding more nearly resembles the capacity to make specific diagnoses than the ability to discover general laws.

Philosopher W. B. Gallie similarly asserts that historical narrative is an alternative to the pursuit of lawlike generalizations as described by Hempel and Nagel. His review of a number of classic studies in the critical philosophy of history leads him to conclude that "not all explanations need be of the applicative Rule/Case/Result pattern made familiar by logical and methodological textbooks. What an explanation is, or can be or ought to be, depends in any given case, upon its context and upon the character of the inquiry in which it occurs."[7] According to Gallie, alternatives to textbook versions of explanation have been suppressed by the dominant Anglo-American philosophical tradition, which at one time did, and in many quarters still does, claim that the only valid form of explanation is the hypothetico-deductive model.

In response, Gallie argues that narrative comprises an exemplary model for the historical understanding. Narrative, he says, emphasizes retrospective intelligibility by demonstrating how later events were conditioned, occasioned, or facilitated by earlier ones. The central questions that inform the historical understanding simply differ from those of formal explanations, which stress prediction and attempt to show how earlier events necessarily produced later ones. In narrative analysis, the sequence of episodes cannot be predicted beforehand but makes sense only after the fact.

Gallie's discussion of narrative concentrates more on reception than production, more on reading than writing. How, he asks, does a reader follow a narrative? Gallie likens following a narrative to following a game of chance and skill. Both readers and spectators are endowed with varying degrees of knowledge, perception, and intelligence: "Every member of a family circle may be listening to the story: but no two of them follow or interpret it in exactly the same way, and no one of them can be said to have followed it perfectly or ideally or completely."[8] Similarly, not all spectators follow the same game in the same manner; certain of them know more, see from a different angle of vision, or make better judgments than others. Spectators bring knowledge and expectations to the game, but they also continuously revise both as the game unfolds because later, as yet unforeseen, developments could require such revisions as well as the reinterpretation of earlier incidents.

For Gallie, following a narrative in large measure involves the apprehension of human agency; that is, the reader's capacity to perceive the protagonists' intentions, desires, and thoughts. At times, he says, readers so completely identify with a story's protagonist that they put themselves in his or her shoes and feel much as he or she does. At other times, they remain "detached inactive observers" who are moved because, from their position, they can only look on helplessly as a character undergoes agonizing life dilemmas, mundane anguish, or impending loss. Indeed, Gallie claims that good readers continuously oscillate between their own positions and those of the protagonists: "It is not, therefore, any subordination of the observer's standpoint to that of the agent, but rather an unusually rapid movement and interplay between the two standpoints that characterizes our appreciation of a story's development."[9] Such readers must have a "double vision" that constantly shifts back and forth between themselves and the protagonists.

Writing after Gallie, historian J. H. Hexter depicts historical narrative more from the writer's than the reader's viewpoint. Writers of history, he claims, attempt to communicate knowledge about the past by writing narratives that explain how events unfolded: "Narrative is the most common mode of historical explanation because it is often the kind of explanatory answer solicited by a kind of question that historians very often ask and that is very often asked of them. Two ordinary forms of this question are 'How did it come about that . . . ?' and 'How did he (or they) happen to . . . ?'"[10] In Hexter's view, historians study unfolding processes more than static structures.

Hexter argues, however, that Gallie's analogy between the historical understanding and a game of chance and skill refers more to readers than to writers. The concept of suspense, for example, pertains to the skills of the former, but not the craft of the latter. "Unless the writer," Hexter says, "has the outcome in mind as he writes the story, he will not know how to adapt the proportions of his story to the actual historical tempo, since that is knowable only to one who knows the actual outcome."[11] Far from being in suspense, writers of history use their knowledge of how the narrative will end to decide how vividly and at what length to portray particular episodes. These features of narrative require conceptual analysis, Hexter says, "if one accepts the view that such attributes of historiography as accessibility, force, vividness, and depth are not merely decorative but have true noetic value."[12] In his view, narrative is a cognitive instrument, not a mere condiment designed to make historical knowledge more palatable.

Although Gallie and Hexter agree that historical narratives continually shift between the observer's and the participants' viewpoints, they differ in their perceptions of what distinguishes the two perspectives. Gallie stresses the position of the reader and underscores the interplay between the closeness of passionate identification versus the distance of detached observation. Hexter, on the other hand, focuses on the position of the writer, and emphasizes the interaction of forward-looking uncertainty versus backward-looking certitude. The protagonists, he claims, stand midstream, looking to the future with no knowledge of how things will turn out; the historian sees the larger flow, looking backward with the wisdom of hindsight. Taken together, the divergent reflections of Gallie and Hexter do not contradict one another. Rather, they underscore the complexity involved in discussing "point of view" in social analysis.

The French philosopher Paul Ricoeur has recently attempted to synthesize studies on the use of narrative in historical studies. He boldly argues that processual analysis must take narrative as its form, rather than more modestly pointing to the affinities between them. Time and narrative are inseparable because, he says, "time becomes human time to the extent that it is organized after the manner of a narrative; narrative, in turn, is meaningful to the extent that it portrays the features of temporal experience."[13] Ricoeur asserts that time and narrative are dialectically related: time becomes human when shaped by narrative form, and narrative becomes meaningful when it depicts human experience in the flow of time. Narratives shape temporal experiences, and temporal experiences in turn embody narratives.

Ricoeur stresses the reader's responses more than the writer's intentions in a manner that allows him to argue that narrative analyses need not be written in narrative form. For him, the exemplary nonnarrative history is Fernand Braudel's monumental history of the Mediterranean world. Although Braudel's history of a "long time-span" explicitly rejects a "narrative history of events," Ricoeur reads it as if it had a plot, central characters, and key turning points. Thus seen as an implicit narrative, Braudel's work tells of "the decline of the Mediterranean as a collective hero on the stage of world history."[14] In this manner, Ricoeur argues persuasively for a theory of narrative analysis based on how a text is read, not on its literal form.

Ricoeur proves less convincing, however, in his one-sided emphasis on the historian's act of synoptic judgment. Rather than follow Gallie and Hexter in stressing the double vision inherent in the interplay between the viewpoint of the observer and that of the protagonists, he argues that the historian alone transforms events into larger patterns of understanding. In his view, the protagonists are so caught up in the flow of events that they make unreliable narrators. Ricoeur speaks, for example, of "the confused and limited perspective of the agents and the eye-witnesses of the events."[15] He emphasizes that historical actors neither know the conditions under which they act nor can foresee the consequences of their actions. Furthermore, he says, the connections among historical events often become apparent only in the long run. Indeed, at times the wisdom of hindsight arrives only after the protagonist's death. In Ricoeur's view, only the historian can apprehend the larger course of human events.

Ricoeur's emphasis on the historian as an omniscient narrator suppresses the analytical import of the protagonists' narratives. He assumes that every protagonist's narrative can be fully incorporated into a unified master narrative. But what if the protagonists' stories reverse Ricoeur's ratio of synoptic judgment and gain in focus what they lose in scope? The strengths and limitations of each vantage point may be quite distinct. What if the various narratives so differ in their plot and their form that a larger synthesis among them cannot be reached? The different versions may well not fit together into a larger whole.

Louis Mink has raised the analytical difficulties Ricoeur refuses to face. "Yet while historical narratives," Mink says, "ought to aggregate into more comprehensive narratives, or give way to rival narratives which will so aggregate, in fact they do not; and here is where conceptual discomfort should set in." [16] Mink illustrates his notion by saying that one history's ending cannot become another's beginning without undergoing a fundamental metamorphosis. Because the historical understanding uses narrative forms, which resist summary in "detachable conclusions" and therefore must be read in detail, different accounts cannot simply be pasted together to make a unified master narrative.

Mink further argues that events can be known only under certain descriptions, not as brute facts: "It is clear that we cannot refer to events as such, but only to events *under a description;* so there can be more than one description of the same event, all of them true but referring to different aspects of the event or describing it at different levels of generality. But what can we possibly mean by 'same event'?" [17] Although Mink refers to historical narratives, his appraisal also applies to the accounts given by the historian's subjects.

Point of View in Social Analysis

Let us return once again to E. P. Thompson's study of English working-class history with a view to exploring the interplay between his narrative and those of his subjects of study. To begin, consider a dramatic moment in which Thompson depicts his central topic, the unity of the radical tradition, by connecting its members along a network that emanates from an English artisan named Thomas Hardy. In a virtuoso verbal performance, Thompson links Hardy and the poet William Blake through an imaginative excursion that reminds one of the great chain of being and of connections among socially disparate characters in nineteenth-century novels. In formal terms, such networks resemble dialectical chains where A is linked to B, and B is linked to C, but A has no connection with C.

Thompson begins forging his chain of affiliations by saying, "Hardy was certainly an artisan." He then explains that, one link away, "The line between the journeyman and the small masters was often crossed." He then moves two links away, saying, "And the line between the artisan of independent status (whose workroom was also his 'shop') and the small shopkeeper or tradesman was even fainter." Finally, he concludes by moving three links away, "From here it was another step to the world of self-employed engravers, like William Sharp and William Blake, of printers and apothecaries, teachers and journalists, surgeons and Dissenting clergy."[18] Although Hardy and Blake inhabited different worlds and never knew one another, the historian has connected them, moving one step at a time, through a series of intervening links that unite the tradition of dissent.

Thompson's breathtaking rhetorical fiction raises a central question for culturally sensitive social analysis. Did the working class become conscious of itself by imagining its unity in chainlike fashion? Or did Thompson himself conceive the step-by-step linkages that make up the network? One suspects the latter. In either case, readers concerned with Thompson's problem of how the English working class "made itself" must be able to discern whether the historian, his subjects, or both invented the cultural conceptions (in Benedict Anderson's fine phrase, the "imagined communities") that played such a key role in forming the radical tradition.[19]

The problem of perspective similarly arises when Thompson depicts working-class struggle in terms of the sentimental heroics of victimization. The reader is left wondering whether or not Thompson's subjects actually used this aesthetic to describe their conduct. The descriptive aesthetic that Thompson uses so artfully clearly belongs to the epoch under analysis and can be found in a range of sites, from working-class theater to the novels of Charles Dickens.

In my view, Thompson's narrative is "melodramatic" in the sense that literary theorist Peter Brooks uses the term. Brooks asserts melodramatic forms of drama have particularly shaped the work of such nineteenth-century novelists as Dickens and Henry James. "Within an apparent context of 'realism' and the ordinary," he says, "they seemed in fact to be staging a heightened and hyperbolic drama, making reference to pure and polar concepts of darkness and light, salvation and damnation. They seemed to place their characters at the point of intersection of primal ethical forces and to confer on the characters' enactments a charge of meaning referred to the clash of these forces."[20] It is in this sense that Thompson's narrative aesthetic often approaches the melodramatic. It presents human events with a distinctive moral intensity that follows the logic of the excluded middle; it portrays conflicts between absolute good and absolute evil. The earnest exaggeration in such narratives evokes the reader's partisan responses. The narrator assumes a moral stance toward the protagonists, the protagonists feel persecuted, and the readers react with horror, panic, or sympathetic pity. These dramas move readers to take sides in a battle between virtue and vice.

Consider, for example, the way Thompson encourages his readers to side firmly with Thomas Hardy. On the book's first page, Hardy enters as the "founder and first secretary" of the London Corresponding Society. One page and two years later his epithet becomes more modest, and he is simply a "shoemaker." Having established Hardy's humble position as a commoner, Thompson engages our sympathy by saying: "Mrs. Hardy died in childbirth as a result of shock sustained when her home was besieged by a 'Church and King' mob."[21] Elsewhere Thompson describes the popular image current during Hardy's trial: "The public found in Hardy once again one of those images of independence in which the 'free-born Englishman' delighted: a firm and dignified commoner, defying the power of the state. The circumstances of Mrs. Hardy's death attracted further sympathy."[22] Readers cannot help but feel sympathy for a common man who has been so brutally wronged by the state.

Thompson's choice to write in a melodramatic mode was astute. As an aesthetic for apprehending dramatic conflicts, no doubt including class struggle, the melodramatic imagination shaped the lives of nineteenth-century working-class Englishmen. Yet Thompson's use of melodramatic modes of composition remains deeply ambiguous. Does he depict working-class suffering as melodrama because of the idiom's diffuse appropriateness for the period? Or is it because particular working people, under certain circumstances, guided their conduct through this idiom? To what extent—and precisely when, where, and for whom—can one describe nineteenth-century English working-class consciousness as melodramatic?

Lest readers imagine that anthropology, perhaps because of its celebrated attention to the "native point of view," has never been plagued by the conceptual problems just outlined, let me now return to Victor Turner's use of the case history. The case history constitutes the main ethnographic precedent for using narrative in social analysis. As I have said, British social anthropology's Manchester School, whose members worked primarily in central Africa after World War II, most fully developed this methodology, particularly through the "extended case method," which enables readers to follow a group of people through a series of incidents. Turner's ethnography on the Ndembu of what was then Northern Rhodesia modifies the extended case method by asserting that the processual form of "social dramas" falls into four regular phases: breach, crisis, redressive action, and either reintegration or recognition of schism.

Turner argues that conflicting structural principles play themselves out in disputes over succession to village headmanship, but, because kinship loyalties inhibit the direct expression of hostilities, struggles over succession are often articulated in the oblique idiom of witchcraft and sorcery. Turner begins his ethnography by depicting a contest for Mukanza village headmanship in which a man named Mukanza Kabinda emerges victorious over a man named Sandombu. Yet no sooner does the victor emerge than Sandombu and a man named Kasonda begin to build their personal followings, each of them hoping to become the next village headman.

The struggle for succession provides the context for Turner's fourth social drama, in which a young bride named Ikubi dies, and a woman named Nyamuwang'a is expelled from her village, under accusation of witchcraft. Immediately after Ikubi's death, her father accused Nyamuwang'a of using witchcraft to kill her. As Turner explains, "It was said that Nyamuwang'a had asked Ikubi for some meat that she had cooked shortly before her illness. Ikubi had said that it was for her parents and that she had not enough to give away. Nyamuwang'a had become very angry with her and had threatened her in an indirect way."[23] As the social drama unfolds, the question of Nyamuwang'a's witchcraft continues to be hotly contested among the villagers.

Nyamuwang'a denies any wrongdoing and attributes the young bride's death to somebody else's vengeance medicine. Convinced that Nyamuwang'a used witchcraft to kill Ikubi, a man loses his temper and begins to beat her. Another man rushes to stop the beating, saying that Nyamuwang'a has been wrongly accused of witchcraft, but he asks her to leave the village anyway because of her troublemaking. Yet another man upholds the original charge and says that Nyamuwang'a must leave the village because no witch should live there. Finally, Sandombu, who by then resides elsewhere, says that Nyamuwang'a's accusers lack proof of their charges and invites her to live on his farm. By so doing, Sandombu threatens to split the village in his ongoing efforts to build a following for his succession to headmanship.

Curiously enough, Turner defines the processual form of his case histories without reference to Ndembu cultural conceptions. In their own narratives, do the protagonists think of events as having climaxes, turning points, or crises? Do Ndembu stories, which both describe and shape action, coincide with Turner's definition of the social drama's universal processual form? Do Turner and the protagonists agree about what constitutes the social drama's chain of events?

The Ndembu protagonists clearly differ among themselves about the causal sequences animating the social drama. The participants disagree about what caused the young bride's death. Some deny the presence of witchcraft altogether; others agree that witchcraft caused the death, but disagree not only about who was responsible but also about the form of witchcraft used. The protagonists interpret the central incidents so differently that the notion of a unified social drama seems, at best, problematic. The participants agree about neither what triggered the sequence of events nor who was involved. In what sense, then, can Turner say that the various protagonists participated in the "same" social drama?

When the social analyst and the protagonists use culturally divergent forms of narrative analysis, the problems of point of view become both clearer and more complex. Clarity emerges from the realization that the protagonists' narratives pose a deeper challenge to the analyst's sovereign viewpoint than Gallie and Hexter allow. Complexity involves grappling with narrative forms that work, say, without our notions of "climax," "turning point," or even "point of view." In other words, the universal centrality of the "double vision" crumbles under its own implications because it forces the analysis to confront radically different narrative forms.

In his studies of *wayang*, or Javanese shadow theater, for example, A. L. Becker argues that Javanese dramas violate "Western" notions of a well-formed plot. "The differences," he says, "with the Aristotelian notion of plot should now be apparent. What in the wayang plot are significant coincidences, in the Aristotelian plot are crudities, violations of the basic notions of unity and causality. In wayang, we might say that Gatsby, Godzilla, Agamemnon, John Wayne, and Charlie Chaplin—or their counterparts—do appear in the same plot, and that is what causes the excitement; that clash of conceptual universes is what impels the action."[24] For the Javanese, significant coincidences bring together different categories of being, different orders of time, and different epistemologies. When battles break out, not only do the protagonists represent what to "us" seem outrageously clashing conceptual worlds but also the fight ends with the restoration of a proper balance among contending forces, rather than by separating the victors from the vanquished.

In cross-cultural studies, the gaps between the analyst's narratives and those of the protagonists often rival the clashes of incongruous epistemologies in Javanese shadow theater. Not only will their stories not fit together into a larger whole, as Mink argues, but the protagonists' narrative forms often lack climaxes, turning points, or a stable narrative point of view. Most writers on the historical understanding sidestep vexing problems of translation by assuming that the analyst and the social actors use approximately the same narrative forms. Even within the "same" culture, however, different actors often use quite different narrative forms. By no means all of "our" culturally available narrative forms foreground plot, climax, and the interplay of narrator and protagonists. Hence the gains and complexities in holding the social analyst's narratives in creative tension with those of the protagonists. Rather than being merely ornamental, a dab of local color, protagonists' narratives about their own conduct merit serious attention as forms of social analysis.

Part Three · Renewal

7 | *Changing Chicano Narratives*

SOCIAL THINKERS MUST TAKE other people's narrative analyses nearly as seriously as "we" take our own. This transformation of "our" objects of analysis into analyzing subjects most probably will produce impassioned, oblique challenges to the once-sovereign ethnographer. Both the content and the idioms of "their" moral and political assertions will be more subversive than supportive of business as usual. They will neither reinforce nor map onto the terrain of inquiry as "we" have known it. Narrative analyses told or written from divergent perspectives, as I have said, will not fit together into a unified master summation. A

147

source at once of insight and discomfort, the dilemma of "incommensurability," or lack of fit among diverse narratives, makes it imperative to attend with care to what other people are saying, especially if they use unfamiliar idioms and speak to us from socially subordinate positions. Taking account of subordinate forms of knowledge provides an opportunity to learn and productively change "our" forms of social analysis. It should broaden, complicate, and perhaps revise, but in no way inhibit, "our" own ethical, political, and analytical insights.

What follows works in the manner of a case history that explores three Chicano narratives with a view to assessing their value as analyses of the concept of culture. The first, *"With His Pistol in His Hand": A Border Ballad and Its Hero,* was published in 1958 by Américo Paredes.[1] It concerns a ballad about a south Texas Mexican man who shoots an Anglo-Texan sheriff and becomes the object of a manhunt. At once a study in folklore and a piece of social criticism, the work now addresses a wider social movement as well as a professional audience. The second, *Barrio Boy,* was published in 1971 by Ernesto Galarza.[2] Written toward the end of a career, the bilingually entitled autobiography tells of an early childhood spent in a village of Nayarit, Mexico, and then of a move north to Sacramento, California. This book appeared shortly after the mobilization of the Chicano movement in the late 1960s. The third, *The House on Mango Street,* was published in 1986 by Sandra Cisneros.[3] Written by a young woman, this short-story cycle speaks with a playful diction that often approaches the nursery rhyme. Rather than telling of the journey "north from Mexico," the protagonist remains stationary in a Chicago neighborhood that changes around her as she comes of age. This work envisions a politics of identity and community not yet realized either in social analysis or in the Chicano movement.

The three narratives tell of the Chicano warrior hero. The first portrays him in a positive light, the second mocks him, and the third displaces him. Despite their differences of tone, these tales of "how we got to be the way we are" follow an Edenic mythic pattern of an idealized initial condition, a fall, and subsequent struggles to survive, and perhaps thrive, into the present. These continuities and changes in Chicano narrative forms reveal shifting conceptions of culture. Once a figure of masculine heroics and resistance to white supremacy, the Chicano warrior hero now has faded away in a manner linked—at least in the texts under discussion—to the demise of self-enclosed, patriarchal, "authentic" Chicano culture. The trajectory of the three narrative analyses moves Chicano identity from bounded cultural purity through the mockery of patriarchs to encounters at the border zones of everyday life.

The Chicano narratives speak to changing conceptions of culture, not only as a concept in social analysis but also as a vital resource for a developing politics of identity and community. For Chicanos, "our" felt oppression derives as much from cultural domination as from the brute facts of poverty. During my junior high school days in Tucson, Arizona, for example, Chicano students could be obliged to bend over and grab their ankles so that teachers could give them "swats" with a board. This punishment somehow fit the "crime" of speaking Spanish in school. Or consider how Anglo-Americans who learn a second language in college become "cultured" and "broaden their horizons," but Chicanos who enter elementary schools already speaking another language suffer from a "deficit" and are labeled "at risk." In "our" everyday lives, cultural domination surfaces as myriad mundane sites of cultural repression and personal humiliation. For "us," questions of culture encompass social analysis, and much more.

The Chicano narratives studied in this chapter weave together laughter, politics, culture, and patriarchy. They prominently include borders as sites where identities and cultures intersect. Their distinctively Chicano forms of irony provoke knowing chuckles more often than belly laughs. When the protagonists speak in self-deprecating voices, their humor can be so understated that its wit, not to mention its barbed edges, often escapes straight-faced readers and listeners. Culturally distinctive jokes and banter play a significant role in constituting Chicano culture, both as a form of resistance and as a source of positive identity.[4] Rather than defusing grievances, the incongruities thus exposed offer analytical insight potentially useful for mobilizing popular resistance based on inequities of race and class.

Americo Paredes: The Chicano Warrior Hero

The author of *"With His Pistol in His Hand,"* Américo Paredes, was a pioneer in the field of Chicano studies. He entered the university after World War II, when he was in his 30s, after having been in succession a singer, a poet, and a journalist. His gift for language shows both in his poetry and in his multifaceted academic writings on folklore, literature, and anthropology. Now an eminent professor emeritus at the University of Texas at Austin, he began his academic career in the mid-1950s, when the Chicano movement had not yet emerged as a widely recognized social phenomenon.

When Paredes wrote *"With His Pistol in His Hand,"* during the 1950s, anti-Mexican prejudice throughout the Southwest and California was even more evident than today. In south Texas, where this prejudice was particularly virulent, it took courage to challenge the dominant ideology of Anglo-Texan racial superiority. José Limón has described the publication of Paredes's book as a struggle against Anglo-Texan white supremacy. Even after the manuscript's publication, Limón says, an ex-Texas Ranger asked the press for Paredes's address, so that he could "shoot the sonofabitch who wrote that book."[5] Paredes, it seems, had touched a nerve. Under the circumstances, one marvels that the book's narrator can speak with a fine blend of scholarly integrity, low-key chuckles, and devastating criticism.

Always reread from ever-changing "present" vantage points, past narratives rarely continue to be the "same" in their cultural meanings. In part, changing readings reflect changing audiences. At the time of its publication, for example, Paredes's work reached local and professional audiences; a decade later, it was inserted into the Chicano movement in a manner neither its author nor its early readers could have foreseen. Thus "relocated," the book took on new cultural significance. Yet again, from the perspective of feminist thought in the late 1980s, Paredes's work now appears dated in its idealization of a primordial patriarchy, and ahead of its time in so clearly seeing the interplay of culture and power. To project a heterogeneous, changing heritage into the future, "we" Chicanos must continually reread past narratives in order to recover courageous early works without reifying them as sacred relics more fit for veneration than dialogue and debate.

Writing in an understated manner, Paredes uses a nostalgic poetic mode to depict his Garden of Eden. He describes a pastoral patriarchy that governed the Rio Grande region from the arrival of Mexican settlers in 1749 to the Mexican-American War of 1848. In a culturally distinctive version of Frederick Jackson Turner's notion of frontier democracy, Paredes asserts that in primordial times benevolent patriarchs maintained a cohesive and egalitarian social order. "Social conduct," he says, "was regulated and formal, and men lived under a patriarchal system that made them conscious of degree. The original settlements had been made on a patriarchal basis, with the 'captain' of each community playing the part of father to his people" (p. 11). If taken literally, Paredes's view of the frontier social order seems both pre-feminist and as implausible as a classic ethnography written and read in accord with classic norms. How could any human society, even one as egalitarian as that of the Ilongots, function without inconsistencies and contradictions?[6] Did patriarchal authority engender neither resentment nor dissent? Read as poetic vision, however, the account of primordial south Texas Mexican society establishes the terms for verbally constructing the warrior hero as a figure of resistance. It enables Paredes to develop a conception of manhood rhetorically endowed with the mythic capacity to combat Anglo-Texan anti-Mexican prejudice.

The treaty following the War of 1848 definitively shattered

the Edenic epoch of primordial pastoral patriarchy. After nearly a century of relatively peaceful existence, the patriarchs were deposed, the united land was divided, and the border was drawn. In mythic terms, Rio Grande Mexicans fell from innocence when their earthly paradise was split asunder: "It was the Treaty of Guadalupe that added the final element to Rio Grande society, a border. The river, which had been a focal point, became a dividing line. Men were expected to consider their relatives and closest neighbors, the people just across the river, as foreigners in a foreign land. A restless and acquisitive people, exercising the rights of conquest, disturbed the old ways" (p. 15). The intrusive border brought a definitive end to the old way of life. From this point onward, primordial pastoral patriarchy (whatever its historical status) definitively survives only as folklore and as an idealized vision of manhood.

Lest there be any confusion, Paredes's narrative about the invasive border tells the history of his own ancestral past. He is not an immigrant. Neither he nor his Mexican ancestors moved after about 1750; instead, military conquest transformed the Rio Grande from a fertile place of gathering together into a barbed line of demarcation. The imposition of the border compelled friends and relatives to become citizens of two distinct nations. Long before his birth, Paredes's ancestral homeland had thus become south Texas. He was born into a world dominated by an aggressive group that spoke a foreign language. But they were the immigrants, not he. Not unlike blacks and Native Americans, Chicanos cannot readily be absorbed to a standard history of immigration and assimilation.

After telling about how the border invaded south Texas, Paredes's tone becomes quietly ironic. "In the conflict along the Rio Grande," he says, "the English-speaking Texan (whom we shall call the Anglo-Texan for short) disappoints us in a folkloristic sense. He produces no border balladry. His contribution to the literature of border conflict is a set of attitudes and beliefs about the Mexican which form a legend of their own and are the complement to the *corrido*, the

Border-Mexican ballad of border conflict" (p. 15). Although Mexicans sing their resistance with fine *corridos*, Anglo-Texans impose their domination with prosaic attitudes and beliefs. Doomed to lose the shooting wars, Mexicans use *corridos* of enduring value to counter Anglo-Texan claims to cultural supremacy. In his social criticism, Paredes speaks obliquely, deftly, pointedly, bilingually.

When Paredes speaks in more detail about border conflict, he plays with ironic parallel constructions that move between the perspectives of Mexicans and Anglo-Texans. He begins with the Anglo-Texan legend about Mexicans. In this view, Mexicans are cruel, cowardly, treacherous, and thieving because their mixed blood (Spanish and Indian) has made them degenerate. Mexicans are said to recognize the superiority of Anglo-Texans, especially the finest of their breed, the Texas Rangers. The Anglo-Texan legend about Mexicans circulated in popular attitudes and beliefs, which were reflected in and reshaped by printed works extending from nineteenth-century war propaganda to twentieth-century scholarship: "The truth seems to be that the old war propaganda concerning the Alamo, Goliad, and Mier later provided a convenient justification for outrages committed on the Border by Texans of certain types, so convenient an excuse that it was artificially prolonged for almost a century. And had the Alamo, Goliad, and Mier not existed, they would have been invented, as indeed they seem to have been in part" (p. 19). Gradually unrolling his punch line, Paredes suggests that the writings of Anglo-Texan scholars not only justified the abuse of Mexicans but were also, in part, invented.

Mexican perceptions of Anglo-Texans, on the other hand, appear in sayings, anecdotes, and ballads about the Texas Rangers rather than in authoritative print. Without American soldiers, the sayings go, Rangers would not dare enter the border region. In this view, the cowardly Rangers never fought face-to-face against armed Mexicans, but shot them in the back or in their sleep. Many a tale tells of how Rangers killed innocent (often unarmed) Mexicans and planted rusty old guns on their corpses to justify their claims to have shot them in self-defense while pursuing thieves. Paredes hastens to say that such perceptions are partisan: "I do not claim for these little tidbits the documented authenticity that Ranger historians claim for their stories. What we have here is frankly partisan and exaggerated without a doubt, but it does throw some light on Mexican attitudes toward the Ranger which many Texans may scarcely suspect. And it may be that these attitudes are not without some basis in fact" (p. 25). His rhetorical tactic nicely parallels and opposes that used to summarize Anglo-Texan perceptions. Once again, he ends by reversing himself, but this time he accents how Mexican perceptions rest on a significant grain of truth, not a large dose of invention.

Throughout his discussion of border conflict, Paredes himself becomes a warrior hero who battles against Anglo-Texan academic opponents. His devastating critique of J. Frank Dobie's and Walter Prescott Webb's influential work on the folklore and history of Texas shows how their (often unreliable) writings celebrate Anglo-Texans and denigrate their fellow citizens of Mexican ancestry.[7] Paredes exposes their work as a version of popular Anglo-Texan white supremacy dressed in academic garb. In being prejudiced and quick on the inference, Dobie and Webb appear to be latter-day incarnations of the Texas Rangers.

In his own good time, Paredes settles down to tell the ballad of Gregorio Cortez. Like his rendition of pastoral patriarchy, Paredes uses a poetic voice to display an updated version of the ancient ideal of manhood: "That was good singing, and a good song; give the man a drink. Not like these pachucos nowadays, mumbling damn-foolishness into a microphone; it is not done that way. Men should sing with their heads thrown back, with their mouths wide open and their eyes shut. Fill your lungs, so they can hear you at the pasture's further end. And when you sing, sing songs like *El Corrido de Gregorio Cortez*. There's a song that makes the hackles rise. You can almost see him there—Gregorio Cortez, with his pistol in his hand" (p. 34). Descendants of the primordial patriarchs, these country men live in the old style. Unaided by microphones, their voices carry across the pasture and make their listeners feel *muy gallo*, literally very rooster, very male like a fighting cock, with rising hackles. The descendants of the warrior hero singing across the pasture probably should be understood more poetically than literally. Like Gregorio Cortez and Américo Paredes himself, the singer of *corridos* becomes a latter-day warrior hero, a figure of masculine heroics and resistance to Anglo-Texan domination.[8]

When Gregorio Cortez himself enters, he does so as a horseman who shouts his name in battle and whose heroic deeds are remembered and sung in ballad form. As Paredes notes, "Cortez sounds not like a Border vaquero [cowboy, or buckaroo] but like an old, name-proud hidalgo [nobleman]. It is this medieval pride in name that is the basis of the challenge as it appears in the Border *corrido*, pride in a name that has been earned through deed and not through birth or wealth" (p. 236). His deeds as a warrior horseman confer the aura of medieval nobility on his person. When he boldly shouts his name in battle ("Yo soy Gregorio Cortes"), he elevates the humble *corrido* until it assumes the grandeur of the medieval epic. The Chicano warrior hero has grown larger than life to combat Anglo-Texan assertions of cultural and racial supremacy. It was grand moment. Yet, as shall be seen in a moment, changing Chicano narratives have dismantled these masculine heroics, and reworked, without destroying, "our" forms of cultural resistance.

Ernesto Galarza: The Mocking of the Warrior Hero

The author of *Barrio Boy*, the late Ernesto Galarza, was a scholar-activist. Like Paredes, he is revered by Chicano scholars and activists. Without holding an academic position, he distinguished himself as an organizer and a writer. Throughout his life he helped organize agricultural workers, and he conducted research on the political economy of agribusiness. He wrote works of scholarship, poetry, and children's stories.

In Galarza's autobiography, both the warrior hero and the Edenic myth occupy central places, but they are mocked rather than treated with poetic reverence. In this respect, Galarza's work at once parallels and subverts Paredes's narrative. The shift in attitudes that separates the works by Paredes and Galarza probably derives as much from changing sociohistorical conditions as from the fact that the former writes as a folklorist and the latter as a student of agricultural economics. The chasm between the virtually unchallenged assimilationism of 1958 and the mobilized Chicano community of 1971 informs the two narratives. Writing about south Texas during the 1950s, Paredes called for Mexican cultural resistance to domination by the numerical minority of Anglo-Texans. For him, the critique of ideology appeared most urgent. In contrast, Galarza urged confrontation with established political authorities that governed the residentially segregated urban barrios of northern California in the early 1970s. For him, the analysis of capitalism and its bureaucratic administrative apparatus seemed most crucial. Shaped by distinct disciplinary predilections and differing historical circumstances, the two writers set complementary yet divergent agendas for social analysis.

Galarza's work has often been read with solemnity, as if it were written in a flat earnest manner. Yet the work is marked by heteroglossia, a play of English and Spanish, and by an understated, often self-deprecating humor through which his political vision becomes apparent.

Barrio Boy opens soberly enough, with an Edenic scene of Mexican rural life. "The pine kindling," Galarza says, "was marvelously aromatic and sticky. The woodsmen of the pueblo talked of the white tree, the black tree, the red tree, the rock tree—*palo blanco, palo negro, palo colorado* and *palo de piedra.* Under the shady canopies of the giants there were the fruit bearers—*chirimoyas, guayabas, mangos, mameyes,* and *tunas*" (p. 6). Life is peaceful. Nature is aromatic, color-ful, and abundant. The praise song of Galarza's pastoral opening makes the primordial environment into a bountiful upland tropical paradise.

However, an extended meditation on the *zopilote*, the tur-key buzzard, interrupts the pastoral opening.

But of all the creatures that came flying out of the *monte*—bats, doves, hawks—the most familiar were the turkey vultures, the *zopilotes*. There were always two or three of them perched on the highest limb of a tree on the edge of the pueblo. They glided in gracefully on five feet of wing spread, flapping awkwardly as they came to rest. They were about the size of a turkey, of a blackish brown color and baldheaded, their wrinkled necks spotted with red in front. Hunched on their perch, they never opened their curved beaks to make a sound. They watched the street below them with beady eyes. Sometimes during the day, the *zopilotes* swooped down to scavange in the narrow ditch that ran the length of the street, where the housewives dropped the entrails of chickens among the garbage. They gobbled what waste the dogs and pigs did not get at first. [p. 6]

As ugly in appearance as it is graceful in flight, this scav-enger becomes a mock national bird for Galarza's natal vil-lage of Jalcocotán, Nayarit, Mexico.

Governed by male heads of family, or *jefes de familia*, Jalcocotán formally resembles Paredes's primordial Rio Grande society ruled by benevolent patriarchs. Yet Galarza introduces the term *jefe de familia* by talking not about the deceased patriarch, Grandfather Félix, but about his suc-cessor, a diminutive matriarch named Aunt Tel:

Doña Esther, my Aunt Tel, as I called her, was a small person. Something over five-feet-five, she was fair-skinned and hazel-eyed. She seldom laughed, for when we came to Jalco she had already had enough grief to last a person a lifetime, the least of which was the responsibility for two younger brothers and a sister after the death of Grandfather Félix. He, too, had been a rigid *jefe de familia*. She had lived all her life under authority but it had not bent her will; standing up to it she was more than a person—she was a presence. When she was alone in the cottage with us she told jokes about animals and foolish, stuck-up persons. She smiled mostly with her eyes. [p. 17]

Endurance, resilience, and her twinkling eyes make the matriarch Aunt Tel an inspiring presence in young Ernesto's life. In his oblique criticism of patriarchal authority, Galarza moves from Aunt Tel to Coronel, the dominant rooster of Jalcocotán. As Paredes suggested in his depiction of the ballad singer, to be *muy gallo* is to be a real man. Fighting cocks are widely celebrated as symbols of manhood in Mexican speech and song, as indicated by Galarza's introduction of the rooster Coronel, challenging all within earshot: "Coronel always held himself like a ramrod, but he stood straightest when he was on top of the corral wall. From up there he counted his chickens, gave the forest a searching look, and blasted out a general challenge to all the world. With his flaming red crest and powerful yellow spurs, Coronel was the picture of a very *jefe de familia*" (p. 23). If Jalcocotán's national bird is a mock eagle, the turkey buzzard, its dominant *jefe de familia* is a mock patriarch, the rooster Coronel.

By interrupting the Edenic scene and by displacing the *jefe de familia*, Galarza sets the stage for a mock cockfight that pits the rooster Coronel against the nameless turkey buzzard. The parodic cockfight occurs in the world of women, children, and animals, without adult male witnesses. In any case, it is all over in a moment, and the turkey buzzard flies off with the prize, a heap of chicken guts, while the rooster Coronel stays behind to claim victory:

Coronel, standing erect among the litter gave his wings a powerful stretch, flapped them and crowed like a winning champ. His foe, five times larger, had fled, and all the pueblo could see that he was indeed *muy gallo*.

Seeing that Coronel was out of danger, Nerón and I dashed to tell the epic story. We reported how our rooster had dashed a hundred times against the vulture, how he had driven his spurs into the huge bird inflicting fatal wounds, Nerón, my dumb witness, wagged his tail and barked. [p. 31]

The cockfight mocks the village's established authorities, the *jefes de familia*, so obliquely that most readers miss its irony. Because it deals with seemingly nostalgic childhood memories about rural village life, the narrative probably appears innocent. Although their self-deprecating postures and their plain speech can be deceptive, Galarza and Paredes freely use irony, satire, mockery, and double meaning.

When Galarza describes a *corrido* songfest, his account must be taken tongue in cheek. It has none of the poetic solemnity of Paredes's depiction of a man who throws his head back as he belts out the *corrido* of Gregorio Cortez:

When some of the *compadres* got drunk, usually on Sundays, there was singing in some corral or in the plaza. Women and children took no part in these affairs, which sometimes ended in fights with machetes. We couldn't help hearing the men's songs, which became louder with the drinking. They sang the *corrido* of Catalino, the bandit who stood off hundreds of *rurales*, the mounted police who chased him up and down the Sierra Madre year in and year out. In his last battle, Catalino was cornered in a canyon. From behind a boulder he picked off dozens of rurales with his Winchester, taking a nip of *aguardiente* between shots, and shouting to his persecutors: "Acérquense, desgraciados, aquí está su padre." The rurales, like anybody else, did not like to be called wretched punks especially by an outlaw who boasted he was their father. In Mexico for such an insult you paid with your life. They closed in until Catalino lay dead. They chopped off his head and showed it in all the pueblos of the Sierra Madre, which made Catalino hero enough to have a ballad composed about him. It was generally agreed that he was from Jalcocotán where the bravest men were to be found, especially on Sunday nights when they were drunk. [pp. 48–49]

Nobody's masculine reputation escapes Galarza's parodic gaze. The *rurales* are mortally insulted by Catalino, who in turn becomes a hero by having his head chopped off. And the village men become the region's best and bravest only during their drunken Sunday night songfests. Galarza's deft, ironic touch deflates an overblown masculine ethic, but leaves the men's humanity intact.

After Galarza's move north to Sacramento, his mockery of patriarchal authority continues, but in a new context and with new consequences. In California, young Ernesto used his English-language education to translate for his elders as they negotiated with established Anglo authorities: "When troubles made it necessary for the *barrio* people to deal with the Americans uptown, the *Autoridades* [authorities], I went with them to the police court, the industrial accident office, the county hospital, the draft board, the county clerk. We got lost together in the rigamarole of functionaries who sat, like *patrones* [bosses], behind desks and who demanded licenses, certificates, documents, affidavits, signatures, and witnesses" (p. 252). Speaking from a bicultural border zone, Galarza juxtaposes the Mexican figures of the *Autoridad* and the *patrón* with North American bureaucratic offices and official documents. The idiom that once mocked *jefes de familia* in a Mexican village now undercuts the authority of state officials in Sacramento. The whimsical sense for incongruities that informs Galarza's vision of Jalcocotán shapes a bilingual text that, unbeknownst to them, verbally transforms Anglo-American authorities into Mexican bosses.

The autobiography's conclusion thus brings into focus Galarza's lifetime concern with Chicano and working-class struggles against Anglo-American capitalist domination. Paredes elevates primordial patriarchs in order to endow their successors with mythic potency for combatting Anglo-Texan prejudice; Galarza mocks Mexican patriarchs in order to gain a critical idiom for subverting Anglo-American political authorities. Although one inflates patriarchy and the other deflates it, both writers displace and transform the primoridal patriarchs so that they can play an emancipatory role in Chicano struggles of resistance.

Sandra Cisneros: The Fading of the Warrior Hero

The author of *The House on Mango Street*, Sandra Cisneros, is a young woman who grew up in the Mexican community of Chicago. A writer and a teacher, she graduated from the Iowa Writers Workshop, and she has taught creative writing at an alternative school for dropouts in Chicago. For her, writing is a craft and a form of empowerment. At once widely accessible and unobtrusively bilingual, her writing reflects concerns at once Chicana, feminist, and broadly political.

Cisneros's work grows out of a wider movement. During the 1980s, the most creative modes of imagining Chicano identity have emerged less often from social thinkers than from creative writers, particularly from short-story cycles authored by women. It is no accident that a marginal genre, such as the short story, should become a site for political innovation and cultural creativity. Literary theorist Mary Louise Pratt has argued, for example, that the short-story cycle's formal marginality (as compared with the novel) makes it a particularly likely arena for experimentation, for the development of alternative moral visions, and for the introduction of women and teenagers as central protagonists.[9] In the case at hand, young Chicana authors have written against earlier versions of cultural authenticity that idealized patriarchal cultural regimes that appeared autonomous, homogeneous, and unchanging.

Esperanza, the central protagonist of *The House on Mango Street*, tells a gender-specific coming-of-age story that develops a distinct strand of her cultural heritage. More matriarchal than patriarchal, her vision reaches back to her great-grandmother and forward to herself. Yet her constant play, her deceptively childlike patter, subverts oppressive patriarchal points of cultural coherence and fixity.

Esperanza does not orient to a remembered ancestral homeland in Mexico or anywhere else. Unlike the works of Paredes and Galarza, Cisneros's narrative invokes neither a primordial pastoral patriarchy nor a primeval tropical village. If Esperanza has a cultural anchor, an Edenic reference point, it is the house of her dreams, paradoxically tucked away in a future that never arrives. "I knew then," she says, "I had to have a house. A real house. One I could point to. But this isn't it. The house on Mango Street isn't it. For the time being, Mama said. Temporary, said Papa. But I know how those things go" (p. 9). The bilingualism of this prose is subtle enough to be ignored by Anglo readers. In her own public readings, however, Cisneros pronounces mango with the 'a' of "all," not that of "hat," and she accents Mama and Papa on the second syllable, not the first. Even life in the *barrio* appears not as near-documentary portraits of grinding poverty but as Esperanza's oblique statement that the American Dream has eluded her; she has no home, not even a room, of her own, and in her childhood she never will.[10]

In one of her short stories, she plays with themes of the warrior hero—the horseman, the name shouted in combat, and the *corrido* which sings of his deeds—destabilizing each as she goes. Let me illustrate by citing "My Name" in its entirety:

In English my name means hope. In Spanish it means too many letters. It means sadness, it means waiting. It is like the number nine. A muddy color. It is the Mexican records my father plays on Sunday mornings when he is shaving, songs like sobbing.

It was my great-grandmother's name and now it is mine. She was a horse woman too, born like me in the Chinese year of the horse—which is supposed to be bad luck if you're born female—but I think this is a Chinese lie because the Chinese, like the Mexicans, don't like their women strong.

My great-grandmother. I would've liked to have known her, a wild horse of a woman, so wild she wouldn't marry until my great-grandfather threw a sack over her head and carried her off just like that, as if she were a fancy chandelier. That's the way he did it.

And the story goes she never forgave him. She looked out the window all her life, the way so many women sit their sadness on an elbow. I wonder if she made the best with what she got or was she sorry because she couldn't be all the things she wanted to be. Esperanza. I have inherited her name, but I don't want to inherit her place by the window.

At school they say my name funny as if the syllables were made out of tin and hurt the roof of your mouth. But in Spanish my name is made out of a softer something like silver, not quite as thick as sister's name Magdalena which is uglier than mine. Magdalena who at least can come home and become Nenny. But I am always Esperanza.

I would like to baptize myself under a new name, a name more like the real me, the one nobody sees. Esperanza as Lisandra or Maritza or Zeze the X. Yes. Something like Zeze the X will do. [pp. 12–13]

Esperanza inhabits a border zone crisscrossed by a plurality of languages and cultures. Multiple subjectivities intersect in her own person, where they coexist, not in a zone of free play but each with its own gravity and density. Moving between English and Spanish, her name shifts in length (from four letters to nine), in meaning (from hope to sadness and waiting), and in sound (from being as cutting as tin to as soft as silver). In contrast to Gregorio Cortez, she does not stand in one place, looking straight ahead, and shout, "Yo soy Esperanza."

Like her grandmother, Esperanza is a horse woman, but not a female imitation of the *hidalgo*, the male warrior horseman. No, she was born, of all things, in the *Chinese* year of the horse; in her heterogeneous cultural world, the Chinese and the Chicano readily come into play together. Both Chinese and Mexicans agree, she says, because neither culture likes its women strong.[11] Her narrative moves, as if along links in a chain of free associations, and great-grandmother Esperanza undergoes a metamorphosis from a rider, the horse woman, to the beast itself, a wild horse of a woman.

Her patrimony, the *corrido*, has been reduced to Mexican records that sound like sobbing. Although she accepts her matronymy (that is, her name), Esperanza refuses to assume her great-grandmother's place by the window. As she concludes the tale, Esperanza yet again turns things topsy-turvy by baptizing her invisible, real self: Zeze the X. Nothing stands still, especially not her name.

Near poems, the short stories evoke twin threats to her

person in the form of sexuality and physical danger. Yet the power of these threats deceptively appears in the patter of "childlike" diction that often imitates nursery rhymes:

> Across the street in front of the tavern a bum man on the stoop.
> Do you like these shoes?
> Bum man says, Yes, little girl. Your little lemon shoes are so beautiful. But come closer. I can't see very well. Come closer. Please.
> You are a pretty girl, bum man continues. What's your name, pretty girl?
> And Rachel says Rachel, just like that.
> Now you know to talk to drunks is crazy and to tell them your name is worse, but who can blame her. She is young and dizzy to hear so many sweet things in one day, even if it is a bum man's whiskey words saying them.
> Rachel, you are prettier than a yellow taxi cab. You know that. But we don't like it. We got to go, Lucy says.
> If I give you a dollar will you kiss me? How about a dollar? [p. 39]

That this is a Chicana version of "Little Red Riding Hood" becomes evident as the bum man asks her to draw nearer, virtually saying, "The better to see you, my dear." His threatening presence echoes the clichéd warning of parents who say to their children, "Don't take candy from strangers." Instead of candy, the bum man offers saccharine words, calls her a pretty girl, praises her shoes, compares her with a yellow cab, and, in the end, offers a dollar for her kiss.

Esperanza depicts her sexual awakening as a process at once sensuous and dangerous. The story entitled "Hips" plays back and forth, metaphorically, between her suddenly present hips and a brand new Buick: "One day you wake up and there they [your hips] are. Ready and waiting like a new Buick with the keys in the ignition. Ready to take you where?" (p. 47). In a later story, she is bursting: "Everything is holding its breath inside me. Everything is waiting to explode like Christmas. I want to be all new and shiny. I want to sit out bad at night, a boy around my neck and the wind under my skirt" (p. 70). Esperanza interweaves her sexuality, her rounding hips, and images of automobiles. Not unlike a car, she is polished and ready to go (where?). In being "bad," she moves toward the sensuous, pleasurable, threatening edges of her world.

In this play of desire and threat, Esperanza meets dangers by gracefully moving on. If her sexuality resembles a new car, her grace is danced. "And uncle," she says, "spins me and my skinny arms bend the way he taught me and my mother watches and my little cousins watch and the boy who is my cousin by first communion watches and everyone says, wow, who are those two who dance like in the movies, until I forget that I am wearing only ordinary shoes, brown and white, the kind my mother buys each year for school" (p. 46). Her grace resides in her person, not in her ordinary shoes. Never standing in one place, she uses the dance to counter male violence and efforts to confine and subordinate her. She just moves on, in her dance of life.

Cisneros opens fresh vistas in what Américo Paredes saw as the inextricably intertwined realms of culture and politics. In her narrative analysis, the concept of culture undergoes a metamorphosis. The warrior hero has seen better days. No longer can he serve as the "unified subject" around which Chicano sagas of masculine heroics revolve. Yet what the concept of culture loses in purity and authenticity, it gains in range and engagement. As embodied in Cisnero's short-story cycle, Chicano culture moves toward the borderlands, the spaces that readily include blacks, Anglos, mundane happenings of everyday life, and heterogeneous changing neighborhoods. Certain border crossings involve literal immigration, in which a number of people move in and out of the neighborhood, or a "wetback" with no last name dies anonymously in an accident, or a fat woman who speaks no English sits by the window and plays homesick songs. Others appear as more figurative border dances through which Esperanza makes her way in a world of desire and threat, budding sexuality and dangerous male violence.

In trying new narrative forms, Cisneros has developed a

fresh vision of self and society; she has opened an alternative cultural space, a heterogeneous world, within which her protagonists no longer act as "unified subjects," yet remain confident of their identities. Esperanza's name itself twists and twirls until it reaches the end of its alphabet, "Zeze the X." In moving through a world laced with poverty, violence, and danger, Esperanza acts at once assertive and playful. She thrives, not just survives, as she dances through her unpredictable world with grace and wit. For all her grace, however, Esperanza does not just take on personas and remove them, as if they were so many old shoes; unlike the less encumbered French literary theorist Roland Barthes, Esperanza feels the weight of the multiple identities that intersect through her person.

On a more reflexive note, I should like to conclude by underscoring the analytical import of the interplay between "their" (Anglo-American) narratives and "ours" (Chicano). In the case at hand, the implications of Sandra Cisneros's short-story cycle came to me quite gradually. It took time— from initially conceiving my article "Grief and a Headhunter's Rage" onward—for the concept of a multiplex personal identity to move in alongside its predecessor, the "unified subject," and for the notion of culture as multiple border zones to find a place next to its predecessor, the "homogeneous community." Yet it would be difficult to exaggerate the major role played by the narrative analyses of Paredes, Galarza, and Cisneros in my charting a path for renewing the anthropologist's search for meaning.

Certain readers may also wish to know that my point of departure in the next chapter, a critique of Max Weber's masculine heroics, followed on the heels of reading Cisneros, but with a major difference. The human and analytical limitations of Weber's passionate detachment struck me all at once, not gradually. This realization left me feeling at once deeply disoriented and excited at new possibilities for the social analyst as a "positioned subject." On the one hand, disciplined work habits went by the wayside because I could do nothing but wander around while things sank in at their own pace. On the other hand, new topics opened up because my attention was somehow drawn to works not usually included in the canon of interdisciplinary works for cultural studies. My inquiry, it seemed, was on a meander. Once absorbed, however, the critique of Weber proved central in organizing my thoughts for much of this book.

8 | *Subjectivity in Social Analysis*

ACCORDING TO ETHNOGRAPHIES written in the classic mode, the detached observer epitomizes neutrality and impartiality. This detachment is said to produce objectivity because social reality comes into focus only if one stands at a certain distance. When one stands too close, the ethnographic lens supposedly blurs its human subjects. In this view, the researcher must remove observer bias by becoming the emotional, cognitive, and moral equivalent of a blank slate. Translated into the ethical terms critiqued in chapter 3, the myth of detachment gives ethnographers an appearance of innocence, which distances them from complicity with imperialist domination. Prejudice and distortion, however, putatively derive from the vices of subjectivity: passionate concern, prior knowledge, and ethical engagement.

If distance has certain arguable advantages, so too does closeness, and both have their deficits. Yet classic social science has endowed the former with excessive virtue, and the latter with excessive vice. Distanced normalizing accounts, as seen in chapter 2, all too often lead ethnographic writings to translate the compelling events of daily life into the routine performance of conventional acts. The present chapter contests the equation of analytical distance and scientific objectivity by arguing that social analysts should explore their subjects from a number of positions, rather than being locked into any particular one.

In my view, social analysts can rarely, if ever, become detached observers. There is no Archimedean point from which to remove oneself from the mutual conditioning of social relations and human knowledge. Cultures and their "positioned subjects" are laced with power, and power in turn is shaped by cultural forms. Like form and feeling, culture and power are inextricably intertwined. In discussing forms of social knowledge, both of analysts and of human actors, one must consider their social positions. What are the complexities of the speaker's social identity? What life experiences have shaped it? Does the person speak from a position of relative dominance or relative subordination? This chapter uses a series of examples to explore the consequences of thus understanding the factors that condition social analysis.

The Heroics of Value-Free Inquiry

Discussions of objectivity in the human sciences ritually invoke Max Weber as their founding ancestor. The Weberian tradition has legitimated research programs that attempt, in the name of value-free inquiry, to clarify the world rather than to change it. Weber's successors have transformed the original demanding ethic of "disinterested-ness" into an orthodoxy widespread in the social sciences that equates objectivity with an attitude of emotional disen-gagement, cognitive distance, and moral indifference.

Weber himself advocated a position that partially over-laps with, but also significantly diverges from, the particu-lar kind of distanced observation so often promoted by his successors. In "Science as a Vocation," for example, he ar-gues that neither the prophet nor the demagogue has any place in the classroom. One should neither preach one's reli-gion nor impose one's politics on a captive audience. Socio-logical analyses provide no scientific grounds for making judgments about whether the phenomena under study are humanly worthwhile. Questions, for instance, about the ulti-mate worth of monastic discipline simply cannot be an-swered within the limits of sociological inquiry. In a histori-cal epoch marked by the "disenchantment of the world," scientific knowledge should not be conflated with ultimate values.

Weber's disciplined neutrality with respect to ultimate values does not imply, however, that scientists should work without passion or enthusiasm: "The idea is not a substitute for work; and work, in turn, cannot substitute for or compel an idea, just as little as enthusiasm can. Both, enthusiasm and work, and above all both of them *jointly,* can entice the idea."[1] In "Politics as a Vocation," Weber speaks in a closely related manner about the ethic of responsibility in the bour-geois state: "For the problem is simply how can warm pas-sion and a cool sense of proportion be forged together in one and the same soul? Politics is made with the head, not with other parts of the body or soul. And yet devotion to politics, if it is not to be frivolous intellectual play but rather genu-inely human conduct, can be born and nourished from pas-sion alone."[2] In other words, warm passion emanates from devotion to a cause, and a cool sense of proportion derives from the detachment that clarifies reality. For Weber, doing good politics has the properties of an oxymoron in that it requires one to be "warm" and "cool" at the same time.

Similarly, doing good science requires a fusion of enthusiasm and work. Weber's polyphonic capacity to hold contradictory or incongruous tendencies in tension bears only a faint resemblance to the ethic of disinterest, verging on boredom, so often attributed to him by orthodox social scientists.

If even a debased version of Weber's vocational ethic has proven compelling to his successors, its hold largely resides in its capacity to endow routinized lives with mythic meaning. In exhorting scientists to live up to a demanding ethic, Weber extends the argument made in his classic study of the Protestant ethic's momentous impact on the development of capitalism. Even in separating science from religion, Weber often describes the former by using concepts from the latter, most notably the terms "vocation," as seen in his title, and "devotion," as seen in the following: "Ladies and gentlemen. In the field of science only he who is devoted *solely* to the work at hand has 'personality.' . . . An inner devotion to the task, and that alone, should lift the scientist to the height and dignity of the subject he pretends to serve."[3] Much in the manner of Calvin's doctrine, Weber's ethic both inspires people to rise above themselves *and* proves impossible for anyone but the virtuoso to live up to.

In mythic terms, Weber's ethic has a venerable genealogy that extends back to quest stories about the pursuit of the unobtainable (say, the Holy Grail) and chivalric romances about absolute devotion to the unattainable (say, the beautiful princess). Although less elevated than a quest story or a chivalric romance, Weber's doctrine remains harsh, manly, and worthy of a warrior figure: "To the person who cannot bear the fate of the times like a man, one must say: may he rather return silently, without the usual publicity build-up of renegades, but simply and plainly. The arms of the old churches are opened widely and compassionately for him."[4] In Weber's view, surrender to the church's (womanly) compassionate embrace is the only alternative for those unable to endure manly devotion to scientific discipline. The masculine heroics of science as an ascetic calling socialize people for service in such latter-day warrior priesthoods as the modern state and its military, religious, corporate, educational, and other bureaucratic regimes.

Like his vision of passionate detachment, Weber's notion of science as a vocation has fallen from its former high standards. It now survives in the daily lives of academics as the "busy-ness ethic." One friend says to another, for example, "Let's get together and talk," whereupon the two of them deploy an obligatory gesture worthy of Radcliffe-Brown's Andaman Islanders: they pull out their appointment calendars. When the appointed hour on the appointed day arrives, they greet one another breathlessly, converse for a while, and excuse themselves, saying they're already late for an important meeting. For many of us, willy-nilly caught in this ethic, the central drama of our all-consuming professional lives has become how-busy-I-am. Woe to those who simply do their jobs without subscribing to the self-aggrandizing, meaning-giving "busy-ness ethic." Neither their colleagues nor their deans will take them seriously.

In my view, however, the notion of one's profession as a calling in the pursuit of perfection produces careers that revolve around the twin poles of great effort and tremendous frustration. Arguably, this vocational ethic promotes not only institutional devotion and human unhappiness but also an overly constricted definition of legitimate sources of knowledge. Weberian knowledge emerges more readily from "manly" strength than "womanly" weakness. Yet sources of knowledge other than absolute devotion to a higher standard also provide certain insights for social analysis.

In the present era, feminist thought has made the limitations of the harsh ethic demanded by the warrior priesthood particularly evident. Weber's "manly" ethic should be loosened because its androcentrism has suppressed valuable sources of insight deemed unworthy by bearers of the high standard. This ethic underestimates the analytical possibilities of "womanly weaknesses" and "unmanly states," such as rage, feebleness, frustration, depression, embarrassment, and passion. Victims of oppression, for example, can provide insights into the workings of power that differ from those available to people in high positions. The welfare mother and the chief of police surely differ in their knowledge and feelings about state power. Arguably, human feelings and human failings provide as much insight for social analysis as subjecting oneself to the "manly" ordeals of self-discipline that constitute science as a vocation. Why narrow one's vision to a God's-eye view from on high? Why not use a wider spectrum of less heroic, but equally insightful, analytical positions?

The Typewriter Incident

Alongside the prevailing orthodoxy, a more classic form of Weber's ethic shapes certain areas of present-day research in the human sciences. Consider, for example, Clifford Geertz's essay, "Thinking as a Moral Act: Dimensions of Anthropological Fieldwork in the New States." Weberian notions of passionate detachment and science as a vocation fairly saturate his argument: "What little disinterestedness one manages to attain comes not from failing to have emotions or neglecting to perceive them in others, nor yet from sealing oneself into a moral vacuum. It comes from a personal subjection to a vocational ethic."[5] For Geertz, doing fieldwork with Weberian disinterestedness involves following a demanding vocational ethic that brings together feeling, thought, and ethics. His analysis, which lends a distinctive cast to the conception, widespread among its practitioners, that cultural anthropology is a calling, in the end uncharacteristically reveals more about the dynamics of power than the workings of culture.[6]

Geertz maintains that fieldwork, where "one must see society as an object and experience it as a subject," virtually requires the fusion of "two fundamental orientations toward reality—the engaged and the analytic—into a single attitude."[7] Fieldwork as a form of conduct involves a tension between scientific understanding and moral perception, between a disciplined form of inquiry and the practical activities of everyday life. Geertz's oxymorons bring together not only the engaged and the analytic but also friends and informants, living and thinking, the personal and the professional, and perceiving cultural values as objects and holding them as a subject. This classic Weberian notion of passionate detachment consists of holding polar orientations in tension, rather than remaining, in the name of scientific impartiality, unmoved by moral concern.

In characterizing the moral tensions between field-workers and their informants, Geertz brings his readers close to fieldwork as a practical activity. He tells a self-parodic anecdote about his relation with a young Javanese man who wrote fiction, worked as a clerk, and served as one of the ethnographer's best informants. Geertz's job, as an ethnographer, involved recording interviews from the young man whose job, as a fiction writer, entailed in turn borrowing the ethnographer's typewriter. The young man borrowed the typewriter more and more often, until the day that the ethnographer wrote a seemingly tactful note saying that he needed the typewriter that day. The note, it turned out, gave offense, and subsequent efforts to make amends only made matters worse. In the end, the misunderstanding between ethnographer and informant terminated their relationship.

Although deeply influenced by the Weberian ethic, Geertz portrays himself in the typewriter episode as a cross-culturally inept figure. His conduct is at odds with that of a warrior priest who systematically subjects himself to the manly discipline of scientific virtue. When Geertz describes his efforts to restore good relations with his informant, for example, he says, "I made some feeble efforts to repair the situation—rendered all the more feeble by my sense of having behaved like an ass—but it was too late."[8] Indeed, his vulnerability becomes a source of insight for the exploration of certain moral dilemmas of conducting fieldwork in Java.

What moral does Geertz find in the story? For him, the rupture exposes the tenuous constructs that shape interpersonal relations in the field. The ruptured relationship, he says, has one set of meanings for the ethnographer, and quite another for his informant. Because he sought friendship, the ethnographer feels jilted. Because he sought collegiality, the young man feels humiliated. Geertz's remarkably candid anecdote reveals that doing fieldwork involves human failings as excruciating as they are mundane. It also reveals the terrible asymmetries that separate field-worker and informant.

Although most professional readers of Geertz would expect him to stress culture above all else, the miniature case history emphasizes power relations at the expense of cultural conceptions. The young Javanese man, as he seeks collegiality and rejects overtures of friendship, appears oddly transparent to American readers. We do not learn, for example, how he expressed his desire to be accepted as a fellow writer. Which Javenese concepts have been translated as "acceptance"? How do they diverge from "our" notion? Moreover, it seems likely that the young man understood Geertz's overtures not in relation to American notions of "friendship" but in terms of distinctively Javanese notions of conduct.

Geertz's typewriter incident shows how feelings that appear unworthy from a strict Weberian perspective can provide insight into relations of inequality. A researcher determined to live up to a high standard would most probably eliminate "feebleness" as a potential source of knowledge because it would appear beneath his or her dignified ethic of masculine heroics. The limits of the analysis at the same time underscore the practical difficulties of doing reflexive narrative analyses that attempt simultaneously to encompass transitional processes, the dynamics of power, and the workings of culture.

A Tent of One's Own

Adherence to the vision of anthropology as a vocation has been widespread but not universal. Notable exceptions do exist, particularly among women ethnographers.

According to her ethnography *Never in Anger: Portrait of an Eskimo Family*, Jean Briggs worked without Weberian pretensions.[9] In conducting her fieldwork, she did not try to elevate herself to the dignified heights of science as a vocation. Instead, she used her own feelings, particularly depression, frustration, rage, and humiliation, as sources of insight into the emotional life among members of an Eskimo group in the Canadian Northwest Territories.

Briggs struggled to do her research and survive under exceptionally difficult conditions. While conducting fieldwork, she suffered from not altogether unrealistic anxieties about freezing to death, nutritional deprivation, and severe illness. Members of the Eskimo community where she resided were caring, even solicitous of her well-being. According to their norms, however, her desires for domestic privacy were opaque, and her emotional outbursts threatened to rip apart their intricately woven social fabric. In a reversal of usual relations between rational Western Man and the emotional rest, the Eskimos lived with a culturally valued degree of emotional control that the culturally more impulsive ethnographer simply could not attain.

Faced with demanding physical and emotional circumstances, Briggs needed a tent of her own, a place where she could renew body and soul. In time, she closeted herself every evening in her tent, and indulged her cravings for familiar food, books, and work. When summer changed to autumn, her hosts advised her to fold up the tent and move in with them, but she resisted: "Could I tolerate the company of others for twenty-four hours a day? In the past month my tent had become a refuge, into which I withdrew every evening after the rest of the camp was in bed, to repair the ravages to my spirit with the help of bannock and peanut butter, boiled rice, frozen dates, and Henry James."[10] Briggs often took her penciled notes into her tent and "sat happily typing" for long hours at a time.[11] When mishaps, such as lumps of slush falling into her typewriter, ended her workday, she responded with emotional outbursts that offended her more emotionally disciplined hosts.[12] Like Geertz, she regarded her typewriter as a sacred object, not to be pro-faned. The typewriter stood for her workspace and her pro-fessional identity.

Briggs's ethnography more nearly resembles the captivity narrative, a tale of deprivation and survival, than the ro-mantic quest, a story of adventure and conquest. In com-menting on her irrepressible cravings for the "solace of oat-meal, dates, boiled rice, and bannock," the ethnographer accurately depicts her experience as one of isolation, de-privation, and risk: "It is hard for anyone who has not expe-rienced isolation from his familiar world to conceive the vital importance of maintaining symbolic ties with that world and the sense of deprivation that results from their absence. One can be driven to lengths that seem ludicrous once one is safely back on home ground." [13] Although the choice was originally her own, Briggs found herself overwhelmed by an alien world. In response to emotional and physical deprivation, she sought consolation through food, and even went so far as to hoard eight sesame seeds in tin foil. The ethnographer was held prisoner, not by the Eskimos but by her determination to succeed in doing fieldwork under demanding conditions.

Briggs's resolve to survive a demanding test had some-thing of the sentimental heroics of victimization found in certain melodramatic nineteenth-century novels (notably including those of Henry James, and perhaps others she was reading at the time). Yet this resolve did not inspire her to follow the model of masculine heroics in which, as Weber says, the devoted scientist rises "to the height and dignity of the subject he pretends to serve." [14] In everyday fieldwork, she never aspired to perfection. Instead, she made mistakes, felt frustrated, broke into tears, had angry outbursts, grew fatigued, and became depressed. On one occasion, a fishing companion warned her to move to a safer spot, but after an initial effort: "Suddenly, something in me gave up. I had no will to struggle further. Dropping to my knees and lowering my head to the ice, I crawled toward home, seething with humiliation and rage but totally unable to stand up. Shielded by the parka and hood that fell over my face, I wept at my ignominy."[15] Even in retrospect, she could not decide whether she fell to her hands and knees because the wind was overwhelming or because she was fatigued from depression. In any case, she survived only by abandoning her dignity and enduring humiliation.[16]

Briggs makes her own depression central to *Never in Anger*. Her final chapter comprises an eighty-two-page case history, depicting the relationship between the ethnographer and her informants as it moved from covert conflicts, through more overt ones, to being shunned. Initially, she was treated as an honored guest, an adopted daughter, a stranger, and a curiosity. Later, she became like a recalcitrant child who oscillated between helpless dependence and mutinous independence. Finally, she suffered the ultimate sanction and was ostracized because, as one Eskimo said in a letter, "she is so annoying, we wish more and more that she would leave."[17]

Briggs explores her fieldwork moods not as an end in itself but as a vehicle for understanding Eskimo family and emotional life. She learned about their conceptions of emotions from their efforts to interpret her unfamiliar ways of acting: "It is possible that in that early period they were watching, weighing, not yet confirming unpleasant judgements but puzzling how to interpret my strange behavior, just as I puzzled how to interpret theirs."[18] Whenever she withdrew from her hosts, they interpreted her behavior by saying she was tired, regardless of whether she felt depressed, cold, or simply in need of solitude. In retrospect, however, Briggs wondered whether the people's caring attention reflected notions about a white woman's feebleness, a perception of emotional fatigue, or both. For the Eskimos, unpredictable tiredness and emotional upset were closely associated.[19] Their perception of her "tiredness" revealed much about their views of emotions, particularly as experienced in the informal practices of everyday life rather than as articulated in abstract context-free statements.

Briggs delineates transitions in ethnographer-informant relations through a reflexive narrative that highlights cultural conceptions more than the dynamics of power. She displays a grasp of culturally shaped emotional lives, both her own and that of the Eskimos. Yet her analysis of power relations stresses her initial status as honored guest and her later childlike dependence without sufficiently acknowledging her place in a system of domination. During the fieldwork period, as she later realized, the ethnographer failed to recognize the burden her possessions imposed on her host, Inuttiaq: "It was only after I had returned to my own country that I saw, in my photographs of a spring move, the contrast between Inuttiaq's sled load and Ipuituq's, the latter over knee high, the former shoulder high. At the time I was blind."[20] Even in retrospect, however, Briggs was able to perceive the cultural shape of emotions with fine insight, but remained relatively blind to the material differences that divided her from her hosts. If Geertz's essay highlights power relations at the expense of cultural meanings, Briggs does the reverse.

Briggs's relationship with the Eskimos was contradictory, at once vulnerable and dominant. In the local setting, she depended on her hosts for basic survival; in the national setting, she was richer and more powerful than they. Her experience among the Eskimos was colored by feelings of vulnerability, yet her treatment as an honored guest in the beginning and the passive resistance of shunning toward the end were doubtless shaped by the power dynamics between the ethnographer and her informants. Neither her experience nor her relations with the Eskimos were as unified as her narrative persona would make them appear.

Multiplex Personal Identities and Social Analysis

Cautionary tales that circulate among field-workers warn against going too far in identifying with the so-called natives. In one such tale, for example, legendary turn-of-the-century North American ethnographer Frank Hamilton Cushing's writings reputedly grew better and better until the day he was initiated into a Zuni secret society. From that time onward, it is said, his ethnography deteriorated. Moral: don't go native. "Going native" is said to mean the end of scientific knowledge. Often traced to Malinowski's legendary fieldwork, this view asserts that the optimal field-worker should dance on the edge of a paradox by simultaneously becoming "one of the people" and remaining an academic. The term *participant-observation* reflects even as it shapes the field-worker's double persona.

The dilemmas of identification as a source of knowledge have been forcefully presented in a recent paper by anthropologist Dorinne Kondo. As a Japanese-American, Kondo was pressured in Japan to conform with norms more fully than other outsiders. In a vivid anecdote, she describes herself on a muggy afternoon in Tokyo, pushing a baby in a stroller and shopping for fish and vegetables: "As I glanced up into the shiny metal surface of the butcher's display case, I noticed someone who looked terribly familiar: a typical young housewife, in slip-on sandals and the kind of cotton shift the Japanese label 'home-wear,' a woman walking with a characteristically Japanese bend in the knees and sliding of the feet. Suddenly I clutched the handle of the stroller to steady myself as a wave of dizziness washed over me—for I realized I had caught a glimpse of nothing less than my own reflection."[21] Kondo felt overwhelmed with anxiety. Had she gone native? Had what Clifford Geertz saw as the tenuous construct shaping field relations become the literal truth? Had she irreversibly become the dutiful daughter of her Japanese "family"? Would she now become a Japanese housewife rather than a Japanese-American academic?

Kondo thought she had gone too far, and she followed disciplinary norms by attempting to gain distance on her situation. She returned to the United States for a month. On returning to Japan, she moved into an apartment next door to her landlady's family. Rather like Jean Briggs, she hoped her new situation would allow her to enjoy "the best of both worlds: the warmth of belonging to a family and the privacy of my own space."[22]

Yet Kondo could only distance herself to a certain degree.

Because of their cultural expectations about a person who looks so like them, the Japanese obliged her to act like a "native." Her near-native persona gave the Japanese-American ethnographer certain advantages, such as rapid incorporation into a number of social groups. But it also inhibited her in other areas. Unlike a more foreign researcher, Kondo could neither ask "indelicate" questions nor speak with people across certain status lines.

The moral Kondo draws from her story is that the process of knowing involves the whole self. The social analyst is at once cognitive, emotional, and ethical. She constructs knowledge through contexts of shifting power relations that involve varying degrees of distance and intimacy. Rather than uphold detachment as the unified standard of objectivity, Kondo argues for the explicit recognition of multiple sources of knowledge in social analysis.

Kondo's proposal to dissolve the detached observer with his "God's-eye view" of social reality makes most classic ethnographers quake. Are there no standards? Where has objectivity gone? Can this be the advent of unbridled chaos that allows nihilism and relativism to walk hand in hand in a land where "anything goes"? In what follows, I argue, to the contrary, that dismantling objectivism creates a space for ethical concerns in a territory once regarded as value-free. It enables the social analyst to become a social critic.

Social Criticism and Multiplex Communities

In general, social critics attempt to use persuasive eloquence and adept social analysis to make oppression morally unacceptable and human emancipation politically conceivable.[23] In so doing, they invoke local cultural values, such as justice, well-being, or cosmic balance. They engage in arguments about social issues where empirical analyses and ethical judgments are inextricably intertwined. In such cultural arenas, human relations are governed more often by conflict than consensus.

In his recent book entitled *Interpretation and Social Criti-*

cism, political theorist Michael Walzer argues that social criticism involves making complex ethical judgments about existing social arrangements.[24] The moral vision so applied emerges, not from the outside, but from within the society under criticism. In all human societies, everyday life and moral standards overlap, but they also, as Walzer aptly stresses, remain to a certain degree at odds with one another: "The moral world and the social world are more or less coherent," he writes, "but they are never more than more or less coherent. Morality is always potentially subversive of class and power."[25] Moral visions grow out of specific forms of life that they both unthinkingly reflect and critically call into question. Social critics thus remain grounded in the local cultures to which they direct their exhortations and invectives.

Ideally, according to Walzer, social critics should be meaningfully connected with, rather than utterly detached from, the group under critique. Like my own argument, his assertion contests the conventional wisdom that idealizes the impartial detached observer. Walzer argues that the critic should be socially connected, probably not at the center of things, but neither a complete stranger nor a mere spectator. In his view, the most powerful members of society make better apologists than critics, and those most marginal either perceive their world through distorted lenses or all too readily cave in to efforts to co-opt them.

Unfortunately, Walzer limits the applicability of his analysis by defining the key word *community* too narrowly. It is as if he accepted classic ethnography's notion that each individual can belong to one, and only one, discrete (unambiguous, nonoverlapping) culture. No doubt certain limiting cases exist where a social critic's audience and community are one and the same discrete group. More frequently, however, one finds precisely what Walzer overlooks: a plurality of partially disjunctive, partially overlapping communities that crisscross between the people social critics address and those for whom they speak.

The complexity of a social critic's "community" emerges with a certain clarity in the work of the celebrated social historian E. P. Thompson. The moral vision that informs his committed history is evident, for example, in the conclusion of *The Making of the English Working Class*, where he sketches a "what if" vision of the past in order to critique the present.[26] What if, he asks, the two cultures of nineteenth-century English radicalism—the craftspeople and the romantics— had united in resistance to Utilitarianism and "the exploitive and oppressive relationships intrinsic to industrial capitalism"?:

After William Blake, no mind was at home in both cultures, nor had the genius to interpret the two traditions to each other. It was a muddled Mr. Owen who offered to disclose the "new moral world," while Wordsworth and Coleridge had withdrawn behind their own ramparts of disenchantment. Hence these years appear at times to display, not a revolutionary challenge, but a resistance movement, in which both the Romantics and the Radical craftsmen opposed the annunciation of Acquisitive Man. In the failure of the two traditions to come to a point of junction, something was lost. How much we cannot be sure, for we are among the losers.[27]

For some fifty years, working-class struggles created and exemplified a "heroic culture" that gave life to the radical tradition. "Their" nineteenth-century failure to unite the two traditions is also "our" twentieth-century failure. As the inheritors of radicalism, "we" have been diminished by the gulf separating romantics and craftspeople. Thompson thus exhorts "us," his readers, to live up to "our" radical heritage by uniting workers, artists, and intellectuals in heroic struggle.

Thompson's shifting use of pronouns indicates the complexity of his identifications. His political communities extend, somewhat ambiguously, to nineteenth-century radicalism; his communities of readers include professional historians and lay radicals. He both distances himself from the nineteenth-century radicals and identifies them as predecessors in "our" tradition of dissent. At the same time, he addresses his social criticism to an international group of present-day historians and radicals, among whom he is an eminent figure.

Let us now juxtapose Thompson's moving conclusion with its rhetorical opposite, the ethnographer Harold Conklin's classic technical paper, "Shifting Cultivation and Succession to Grassland Climax."[28] This nonobvious comparison underscores the importance of distinguishing the remaking of social analysis from the use of any particular rhetorical form. The attempts of a renewed social analysis to grasp the interplay of culture and power require not only experimentation in writing but also changes in the norms for reading. To maintain older habits of reading is willy-nilly to assimilate new forms of social analysis to the classic period's conventional wisdom. If readers shift their practices, on the other hand, they can recover certain works written in distanced normalizing discourse.

By contrast with Thompson's explicit moral passion, Conklin tacitly claims a "guest membership" in the ethnic Hanunoo community of the Philippines, where he resided for an extended period and whose language he speaks fluently. His paper describes Hanunoo agriculture to an international scientific elite, a community in which he is a prominent member. His communities range as widely in geopolitical terms as his memberships in them vary in their definitions.

When Conklin meticulously attends to culturally relevant discriminations made by Philippine shifting cultivators, his voice remains scrupulously dispassionate and scientific:

Where climatic and terrain conditions are ideal for swidden agriculture, a single firing of cut jungle does not—by itself—start a succession to grassland. However, repeated firing of the same site during the following and successive years, for recultivation or by accident, may kill many of the coppicing stumps and young tree seedlings, and discourage the growth of broadleafed shade-providing shrubs, while favoring the spread of erect grasses (especially *Imperata*) whose extensive stoloniferous rhizomes and deep roots are left uninjured.[29]

In other words, under ideal conditions swidden or shifting cultivation (popularly known as "slash and burn") does not start a process that results in the replacement of forest with agriculturally unusable grassland. Ideally, shifting cultivators burn off the forest cover, cultivate the spot for about two years, and then allow the forest to regenerate over an extended fallow period. Such factors as cattle grazing and the dispersal of gardens increase the likelihood of an ideal process. The ecologically destructive succession to grassland climax, in contrast, is associated with such variables as cultivating ridges and hilltops, the simultaneous clearing of adjacent plots, repeatedly burning grass for hunting, and planting grain crops for more than two successive years on a single plot. In its form and content, the analysis appears detached and balanced.

From another angle of vision, however, Conklin's technical article appears as a passionate plea for the ecological soundness of Hanunoo agriculture. In the Philippines, shifting cultivation has long been under assault by public opinion, the media, and governmental policy. The dominant lowland view holds that such agricultural systems, in all times and in all places, destroy the ecological balance by starting a succession to grassland climax. Conklin has chosen a rhetoric designed to persuade an audience of ethnographers, botanists, and agronomists, who conceivably could in turn convince policymakers. Read in this context, the ethnographer emerges as an advocate for the Hanunoo and as a critic of dominant national policy. Like other ethnographers, the author identifies with the underdogs, the people under study. His apparently neutral article has its partisan side. It combines descriptive ethnography, advocacy, and social criticism.

Thus understood, Conklin's technical article becomes an example of committed social analysis. The tacit implications of his article reflect a politics grounded in notions of human well-being and ecological concern. To the extent that "Shifting Cultivation" addresses policymakers, it enters an arena of partisan debate where power, knowledge, feeling, and judgment are at play. Those who enter the debate do so from particular positions with complex stakes in the struggle. In this context, Conklin's neutrality and omniscience become a rhetorically strategic means for assuming the authoritative high ground of scientific knowledge divorced from human interests. He appears simply to report the facts, letting the chips fall where they may, but hoping in this manner to convince Filipino politicians to overcome their prejudice and vested interests.

Despite obvious differences of explicitness, politics, and rhetoric, Conklin's "scientific" ethnography compares, in its serious tone and its persuasive moral vision, with the celebrated committed history of E. P. Thompson. Conklin uses self-effacing detachment and scientific authority on behalf of Hanunoo shifting cultivators; Thompson uses flamboyant identification and a compelling moral vision to benefit the working class. Both attempt to give voice to the voiceless. In a dissenting mode, the ethnographer and the social historian aim to articulate the interests and the aspirations of the dispossessed. Where Conklin demands high ethical and scientific standards of his fellow ethnographers and policymakers, Thompson exhorts equally much from his fellow historians and English radicals. As advocates for subordinate groups, they both develop critiques of social domination. As social critics, the "outsider" speaks the universal language of science, and the "insider" uses the orator's impassioned exhortations.

Subaltern Social Analysis

Let us return briefly to Walzer's discussion of social criticism with a view to considering a problem related to that of whether communities are unitary or multiplex. What should the critic's social position be? Rather surprisingly,

Walzer's ideal social critic appears to be an oppositional member of the ruling class. Such a person's task, as he sees it, is to persuade dominant social groups to improve the lives of socially subordinate groups. The two paradigmatic figures he discusses at length as exemplary social critics are John Locke, who had friends in power, and the prophet Jonah, who was a member of his society's dominant group. One can almost infer that Walzer would advise members of subordinate groups not to speak for themselves because their only hope resides in seeking out a socially prominent spokesperson. Fortunately, one passage, rather at odds with his general argument, concedes that the dispossessed can articulate their own grievances and aspirations: "It may be that a critic from the ruling classes learns to see society through the eyes of the oppressed, but one of the oppressed who sees through his own eyes is no less a social critic." [30] Walzer, however, provides neither further discussion nor any exemplary figure to explore what happens when the oppressed speak for themselves.

Let us now further pursue the opening provided by Walzer's momentary discussion of the social critic who speaks from a subordinate position. Consider the writings of Frantz Fanon, a psychiatrist, revolutionary, and social thinker, who, not altogether unlike Conklin and Thompson, moved between interconnected worlds. His readers and his subjects resided in Algeria, black Africa, and Paris; they were multiracial, multicultural, and multinational. Born in and raised in Martinique, he studied medicine in Paris and went to a position as head of psychiatry in an Algerian hospital. When the revolution against the French colonial regime broke out in 1954, Fanon became pro-Algerian and participated extensively in the anticolonial struggle until he died of leukemia in 1961, at the age of thirty-six. Through his life experiences and his political participation, he came to speak both for himself and for the racially oppressed with a message that the powerful had to confront. [31] In time, and in a manner he could not have fully foreseen, his works came to speak forcefully to those involved in the civil rights struggles of the 1960s in the United States.

In a remarkable passage from *Black Skin, White Masks*, Fanon imagines the jolts he, as a black man, would suffer in everyday encounters with whites if he were to conduct the social experiment of trying to ignore his skin color. When he envisions himself as a neutral figure in a public place, his reverie is interrupted by a white child who notices him and calls out:

"Look, a Negro!" It was an external stimulus that flicked over me as I passed by. I made a tight smile.

"Look, a Negro!" It was true. It amused me.

"Look, a Negro!" The circle was drawing a bit tighter. I made no secret of my amusement.

"Mama, see the Negro! I'm frightened!" Frightened! Frightened! Now they were beginning to be afraid of me. I made up my mind to laugh myself to tears, but laughter had become impossible.[32]

In this anecdote, Fanon shows that, in relation to the white child, he, as a black man, undergoes a shattering transition. His initial attempts to be amused dissolve into a feeling beyond laughter and tears. The black man has reason for discomfort, even apprehension, but why is the white child frightened of him? Evidently, the white child came to the encounter not as a blank slate but already filled with stories that caused a fear of black people.

Although Fanon's anecdote makes the force of racism wrenchingly vivid to me, one of my colleagues dismissed it as merely anecdotal because "it just says that it takes one to know one." In this view, oppressed people's analyses of their own oppression should be ignored because they are so much in the thick of things that they cannot help but distort reality. Disciplinary norms instead require that a cultural gap separate analysts from their subjects. Without a certain distance, it seems, one cannot see things clearly. My argument, of course, is that social analysis can be done—differently, but quite validly—either from up close or from a distance, either from within or from the outside. Ideally, perhaps, analysts should work from one position and try to imagine (or consult with others who occupy) the other.

Lest Fanon's anecdote seem simply implausible, and hence dismissable, one can turn, among other places, to the more dispassionate but strikingly similar report of Floyd H. Flake, the Democratic representative from Queens. A black man, Flake tells of a busy day when he left a speaking engagement and decided to stop and eat at a local ice cream parlor. When he and his aides entered the shop, they encountered a bewildered looking waitress:

> After a few moments of eyeing us suspiciously, she moved cautiously behind the counter and asked: "Who are you? Why are you in Howard Beach? And why are you dressed in suits and ties?" My administrative assistant replied, "This is your congressman!" Her response: "I don't believe you." This issue of whether or not I was really her congressman was discussed for the next five minutes. During this time, one of my aides moved away to look at baked goods at the other end of the counter. The waitress asked, "Who is he and does he have a gun?"[33]

A short time later Flake and his aides laughed about what had happened. Afterward, they felt angry. In the end, Flake himself felt an enduring diffuse sense of ill ease about his experience of raw prejudice.

Studies of the dynamic interplay of culture and power should prominently include analyses by those most involved in the social processes under study. Flake's and Fanon's encounters invite analyses from the subject positions, respectively, of the white waitress, the black aides, and the black man, and of the white child, the white mother, and the black man. The discipline only stands to lose by ignoring how the oppressed analyze their own condition. Indeed, the dominated usually understand the dominant better than the reverse. In coping with their daily lives, they simply must. Hegel's analysis of the master's imaginative leap to discover slave consciousness, for example, remains incomplete until it includes the fact that the slave, for reasons of workaday survival, already knows what's on the master's mind.

Wit as a Weapon in Subaltern Social Analysis

Fanon's direct expression of outrage represents only one end of the spectrum and cannot be taken as the norm for subaltern social analysis. In many cases, the oppressed fail to talk straight. Precisely because of their oppression, subordinate people often avoid unambiguous literal speech. They take up more oblique modes of address laced with double meanings, metaphor, irony, and humor. They often hone their skills through repartee and the form of taunting banter that blacks, for example, call "playing the dozens." The subversive potential and the sheer fun of speech play go hand in hand. Wit and figurative language enable not only the articulation of grievances and aspirations under repressive conditions but also the analysis of conflicts and ironies produced by differences of class, race, gender, and sexual orientation.

In the second part of "On the Jewish Question," for example, Karl Marx uses anti-Semitic stereotypes in a manner that should not be, but often has been, taken literally. Indeed, a number of Marx's sympathetic commentators have felt evident discomfort at the essay's flamboyant "anti-Semitism." Does he literally mean what he says? Has he internalized German anti-Semitism to the point of lacerating self-hatred? Is Karl Marx an anti-Semite? In his fine biography of Marx, for example, historian Jerrold Seigel agonizingly answers these questions with a yes and a no: "If, on balance, it is not possible to describe Marx's relationship to Jewishness—his own or others—in the simple terms of anti-Semitism, it is essential to recognize that Marx felt a deep ambivalence toward Jews and Judaism."[34] Seigel takes Marx literally, at his word, in full earnest. His commentary speaks in Freudian terms about Marx's ambivalence.

Although Seigel's assessment of Marx's personality could well be correct, he fails to consider the tone of the text, its mockery and satire. By and large, one cannot read Marx straight. Designed to grip and persuade a reader, his prose is often flamboyant, at times dripping in sarcasm, and often drawn as caricature in order to bring home a political or analytical point.

Admittedly, the humor in Marx's use of anti-Semitic stereotypes does not make one laugh out loud, particularly not after the Holocaust, but his rhetorical strategy can nonetheless be made apparent. Let us begin with a passage that, taken out of context, sounds like virulent anti-Semitism:

> What is the secular basis of Judaism? Practical need, selfishness.
> What is the secular cult of the Jew. Haggling. What is his secular god? Money.
> Well then, an emancipation from haggling and from money, from practical, real Judaism would be the self-emancipation of our age.[35]

Yet the passage ends on a peculiar note. It equates the specific emancipation from "practical, real Judaism"—selfishness, haggling, the cult of money—with the general emancipation of the age. In other words, Marx equates Christianity with "practical, real Judaism."

The passage about "practical, real Judaism" takes on a quite different significance in the context of Marx's larger argument. He asserts that the Christian state has created an opposition between political life and civil society. In the process, the more communitarian "species-bonds" of political life have been lost, and civil society has dissolved into a world of mutually hostile, selfish monads. For Marx, the state and the market created human beings who behave like stereotypical Jews, and only by abolishing the capitalist state can these human beings achieve their full emancipation. In this context, he says:

> Christianity had its origin in Judaism. It has dissolved itself back into Judaism.
> The Christian was from the beginning the theorizing Jew; the Jew is therefore the practical Christian, and the practical Christian has become the Jew again.[36]

Marx uses a time-honored tactic of repartee and invective as he half-seriously, half-mockingly turns anti-Semitic stereotypes back against their perpetrators.

Because such texts have been endowed, at least in retrospect, with an aura of high seriousness, readers often take them much too earnestly, ignoring figurative language, sarcasm, caricature, and double meaning. Like certain works (such as Conklin's) cast in an objectivist mold, these writings need to be reread at the same time that social analysis expands its use of language so as to include verbal play, wit, banter, and invective.

Consider, as a concluding example, Zora Neale Hurston's recollections of her brief New York years (1925–27), when she was at once a literary figure in the Harlem renaissance and a student of anthropology at Barnard. During this period, before she wrote her major novels and her studies on Afro-American folklore, Hurston studied with noted anthropologists Gladys Reichard, Ruth Benedict, and Franz Boas. Her biographer, Robert Hemenway, cites a phrase from her autobiography in characterizing her Barnard days as virtually free from prejudice: "She was very quickly recognized in a number of New York circles as a special person. Not only was she Barnard's 'sacred black cow,' so cultivated by her classmates that she encountered little overt prejudice, but she was also a published writer, and secretary to a famous novelist."[37] In her autobiography, however, Hurston describes her Barnard years in a rather different key:

I have no lurid tales to tell of race discrimination at Barnard. I made a few friends in the first few days. . . . The Social Register Crowd at Barnard soon took me up, and I became Barnard's sacred black cow. If you had not had lunch with me, you had not shot from taw. I was secretary to Fannie Hurst and living at her 67th Street duplex apartment, so things were going very well with me.[38]

Hemenway takes Hurston's statements about the absence of prejudice at Barnard all too literally. Surely as the object of worship, the "sacred black cow," Hurston feels a certain discomfort with her place on the pedestal. Like a classic form of sexism doubtless well known to her, the cult of the black cow derives from white supremacy manifest not as brutal degradation but as patronizing elevation.

When she describes herself as a "sacred black cow," Hurston takes prejudice and redirects it toward its perpetrators. Like Marx's conversion of Christian Germans into Jews, Hurston's verbal transformation of middle-class New Yorkers into worshippers of the sacred black cow contains a critique of racial oppression. She uses biting self-mockery to mock the congregation that dares worship a profane animal. Ever playful, her tone aptly conveys the relative lightness of the racial condescension she suffered as compared with the fate of those of her contemporaries who were spat upon or lynched for their blackness. Hurston's ironic self-portrait enables her to depict the two-sidedness of her status elevation without losing a critical edge.

Recapitulation

Using objectivism as a foil, I have contested the masculine heroics of Weber's devotion to "science as a vocation." His passionate detachment brings together thought and feeling in a manner that accomplishes much, but too severely restricts the legitimate sources of knowledge for social analysis. The scientist's twin standards of discipline and dignity exclude insights from "lesser" sources of knowledge, ranging from Geertz's "feebleness" and Brigg's "depression" to Fanon's "rage" and Hurston's "irony."

The analyst's position depends, in part, on the interplay of culture and power. Geertz's "feebleness" resulted from his becoming attuned to the power dynamics at play between himself and his Javanese subjects. The goals of the two parties became more and more painfully incongruous. Briggs's "depression" emerged from her sensitivity to the culturally distinctive emotional lives of her Eskimo hosts. Her impulsiveness came to be increasingly at odds with her infor-

194 | CHAPTER EIGHT

mants' self-control. Although one emphasizes power and the other culture, both ethnographers underscore the interaction of their feelings, their observations, and their fieldwork situations.

Kondo's parable of the researcher who looks into a mirror and sees not her analytical self but a Japanese housewife shuffling along the sidewalk argues for using the plural to speak of an observer's identities. More a busy intersection through which multiple identities crisscross than a unified coherent self, the knowing person not only blends a range of cognitive, emotional, and ethical capabilities but her social identities also variously include being a woman, a researcher, and a Japanese-American. That these identities themselves change during fieldwork appears to be the moral of Kondo's deepening awareness of her aversion to becoming a Japanese housewife.

The social analyst's multiple identities at once underscore the potential for uniting an analytical with an ethical project and render obsolete the view of the utterly detached observer who looks down from on high. In this respect, my argument parallels Walzer's discussion of social critic who is connected to a community, not isolated and detached. Rather than work downward from abstract principles, social critics work outward from in-depth knowledge of a specific form of life. Informed by such conceptions as social justice, human dignity, and equality, they use their moral imagination to move from the world as it actually is to a locally persuasive vision of how it ought to be. Because different communities differ in their problems and possibilities, such visions must be more local than universal.

Walzer's discussion of the "connected critic" goes down the wrong path, however, when it assumes that each individual belongs to only one discrete community. The work of Kondo, Thompson, Conklin, and Fanon indicates that individuals often belong to multiple, overlapping communities. Consider how one can be a member of distinct communities of birth, ethnicity, socialization, education, political participation, residence, research, and readership.

In emphasizing the relatively privileged social critic who acts as a broker for the oppressed, Walzer glosses over social criticism made from socially subordinate positions, where one can work more toward mobilizing resistance than persuading the powerful. Such subordinate critical perspectives range from Fanon's uncompromising rage through Flake's modulated anger to Marx's and Hurston's more oblique modes, where wit becomes a tool for apprehending social incongruities and a weapon for use in social conflict.

9 | *Border Crossings*

OFFICIAL ANTHROPOLOGICAL DOCTRINE holds that each human culture is so unique that no yardstick can measure one against another. No one of them is higher or lower, richer or poorer, greater or lesser than any other. One cannot say, for example, that the Balinese have a better or worse form of life than the Navahos. Similarly, official dogma holds that all human conduct is culturally mediated. No domain of life is more or less cultural than any other. Culture shapes the ways that people eat their meals, do politics, and trade in the marketplace as much as it forms their modes of writing poetry, singing *corridos*, and enacting *wayang* dramas. Not only do people act in relation to perceived reality, but it makes no sense to speak of "brute" reality indepen-

196

dent of culture. The myriad modes of perceiving and organizing reality are culture-specific, not panhuman.

Although the official view holds that all cultures are equal,
an informal filing system more often found in corridor talk
than in published writings classifies cultures in quantitative
terms, from a lot to a little, from rich to poor, from thick to
thin, and from elaborate to simple. Such variables as institutional complexity, kinship intricacy, and cosmological
density define greater and lesser "degrees" of culture in a
manner that tacitly derives from notions of "high culture"
as measured in opera houses, art museums, and canonical
lists of great works.

Allow me to make the problem of cultural invisibility
rather more concrete by telling about what happened when
I was a graduate student contemplating fieldwork in the
Philippines. A teacher warned me that Filipinos are "people
without culture." Meaning to be helpful, he suggested doing
fieldwork in Madagascar because people there have "rich"
cultures. Once in Manila, I found that his prophecy appeared to be confirmed by the standard Filipino half-joke
about their "poor" culture. Unlike Indonesia, they explained,
the Philippines never had Hindu-Buddhist temples and
other signs of ancestral high culture. What could one expect,
they added with a faint twinkle, from people who had spent
more than three hundred years in a monastery (Spanish colonial rule) and nearly a half century in Hollywood (American colonial rule)? My first encounter with the Ilongots was
much as predicted. They appeared to be "people without
culture." They lacked the ethnographic staples of the day:
lineages, villages, men's houses, elaborate rituals, and ma-
trilateral cross-cousin marriage.

Michelle Rosaldo and I knew better. We knew that the notions of "people without culture," or with "more" or "less"
culture than others, made no sense. Yet we continued to
speak as if both "civilized" lowland Filipinos and "savage"
Ilongots were alike in that they require no cultural analysis
beyond that provided by "our" commonsense categories.
The gap between explicit and tacit disciplinary norms pro-

duced the inconsistency between anthropological theory and the practices of doing fieldwork. On a practical plane, certain human phenomena seemed more readily amenable to cultural analysis than others. Despite official doctrine, the concept of culture stood on such a narrow foundation that it excluded a number of human groups from its purview.

This book argues that the remaking of social analysis has created not only new methods but also new topics for study. This chapter's oblique recapitulation of my larger argument will attempt to show how zones that classic norms defined as "culturally invisible" have now come so much into focus that they pose central problems for social analysis. What follows builds on the notion that objectivism's practice of using the "detached observer" to make "ourselves" invisible to ourselves has been debilitating. Throughout this chapter I discuss a number of conceptual difficulties with the notion that "they" have culture and "we" do not. Let me proceed by first considering the static class of "people without culture" and then moving on to the more dynamic category of "people between cultures."

Cultural Visibility and Invisibility

One can readily map zones of cultural visibility and invisibility onto the spatial organization of Mexico, the Philippines, and the United States. In "our" own eyes, "we" appear to be "people without culture." By courtesy, "we" extend this noncultural status to people who ("we" think) resemble "us." What are the analytical consequences of making "our" cultural selves invisible? What cultural politics erase the "self" only to highlight the "other"? What ideological conflicts inform the play of cultural visibility and invisibility?

In the nations under discussion, full citizenship and cultural visibility appear to be inversely related. When one increases, the other decreases. Full citizens lack culture, and those most culturally endowed lack full citizenship. In Mexico, Indians have culture and "ladinos" (neighboring

199 | *Border Crossings*

monolingual Spanish speakers) do not. In the Philippines, "cultural minorities" have culture, and lowlanders do not. Ladinos and lowlanders, on the other hand, are full citizens of the nation-state. They work for wages, pay taxes, and sell their wares in the local market. People in metropolitan centers classify them as civilized, in contrast with Indians and cultural minorities, who are cultural, not "rational." To the ethnographic gaze, "civilized" people appear too transparent for study; they seem just like "us"—materialistic, greedy, and prejudiced. Because "their" worlds are so down-to-earth and practical, "our" commonsense categories apparently suffice for making sense of their lives.

Those people who have culture also occupy subordinate positions within the nation-state. In Mexico, Indians inhabit geographical zones that the Mexican anthropologist Gonzalo Aguirre Beltrán calls refuge regions.[1] In other words, the people with culture have been confined to marginal lands. Their cultural distinctiveness derives from a lengthy historical process of colonial domination; their quaint customs signal isolation, insulation, and subordination within the nation-state.

In the Philippine case, the "people without culture" occupy both ends of the social hierarchy. Roughly speaking, Negrito hunter-gatherer groups are on the bottom and lowlanders are on top. The difference between the two ends of the spectrum is that the Negritos are precultural and the lowlanders are postcultural. The Philippine case differs from the Mexican one above all in its overall explicitness. Schemas crystalized during the American colonial era and still current in Philippine popular culture order the nation's peoples along a scale arranged from lesser to greater: Negritos, hunter–dry-rice cultivators, dry-rice cultivators, wet-rice cultivators, and lowlanders.[2] In spatial terms, Negrito hunter-gatherers occupy the most marginal lands; dry-rice and wet-rice cultivators tend to be upland, upriver, or in the interior; lowlanders, as their name suggests, reside in the valleys. In this pseudoevolutionary ladder, people begin without culture and grow increasingly cultured until they reach that point where they become postcultural and therefore transparent to "us."

Within the schema just outlined, Ilongots stand just one rung above the Negritos, hence their relative "lack" of culture. I should add that to a certain extent Ilongots and their neighbors share the ideological perception of degrees of culture. When, for example, the Ifugaos, a group of terraced wet-rice cultivators, entered Ilongot territory as settlers, they proudly proclaimed their cultural superiority to the people whose land they were taking. Measuring their greater degree of culture in elaborate rituals, material culture, and terraced wet-rice agriculture, the Ifugaos claimed that Ilongots lacked culture. Ilongots, who did not fully share this schema, were more impressed with the Ifugaos' physical prowess in fishing and hunting than with their cultural achievements in ritual and agriculture.

In contrast, lowlanders, who are linked to national educational and political institutions, form a (formally) mobile labor force that makes "rational" choices to go where the jobs are. They have been educated; they make decisions about wage labor in accord with an economically rational calculus. They are more rooted in their labor than in their territory. Like Mexican ladinos, lowland Filipinos appear to have entered a system that "we" understand because it is "our" own advanced capitalism. Their colonial heritage has made lowlanders transparent to "us." Initially evangelized under the Spaniards and later educated under the Americans, their colonial experience has disciplined them and made them, like "us," fit to live in a city, work in a factory, serve in a penitentiary, or undergo confinement in an asylum.

Although these social hierarchies seemingly remain static, they are linked to tacit notions of social mobility. This classic model of social structure holds that, although individuals or social groups may move upward or downward, the rungs of the social ladder remain unchanging. In this view, those most down and out, such as Negritos and Ilongots, appear to lack culture. Social mobility from the "bottom" brings people into zones where culture flourishes, such as Mexican refuge regions and Philippine upland and upriver areas. As one approaches the top rungs on the ladder of social mobility, however, the process reverses itself. At this point one begins a process of cultural stripping away, in which Mexican Indians and Filipino cultural minorities become incorporated into the nation-state as peasants and workers. Curiously enough, upward mobility appears to be at odds with a distinctive cultural identity. One achieves full citizenship in the nation-state by becoming a culturally blank slate.

Seen from a distinct but related angle of vision, the conceptual difficulties that have created zones of relative cultural visibility and invisibility derive in large part from tacit methodological norms that conflate the notion of culture with the idea of difference. In this sense, the term *cultural difference* is as redundant as that of *cultural order*, discussed in chapter 4. Consider the case of the field-worker who follows classic norms and goes halfway around the world to record coherent, patterned cultural worlds enclosed within discrete territories, languages, and customs. In their more grouchy moods, such ethnographers grumble that they did not risk their health to dysentery and malaria only to discover that people in Tahiti and Des Moines are, in certain respects, quite alike. From this perspective, to pursue a culture is to seek out its differences, and then to show how it makes sense, as they say, on its own terms.

The problem of cultural purity brings to mind the story that a noted Spanish philologist told about a German colleague who rejected most of his Galician linguistic informants because they did not speak the "pure" dialect of Gallego-Portuguese. Rather like tourists who seek out the exotic and call it typically Galician, the philologist claimed that only a tiny minority of the region's inhabitants spoke the authentic dialect. Most Galicians, he imagined, had been linguistically "corrupted" by Castilian. In other words, the less it resembled its neighbors, the greater the dialect's purity and authenticity. Like culture, this speech community was defined both by its internal homogeneity and by its difference from others.

Although the notion of "difference" has the advantage of making culture particularly visible to outside observers, it poses a problem because such differences are not absolute. They are relative to the cultural practices of ethnographers and their readers. Such studies highlight cultural forms that diverge from (tacitly normative) North American upper-middle-class professional ones. Social analysts commonly speak, for example, as if "we" have psychology and "they" have culture. Current discussions about the cultural reasons that other cultures "somatize" (experience "their" afflictions in bodily ways) must be understood in relation to the unstated norm that human beings should "psychologize" (as Anglo-Americans, or at any rate their therapists, presumably do). The temptation to dress one's own "local knowledge" of either the folk or professional variety in garb at once "universal" and "culturally invisible" to itself seems to be overwhelming.

In practice, the emphasis on difference results in a peculiar ratio: as the "other" becomes more culturally visible, the "self" becomes correspondingly less so. Social analysts, for example, often assert that subordinate groups have an authentic culture at the same time that they mock their own upper-middle-class professional culture. In this view, subordinate groups speak in vibrant, fluent ways, but upper-middle-class people talk like anemic academics. Yet analysts rarely allow the ratio of class and culture to include power. Thus they conceal the ratio's darker side: the more power one has, the less culture one enjoys, and the more culture one has, the less power one wields. If "they" have an explicit monopoly on authentic culture, "we" have an unspoken one on institutional power. This ratio's dark side underscores the urgency of rethinking social analysis in such a manner that at once considers the interplay of culture and power and makes "ourselves" more culturally visible.

The cultural invisibility within which the North American upper middle class hides itself from itself has been vividly portrayed by journalist Frances FitzGerald.[3] Her recent book on intentional communities shows how four quite different groups have attempted to make their lives conform with a particular version of the "American dream." These communities share utopian fantasies about making new beginnings and living in a world without precedents. The retirement village of Sun City, for example, appears extraordinary more because of the past and present homogeneity of its residents than because it has succeeded, as its own mythology would have it, in erasing cultural diversity. "Sun Citians," FitzGerald writes, "are a remarkably homogeneous group; in particular, those who live in Sun City proper occupy a far narrower band on the spectrum of American society than economics would dictate. . . . The men are by and large retired professionals. . . . Most of the women were housewives. . . . Most Sun Citians are Protestants. . . . Politically, they are conservative and vote Republican."[4] Yet the sources of this uniformity remain largely invisible to Sun Citians. To themselves, Sun Citians appear to be so many self-made, rootless monads whose social origins are quite diverse. For them, their current circumstances have produced their cultural transparency.

One Sun City couple affably remarked on how its residents live in the present and appear to have erased their pasts: " 'No one gives a hang here what you did or where you came from,' Mrs. Smith said. 'It's what you are now that matters.' Later, in a different context, her husband said much the same thing, adding that the colonels refused to be called 'Colonel.' "[5] In remarking on the irrelevance of social origins, the Smiths failed to notice the striking absence of working-class people, blacks, Chicanos, Puerto Ricans, and Native Americans in Sun City. In this North American rootless utopia, some pasts evidently matter more than others.

The attempt of Sun Citians to become transparent and erase their pasts, to make themselves postcultural and post-historical, bears a striking resemblance to objectivism's efforts to make the detached observer omniscient, innocent, and invisible. In both cases, the people involved are largely white, upper-middle-class professionals whose myth of detachment conceals their dominant class position. In North America, this group rarely knows itself as ethnic, cultural, or powerful. Much as nobody in Sun City uses titles, classic social analysts pretend to speak either from a position of omniscience or from no position at all. Yet even lone monads who claim to succeed on their own lead lives that are just as culturally shaped as people with more collective senses of identity.

Relational Knowledge

Although professionals often fancy that their "enlightenment" makes them quite different from lay members of their society, North American field-workers nonetheless share certain cultural values with Sun Citians. When ethnographers implausibly maintain, for example, that learning a second culture follows the same patterns as learning the first, they verbally fashion themselves as children learning their cultures of birth. This rhetorical tactic allows them to appear ethically innocent and culturally invisible. In this regard, I have been no exception, and can speak on this subject from personal experience.

While learning Ilongot, I constantly likened myself to a child. My first transcriptions of their texts were written in awkward, large, bold script, peculiarly like my son's efforts in first grade to squeeze the "b" or the "p" between the wide lines. His teacher tells me that Manny's trouble is small motor coordination, but I don't know quite how to describe my problem while initiating ethnographic fieldwork. Perhaps voluntary infantilization will do.

The field-worker's task as a version of early childhood enculturation seemed so natural to me that I eagerly endowed Ilongots with the same perception. When Ilongots decided to teach us their language, I noticed that they did so by commanding (*tuydek*) us to get things, and I inferred that they were following patterns they used with their own children.[6] After all, they often said that children showed their knowledge of a word by correctly fetching the object of a *tuydek*. In my imagination, they and I agreed with the North American ethnographer's notion, which I took for a transparent human universal, that my efforts to learn their language were the same as those of their own children.

In retrospect I find that my presuppositions were most thrown into jeopardy where I thought they were most confirmed: in a life history that I recorded from my Ilongot "brother," Tukbaw.[7] The early portions of his life history reflect Tukbaw's efforts to teach me his language. In fact, his early texts contain multiple *tuydek*—"go and get" this or that—of the sort that adults use with children as well as with other adults. "We are making a house," Tukbaw said, "a new house. Come here, we are going to cut down some trees. Now we are going to put it into the ground. I am going to cut and scrape the earth clean and we will see if we do not put up the house tomorrow. Raise up the house posts. Go and get some people. Go and get some rattan that we can use for tying it together. Also, get some grass for the roof." Although Tukbaw's narrative contains multiple *tuydek*, he clearly did not think that I resembled a child. Tukbaw's words were spoken more as man to man than as man to child. In fact, the task of tying knots on houses involves skills so difficult to achieve that Ilongots regard it as an indication that a boy has achieved the status of adult manhood. Tukbaw's other early texts described such adult activities as visiting, fishing, hunting, and drinking.

At this point it is probably salutary to introduce historian of anthropology James Clifford's depiction of French ethnographer Marcel Griaule as he conducted field research among the Dogon of West Africa. Griaule's notions of fieldwork serve as a foil whose contrasting contours illuminate the cultural distinctiveness of North American field-workers: "Griaule never presented fieldwork as an innocent attainment of rapport analogous to friendship. Nor did he natu-

ralize the process as an experience of education or growth
(child or adolescent becoming adult), or as acceptance into
an extended family (a kinship role given to the ethnographer). Rather, his accounts assumed a recurring conflict of
interests, an agonistic drama resulting in mutual respect,
complicity in a productive balance of power."[8] Griaule's desire to engage the Dogon in agonistic man-to-man combat
highlights the cultural peculiarity of North American field-
workers who want to gain acceptance as a friend and become "one of the people."

Griaule's example reinforces my sense that I failed to apprehend the meaning of Tukbaw's instructional use of *tuydek*
because my own cultural practices as a field-worker remained invisible to me. In addition, however, I failed to see
Tukbaw's relation to me as a significant area of investigation. Although anthropologists often talk about seeing
things "from the native point of view," the phrase usually
denotes such culturally distinctive notions as honor, shame,
the person, marriage, the family, kinship, hierarchy, and
even history.[9] It less often refers to how other people judge
"our" conduct or think in general about "the interpretation
of cultures." Anthropologists rarely consider how members
of other cultures perceive their ethnographers, or how they
conceive questions of cross-cultural understanding. How do
they interpret the cultures of their neighbors, their ethnographers, or their missionaries? Just how Ilongots "put
themselves in somebody else's shoes," or "see things from
the native point of view," or whether such terms even make
sense to them, remains unclear.

Granting the so-called native's interpretations of the ethnographer's conduct a central place in the discipline will
also make the researcher's upper-middle-class professional
persona culturally visible. The study of differences, formerly
defined in opposition to an invisible "self," now becomes the
play of similarities and differences relative to socially explicit identities. How do "they" see "us"? Who are "we"
looking at "them"? Social analysis thus becomes a relational form of understanding in which both parties actively

engage in "the interpretation of cultures." Rather than being perspectival, inscribed from within a single point of view, such forms of human understanding involve the irreducible perceptions of both analysts and their subjects. Much as two narratives usually do not map neatly onto one another, one party's analysis can only rarely be reduced to the terms of the other.

The notion of relational knowledge presented here has been woven from concepts developed through previous chapters of this book. Consider how the introductory notion of the "positioned subject" anticipates the idea of "imperialist nostalgia," in which the "detached observer" appears as a complicit actor in human events rather than as an innocent onlooker. Furthermore, recall how narrative analysis requires a "double vision" that moves between narrator and protagonist and how my discussion of "subjectivity in social analysis" emphasizes the insights offered by "subordinate knowledge." Throughout, I have stressed, first, that the social analyst is a positioned subject, not a blank slate, and second, that the objects of social analysis are also analyzing subjects whose perceptions must be taken nearly as seriously as "we" take our own.

Culture in the Borderlands

The remaking of social analysis has not only redefined the position of the "detached observer" but has also brought new objects of study into focus. One can now ask, for example, about how cultural forms shape and are shaped by human conduct, regardless of whether they are relatively "pure" or blended from two or more "cultures." In this context, the fiction of the uniformly shared culture increasingly seems more tenuous than useful. Although most metropolitan typifications continue to suppress border zones, human cultures are neither necessarily coherent nor always homogeneous. More often than we usually care to think, our everyday lives are crisscrossed by border zones, pockets, and eruptions of all kinds. Social borders frequently become salient around such lines as sexual orientation, gender, class, race, ethnicity, nationality, age, politics, dress, food, or taste. Along with "our" supposedly transparent cultural selves, such borderlands should be regarded not as analytically empty transitional zones but as sites of creative cultural production that require investigation.

The salience of new topics for study created by the remaking of social analysis requires a concept of culture capacious enough to encompass both work guided by classic norms and projects previously excluded or rendered marginal. Such previously excluded topics prominently include studies that seek out heterogeneity, rapid change, and intercultural borrowing and lending. My exploration of what the classic period regarded as "empty spaces" and zones of cultural invisibility has been undertaken with a view toward redefining the concept of culture.

The blindspots of classic norms come home to me with particular force when I reflect on the efforts Michelle Rosaldo and I made to grasp the drastic processes of change Ilongots were undergoing during the late 1960s and early 1970s. At the beginning of our second period of field research in 1974, for example, Michelle Rosaldo wrote in her field journal that we both felt "sad and nervous because there's no hint that we'll find more 'culture' than last time and every reason to think that there'll be less." She went on to talk about the impossibility of doing cultural anthropology in the midst of catastrophic changes imposed by settlers and missionaries: "Some good things are sure to come out of this . . . but the overwhelming fact that things are changing so quickly, settlers impinging, choices being made between possible lowland allies, padi fields being built which don't work, people rejecting their past for a Pollyannaish idea of religion—all that is something I have absolutely no sense of how to understand. (It has to be interesting, but when I think about it, all I've got are boring, depressing thoughts.)"

Evidently, the then-fading classic concept of culture did not readily apply to flux, improvisation, and heterogeneity. Weren't these changes, after all, robbing Ilongots of their culture? What was so cultural about a brutal, all-too-familiar, apparently transparent process of land grabbing, exploitaton, and "incorporation" into the nation-state? We knew that the processes of "cultural jolt" suffered by the Ilongots should, in principle, be as amenable to cultural description as kinship, subsistence, or ritual, but we could not think of what to say about them, beyond the "brute" facts of the matter.

The broad rule of thumb under classic norms to which Michelle Rosaldo and I still ambivalently subscribed seems to have been that if it's moving it isn't cultural. In emphasizing social hierarchies and self-enclosed cultures, the discipline encouraged ethnographers to study the crystalline patterns of a whole culture, and not the blurred zones in between. Social analysts sat at the "postcultural" top of a stratified world and looked down the "cultural" rungs to its "precultural" bottom. Similarly, the borders between nations, classes, and cultures were endowed with a curious kind of hybrid invisibility. They seemed to be a little of this and a little of that, and not quite one or the other. Movements between such seemingly fixed entities as nations or social classes were relegated to the analytical dustbin of cultural invisibility. Immigrants and socially mobile individuals appeared culturally invisible because they were no longer what they once were and not yet what they could become.

North American notions of the "melting pot" make immigration a site of cultural stripping away. Seen from the dominant society's point of view, the process of immigration strips individuals of their former cultures, enabling them to become American citizens—transparent, just like you and me, "people without culture." Often called acculturation (though deculturation seems more apt), this process produces postcultural citizens of the nation-state. In this view, social mobility and cultural loss become conflated, for to become middle class in North America is purportedly to become part of the culturally invisible mainstream. The immigrants, or at any rate their children or grandchildren, supposedly become absorbed into a national culture that erases their meaningful past—autobiography, history, heritage, language, and all the rest of the so-called cultural baggage. Where José Rizal and Gregorio Cortez once stood, there shall be George Washington and the Texas Rangers.

The myth of immigration as a cultural stripping away recently appeared in a newspaper story about so-called illegal aliens. Published shortly after Congress passed the new immigration bill, the story begins by depicting remarkable diversity among the undocumented: "Their stories are as diverse as America. Some entered this country swimming naked through the Rio Grande, others with tickets aboard jet liners. They are laborers, classical pianists, secretaries, dishwashers, restaurant owners, high school students." [10] The writer goes on, however, to celebrate the essential unity underlying this apparent cultural diversity: "They come from almost every conceivable country—Mexico, El Salvador, Japan, Vietnam, Korea, Haiti, Ethiopia, Iran, Poland, New Zealand. For all their cultural differences, they have shared a semi-secret life in their chosen land, forming a kind of shadow economy and culture in which any day could end in arrest and deportation." [11] In the writer's view, the shared experience of living the "same" secret lives homogenizes the new immigrants. They seemingly are well on their way to becoming "people without culture." Verbally at least, the undocumented have been absorbed into the mainstream.

Apparently, images of "illegal aliens" have been manufactured for the consumption of North American readers who at once see themselves as culturally transparent and feel threatened by differences of class and culture. In this context, we should perhaps listen for a moment to the "illegal aliens" who stand teetering on the brink of North American citizenship. It is tempting to assume that monopoly capitalism inexorably commodifies people, turning them into so many perfectly identical rational decision-making individuals. But a certain irrepressible something about the "illegal aliens" bubbles over the rim of the melting pot:

(*Lan Thiet Lu, from North Vietnam*) "I feel I belong here. I want to belong here, especially because I don't have my country any more."

(*Shunsuke Kurakata, from Japan*) He has not decided if he will seek American citizenship. "I just don't know yet," he said. "It's not all real yet."

(*Marcelino Castro, from Mexico*) He has learned a passable version of English and exhibits a certain fatalism about his life. "Ni modo," he says, roughly "what could I do?" when describing his troubles. . . . Now he wants to start his own business and become an American citizen. He already owns two color television sets and a cordless telephone and is a fervent Dallas Cowboys fan.[12]

The undocumented speak with a measure of irony as they simultaneously accede to and resist their cultural homogenization. The Vietnamese woman feels she belongs here, but notes that she has no choice because her native country has vanished; the Japanese musician finds possible citizenship so unreal that he can't even decide whether or not to apply; the Mexican has a cordless telephone and roots for the Dallas Cowboys, but speaks only passable English, spiced with "Ni modo." Even as they move toward cooptation, the undocumented prove unassimilable by refusing the absolute surrender of their "differences."

Elsewhere in the story, it becomes clear that the writer's prejudice and the resistance of the undocumented combine to muddy further the clear waters of compliance and assimilation. In this contradictory process of absorption and rejection, the writer cannot resist indulging his prejudices: his Vietnamese appears inscrutable, his Japanese successful, and his Mexican fatalistic—"Ni modo." In response to the writer's stereotypes, the undocumented both comply and deviate, bobbing and weaving between assimilation and resistance. They neither remain what they once were nor become fully absorbed into the culturally transparent Anglo-American middle class.

More generally, race relations in North America involve a blend of assimilationist efforts, raw prejudice, and cultural containment that revolves around a concerted effort to keep each culture pure and in its place. Members of racial minority groups receive a peculiar message: either join the mainstream or stay in your ghettos, barrios, and reservations, but don't try to be both mobile and cultural. During recent years, the two-edged practices of racial domination have been vividly displayed on the popular television series *Miami Vice*. Low-pitched mood music, prolonged chase scenes, and carefully chosen color schemes combine to create an entertaining, sensuous, violent, eroticized world where threatening forces are at large. The show warns viewers to beware of, and urges them to become aware of, the Third World's implosion into the First.

Much as the radical right these days often masquerades as the left, *Miami Vice* disguises itself as affirmative action heaven, with blacks, Latinos, and whites, all playing cops and robbers, vibrantly policing and trafficking drugs together. Yet the show teaches (or reinforces) forms of prejudice that North American viewing audiences will find increasingly useful during the coming decades (if current demographic projections can be believed). In one episode after another, stereotypical Latino figures abound. To varying degrees and in varying combinations, they appear flamboyant, impulsive, slimy, lazy, and cowardly. *Miami Vice* attempts, literally and figuratively, to arrest and confine diversity rather than to promote its value.

The "good guys" on the show are vice squad members Crockett and Tubbs. They are partners, but rather unequal ones. Their relationship involves a play of racial dominance and subordination more subtle but no less demeaning than that between the Lone Ranger and Tonto. During the 1984–1986 seasons, the black cop Tubbs consistently acted overly emotional; he appeared irrational, hence inferior. His white partner, Crockett, consistently restrained and guided him; he appeared rational, hence superior. During the 1986–1987 season, the locus of irrationality shifted from Tubbs to Crockett. But this time when the white cop acted crazed, his black partner nurtured him. This minidrama was a displaced version of the relationship between a nanny (Tubbs) and her master's child (Crockett). Despite the reversal in the locus of irrationality, the lines of dominance and subordination between the two partners remained constant. The white cop remained "superior" to his black partner.

The issues of containment that so pervade *Miami Vice* unexpectedly surfaced in a local newspaper story where "real life" under advanced capitalism appears to follow after television precedents. The story involves a play of stereotypes at once spatial and racial in which the South is invading the North, Los Angeles is infiltrating the Bay Area, and Latino cocaine traffickers are infesting middle-class neighborhoods:

> A massive cocaine-selling ring uncovered in Foster City last week was a model of sophisticated Colombian-run operations common in Southern California but only recently surfacing on such a large scale in the Bay Area.
>
> Some believe this wholesaling of cocaine, already firmly established in Southern California, is moving north.
>
> In a typical scenario, some inconspicuous, very middle-class-looking people—often unarmed middle-aged women—move into a comfortable neighborhood and rent a condominium by putting down a hefty deposit.
>
> But inside the condos they are guarding huge amounts of cocaine.[13]

Evidently socially invisible Colombians, perhaps living next door, strike terror in suburban souls whose perceptions have been shaped by television reality.

Like "illegal aliens," Colombian cocaine peddlers cannot be contained within the dominant society's vision of citizenship and assimilation. The immigrants who most appear to fit right in—Foster City's cocaine traffickers—are in fact the most alien and threatening. "Contrary to the stereotype depicted in television shows like 'Miami Vice,'" the reporter says, "the suspects in many cases drive new but not flashy cars and refrain from displays of weaponry, exotic or other-wise."[14] Mundane reality appears more threatening than the television fantasy that informs it.

The nightmare vision of invasion from the south and the threat of subsequent Latino cultural hegemony has a vener-able genealogy. Ronald Reagan revived it when he spoke about Nicaragua's proximity to south Texas; it gave the new immigration bill a boost; it assisted California's overwhelm-ing passage of the "English only" initiative; it informs *Miami Vice*. Official celebratory pronouncements about the "de-cade of the Hispanic" hardly conceal diffuse anxieties about the impending impact of projected demographic changes in the Latino population of the United States.[15] Even conser-vative projections predict, for example, that in twenty years California's population will be 40 percent Mexican origin, 20 percent other nonwhite, and 40 percent white. If these pro-jections are correct, in two decades the state's dominant ma-jority will become its numerical minority.

New Subjects of Analysis

Official anxiety about the increasing Latino popu-lation obscures the cultural identities of the so-called invad-ers. "They" become anonymous brown hordes about to engulf Los Angeles and a number of other North American metropolitan centers. In official versions, the brown invad-ers come bearing not culture but poverty, drugs, illiteracy, and crime. Yet by now it should be clear that social analysts who study unequal relations must explore both dominant *and* subordinate forms of knowledge. Because culture and power are always at play with one another, social analysts have learned to inspect not only what was said but also who was speaking to whom under what circumstances. What, one wonders, do down-and-out, unschooled Latino youths have to say for themselves? Do they see themselves as invad-ing hordes, caught "betwixt and between," with no culture to call their own? How do they interpret their distinctive street-wise style?

Let us ask our questions of "El Louie," the protagonist of José Montoya's poem, which now has near-legendary status among its Chicano readers. Published in the early 1970s, the poem waxes sentimental in portraying a *pachuco*, an urban Chicano youth who died in the late 1950s. Shortly after its publication, Montoya's poem provoked extensive debate, which revolved around questions of authentic urban resistance, identity confusion, and the cultural degradation of the underclass's most marginal members.[16] In initial discussions, the cultural significance of El Louie fell victim to classic norms, which asked him, on the one hand, to be a more elevated figure and, on the other, to embody the values of a pristine, authentic culture.

Yet precisely his subordinate status and his capacity to blend cultures make El Louie a central figure in the renewal of the anthropologist's search for meaning. From the present perspective, El Louie requires discussion as a playful persona whose whimsical fantasies join together old things in new ways. His distinctive cultural practices personify a certain Chicano gift for improvisation and recombination within an array of disparate cultural elements that has been called "transculturation." In the following passage, for example, El Louie plays what "we" Chicano teenagers in Tucson during the late 1950s used to call "the role":

> En Sanjo you'd see him
> sporting a dark topcoat
> playing in his fantasy
> the role of Bogart, Cagney
> or Raft.
> * * *
> An Louie would come through—
> melodramatic music, like in the
> mono—tan tan taran!—Cruz
> Diablo, El Charro Negro! Bogart
> smile (his smile as deadly as
> his vaisas!) He dug roles, man,
> and names—like "Blackie," "Little
> Louie . . ."

> Ese, Louie . . .
> Chale, man, call me "Diamonds!"[17]

"El Louie" seeks out the incongruity of such unlikely juxtapositions as Cagney and El Charro Negro, Bogart and Cruz Diablo. "Postmodern" before its time, the poem celebrates multiculturalism in a polyglot text that depicts Anglo, Chicano, and Mexican elements dancing together. The result is not identity confusion but play that operates within, even as it remakes, a diverse cultural repertoire. Creative processes of transculturation center themselves along literal and figurative borders where the "person" is crisscrossed by multiple identities.

In *Borderlands/La Frontera,* a recent work written from a Chicana lesbian perspective, Gloria Anzaldua has further developed and transformed the figure at the crossroads in a manner that celebrates the potential of borders in opening new forms of human understanding. "The new *mestiza* [person of mixed ancestry]," she says, "copes by developing a tolerance for contradictions, a tolerance for ambiguity. She learns to be Indian in Mexican culture, to be Mexican from an Anglo point of view. She learns to juggle cultures. She has a plural personality, she operates in a pluralistic mode—nothing is thrust out, the good the bad and the ugly, nothing rejected, nothing abandoned. Not only does she sustain contradictions, she turns the ambivalence into something else."[18] In making herself into a complex persona, Anzaldua incorporates Mexican, Indian, and Anglo elements at the same time that she discards the homophobia and patriarchy of Chicano culture. In rejecting the classic "authenticity" of cultural purity, she seeks out the many-stranded possibilities of the borderlands. By sorting through and weaving together its overlapping strands, Anzaldua's identity becomes ever stronger, not diffused. She argues that because Chicanos have so long practiced the art of cultural blending, "we" now stand in a position to become leaders in developing new forms of polyglot cultural creativity. In her view, the rear guard will become the vanguard.

Figures such as El Louie and Gloria Anzaldua demand study more as complex sites of cultural production than as representatives of a self-contained, homogeneous culture. Through the remaking of social analysis, such figures have come into sharp focus because "we" now stand prepared to study cultural practices and processes of cultural mediation. A renewed concept of culture thus refers less to a unified entity ("a culture") than to the mundane practices of everyday life. "Our" inquiry now seeks meanings that are more pragmatic than formal; it models itself more on semantics than syntax and grammar. Ethnographers look less for homogeneous communities than for the border zones within and between them. Such cultural border zones are always in motion, not frozen for inspection.

In the present postcolonial world, the notion of an authentic culture as an autonomous internally coherent universe no longer seems tenable, except perhaps as a "useful fiction" or a revealing distortion. In retrospect, it appears that only a concerted disciplinary effort could maintain the tenuous fiction of a self-contained cultural whole. Rapidly increasing global interdependence has made it more and more clear that neither "we" nor "they" are as neatly bounded and homogeneous as once seemed to be the case. The stock market crash of October 1987, for example, was global, not local. News from Tokyo and Hong Kong mattered as much as word from New York and London. Similarly, Latin American and African fiction influence and are influenced by French and North American literary production. All of us inhabit an interdependent late-twentieth-century world marked by borrowing and lending across porous national and cultural boundaries that are saturated with inequality, power, and domination.

Epilogue · A Raging Battle

ALTHOUGH THE IMPORT of academic warfare can be exaggerated, it can also be trivialized. The issues do matter. One should not be misled by the false modesty of academics who mock university politics by pretending to correlate the intensity of conflicts with the smallness of the stakes (compared with corporate and electoral politics). The material stakes in such battles variously include office space, funding for programs, curriculum development, and faculty positions. More broadly at stake in the battle, however, are competing political and intellectual visions. What should count as knowledge and critical thought in the education of our country's future generations? How can we prepare stu-

218

dents to enter the changing multicultural world of the coming century?

In playing itself out in university arenas, the battle's weapon of choice has been the epithet. The name calling has pitted "objectivists" against "relativists," "presentists" against "historicists," and "foundationalists" against "interpretivists." The two parties (or at any rate, the two loosely organized coalitions) appear to be divided, among other things, over forms of analysis that stress constancy versus change and universality versus difference. These are legitimate grounds for conflict, but one wonders at the intensity of debate. What is really at stake?

The partisan evangelical fervor of the conservative agenda's implementation during the 1980s has had somewhat different consequences for the social sciences and the humanities. In the social sciences, it has favored explanations that deal in timeless eternal principles. Hence the "objectivist" emphasis found most prominently in sociobiology and cognitive science, including certain areas of ecology, neurology, ethology, artificial intelligence, generative linguistics, and experimental psychology. In the humanities, it has favored high culture, with its canon of Western culture's great works understood as enduring, sacred objects of worship. In this "monumentalist" view of culture, "Western" refers to the ancient classical world and northern Europe. Ironically, this purported effort to transmit "our" heritage to undergraduate students renders marginal not only the works of American minorities and Third World writers but also classic American texts.

What, one wonders, could unite such strange bedfellows as the "objectivists" and "monumentalists" (to use epithets yet once again)? The two camps have been able to present a united front because "hard-core" objectivists from the natural sciences seek to forge alliances, on the one hand, with social scientists whose research programs most nearly resemble their own and, on the other hand, with humanists whose literary agendas most diverge from their own. Objec-

220 | EPILOGUE

tivist social scientists make strong allies because the large grants required for their brand of research raise considerable overhead for the university and give them corresponding institutional power. Monumentalist humanists disguise the cross-disciplinary alliance that has taken place on the level of institutional politics by perpetuating the myth that an absolute divide separates the humanities from the natural sciences. For example, they often promote (or at any rate are complicit in creating) the conceptual gap between doing serious (scientific) work by day versus the "frill" of playing the violin or otherwise cultivating felicitous (humanist) self-expression in the evening. In the "objectivist-monumentalist" alliance, the natural scientists are almost always the senior partners.

The objectivist-monumentalist coalition oppresses not so much by what it includes as by what it excludes—particularly culture, history, and inequality. How can the objectivists justify developing research paradigms that exclude social struggles revolving around issues of class, race, gender, and sexual orientation? How can the monumentalists justify ignoring radical cultural difference as a means of preparing students to inhabit an increasingly global environment?

These questions are not intended to deny the potential value of objectivist and monumentalist projects. How could an antiobjectivist deny, for example, that we are biological as well as cultural beings? Problems arise, however, when born-again objectivists insist on reducing all human history to its so-called biological foundations. How could an antimonumentalist deny students the opportunity to read Shakespeare? Problems arise here when hard-core monumentalists flatly deny the worth of any cultural artifact that fails to appear among the canonical great works.

When empowered by the conservative agenda, the objectivist-monumentalist axis begins to display totalitarian tendencies. It claims a monopoly on truth that excludes other ways of thinking about the world. In its hegemonic phase, the "truth" of the objectivist-monumentalist worldview becomes self-confirming. It increasingly resembles forms of prejudice produced when (often well-meaning) like-minded people gather together and reach a consensus on the issues of the day. In their so-called consensus, such groups simply ignore the views of people they never invited to the meeting.

My account of the current conflict in American universities is frankly partisan. It makes no claims for neutrality, impartiality, or detachment. Intellectuals at times speak to a perceived consensus about shared understandings, but when social formations erupt into battle zones, as they often do, one cannot help but take sides. The objectivists and monumentalists, on the other hand, prefer to stand above the fray, where they can assume a position of omniscience, and work in the "clean" realm of detachment and ethical neutrality. To me, the attitudes embodied in their "standing above it all" range from mild condescension through active surveillance to brute domination; to them, their position is one of impartiality and their distance works in the service of objectivity. To me, one rarely studies culture from a neutral position, so analysts should be as explicit as possible about partisanship, interests, and feelings; to them, scholarship is disinterested inquiry in the service of truth and knowledge. The debate by now almost follows a script that pits "us" against "them."

Let me illustrate how this script runs by telling readers about a relatively obscure event. In late 1986 and early 1987 a minor chorus of praise songs greeted the publication of Thomas Sowell's *A Conflict of Visions*, a work that claims to provide an objective appraisal of two competing schools of social thought. More telling than the book itself, which has relatively little import, was its reception. The reviews revealed the political and ethical fault lines of an intense conflict in the human sciences that is often waged in more neutral or abstract language.

One reviewer, for example, described Sowell as "a free-market economist and perhaps the leading black scholar among conservatives."[1] He credited the book with having developed a fair and balanced characterization of two visions, the "constrained" and the "unconstrained." According to the reviewer, Sowell "prefers the constrained vision, yet there is nothing tendentious or one-sided about his argument." Before hearing anything more about the book or its review, however, I already find the very terms of the opposition, "constrained" and "unconstrained," tendentious and one-sided. The words themselves betray Sowell's bias. "Constrained" invokes a safe, finite space where sober, responsible, realistic citizens go about earning their daily bread. They're doing nothing millenarian; they are just getting on with the difficult job of everyday life. "Unconstrained" suggests a dangerous, intoxicating space where "anything goes," "all hell will break loose," and before you know it people will be doing "it" in the streets.

Before drawing their own conclusions, readers had best inspect the reviewer's version of Sowell's opposing visions:

Mr. Sowell says there are two basic visions in human history, the constrained and the unconstrained. These obviously conflict, thus the title of his book. The constrained vision sees man as hopelessly flawed. The best he can accomplish is a perilous peace and fragile prosperity, and these only by following the collective wisdom of society and tradition ("systematic knowledge," Mr. Sowell calls it) rather than pursuing heaven on earth. The unconstrained vision rejects the idea of inherent limits on man. Through will and reason, he can perfect himself and eradicate social evils. As you might guess, the civil rights movement draws from the unconstrained vision.[2]

A political conservative similar to Sowell himself, the reviewer displayed his predilections in the "reasonable" tone he used in speaking about human imperfection and the consequent need for social constraint. For him, human wisdom resides in following tradition, in doing today as was done yesterday.

One marvels at the reviewer's depiction of Sowell's version of the "unconstrained" vision. Did most members of the civil rights movement really reject the idea of human limits? Or were they making a much more specific demand for social change? An enormous gap separates saying (*a*) white supremacist social arrangements are morally unacceptable and must be altered and (*b*) human beings can, without limits, perfect themselves and eradicate social evil. The bad faith of conflating a concerted effort to ameliorate social arrangements with a doctrine of human perfectibility probably speaks for itself.

In my view, the reception of Sowell's work derives from the politics of the 1980s. During this period, the nationally dominant conservative agenda has distorted a once-healthy debate by creating a climate of holy war and tilting the balance of power and resources far to one side. Decisions made in Washington have included not only the nation's massive militarization, the Star Wars initiative, and the restriction of civil rights advocacy but also the reduction in funding for social science research and the promotion of a conservative vision for the humanities.

My intent in speaking (with deliberate satire) about objectivists and monumentalists has been to uncover the covert polemics in which Sowell and his reviewer have engaged. In my view, people who differ over what W. B. Gallie has called "essentially contested concepts" should sharpen debate on issues that divide them rather than pretend to be bedfellows. Rhetorically, objectivists and monumentalists deploy their oppositional visions as scare tactics to discredit research programs they deem unworthy. In the process, they attack extreme versions of relativism, subjectivism, historicism, and assorted other "unconstrained" visions. These are positions that very few, if any, people actually hold.

In response to such assaults, Clifford Geertz has tried to clarify matters by considering the case of relativism. He does not defend relativism (which, in any case, is barely recognizable in its attackers' versions). Instead, he launches a persuasive attack on the rising tide of antirelativism. Geertz explains his stance by using a revealing analogy:

Those of us who are opposed to increased legal restrictions on abortion are not, I take it, pro-abortion, in the sense that we think abortion a wonderful thing and hold that the greater the abortion rate the greater the well-being of society; we are "anti

anti-abortionists" for quite other reasons I need not rehearse. In this frame the double negative doesn't work in the usual way; and therein lies its rhetorical attractions. It enables one to reject something without thereby committing oneself to what it rejects.[3]

Geertz thus can attack "antirelativism" without committing himself to their version of "relativism," or any other variety of the "unconstrained" vision. His critique frees interpretive social scientists from trying to defend positions attributed to them that they never held in the first place. Those of us who want to decenter objectivism have not been advocates of its supposed opposite—subjectivism, relativism, or whatever red-flag word is being waved at the time.

My seriously intended political satire provides a broader context for this book. In my view, the current battle about how best to prepare students for life in the twenty-first century revolves around questions of the degree and significance of human differences, whether change or stasis is the natural state of society, and to what extent struggle shapes the course of human events. At the level of interdisciplinary cultural studies, the debate has to do with competing research programs that differ in their aims, what they want to know and, not simply in their methods, how they come to know what they know. The choice of what we want to know is primarily political and ethical, hence the intensity of feelings brought to and aroused by the conflict.

Notes

Introduction

An earlier version of this chapter appeared as "Grief and a Head-hunter's Rage: On the Cultural Force of Emotions," in *Text, Play, and Story: The Construction and Reconstruction of Self and Society*, ed. Edward M. Bruner (Washington, D.C.: American Ethnological Society, 1984), pp. 178–95.

1. In contrasting Moroccan and Javanese forms of mysticism, Clifford Geertz found it necessary to distinguish the "force" of cultural patterning from its "scope" (Clifford Geertz, *Islam Observed* [New Haven, Conn.: Yale University Press, 1968]). He distinguished force from scope in this manner: "By 'force' I mean the thoroughness with which such a pattern is internalized in the personalities of the individuals who adopt it, its centrality or marginality in their lives" (p. 111). "By 'scope,' on the other hand, I

225

mean the range of social contexts within which religious considerations are regarded as having more or less direct relevance" (p. 112). In his later works, Geertz developed the notion of scope more than that of force. Unlike Geertz, who emphasizes processes of internalization within individual personalities, my use of the term *force* stresses the concept of the positioned subject.

2. Anthropologists have long studied the vocabulary of the emotions in other cultures (see, e.g., Hildred Geertz, "The Vocabulary of Emotion: A Study of Javanese Socialization Processes," *Psychiatry* 22 (1959): 225–37). For a recent review essay on anthropological writings on emotions, see Catherine Lutz and Geoffrey M. White, "The Anthropology of Emotions," *Annual Review of Anthropology* 15 (1986): 405–36.

3. The two ethnographies on the Ilongots are Michelle Rosaldo, *Knowledge and Passion: Ilongot Notions of Self and Social Life* (New York: Cambridge University Press, 1980), and Renato Rosaldo, *Ilongot Headhunting, 1883–1974: A Study in Society and History* (Stanford, Calif.: Stanford University Press, 1980). Our field research among the Ilongots was financed by a National Science Foundation predoctoral fellowship, National Science Foundation Research Grants GS-1509 and GS-40788, and a Mellon Award for junior faculty from Stanford University. A Fulbright Grant financed a two-month stay in the Philippines during 1981.

4. Lest the hypothesis Insan rejected appear utterly implausible, one should mention that at least one group does link a version of exchange theory to headhunting. Peter Metcalf reports that, among the Berawan of Borneo, "Death has a chain reaction quality to it. There is a considerable anxiety that, unless something is done to break the chain, death will follow upon death. The logic of this is now plain: The unquiet soul kills, and so creates more unquiet souls" (Peter Metcalf, *A Borneo Journey into Death: Berawan Eschatology from Its Rituals* [Philadelphia: University of Pennsylvania Press, 1982], p. 127).

5. R. Rosaldo, *Ilongot Headhunting, 1883–1974*, p. 286.

6. Ibid., p. 288.

7. M. Rosaldo, *Knowledge and Passion*, p. 33.

8. See A. R. Radcliffe-Brown, *Structure and Function in Primitive Society* (London: Cohen and West, Ltd., 1952), pp. 133–52. For a broader debate on the "functions" of ritual, see the essays by Bronislaw Malinowski, A. R. Radcliffe-Brown, and George C. Homans, in *Reader in Comparative Religion: An Anthropological Approach* (4th ed.), ed. William A. Lessa and Evon Z. Vogt (New York: Harper and Row, 1979), pp. 37–62.

9. Max Weber, *The Protestant Ethic and the Spirit of Capitalism* (New York: Charles Scribner's Sons, 1958).

10. A key antecedent to what I have called the "positioned subject" is Alfred Schutz, *Collected Papers*, vol. 1, *The Problem of Social Reality*, ed. and intro. Maurice Natanson (The Hague: Martinus Nijhoff, 1971). See also, e.g., Aaron Cicourel, *Method and Measurement in Sociology* (Glencoe, Ill.: The Free Press, 1964) and Gerald Berreman, *Behind Many Masks: Ethnography and Impression Management in a Himalayan Village*, Monograph No. 4 (Ithaca, N.Y.: Society for Applied Anthropology, 1962). For an early anthropological article on how differently positioned subjects interpret the "same" culture in different ways, see John W. Bennett, "The Interpretation of Pueblo Culture," *Southwestern Journal of Anthropology* 2 (1946): 361–74.
11. Clifford Geertz, *The Interpretation of Cultures* (New York: Basic Books, 1974) and *Local Knowledge: Further Essays in Interpretive Anthropology* (New York: Basic Books, 1983).
12. Although anger appears so often in bereavement as to be virtually universal, certain notable exceptions do occur. Clifford Geertz, for example, depicts Javanese funerals as follows: "The mood of a Javanese funeral is not one of hysterical bereavement, unrestrained sobbing, or even of formalized cries of grief for the deceased's departure. Rather, it is a calm, undemonstrative, almost languid letting go, a brief ritualized relinquishment of a relationship no longer possible" (Geertz, *The Interpretation of Cultures*, p. 153). In cross-cultural perspective, the anger in grief presents itself in different degrees (including zero), in different forms, and with different consequences.
13. The Ilongot notion of anger (*liget*) is regarded as dangerous in its violent excesses, but also as life-enhancing in that, for example, it provides energy for work. See the extensive discussion in M. Rosaldo, *Knowledge and Passion*.
14. William Douglas, *Death in Murelaga: Funerary Ritual in a Spanish Basque Village* (Seattle: University of Washington Press, 1969); Richard Huntington and Peter Metcalf, *Celebrations of Death: The Anthropology of Mortuary Ritual* (New York: Cambridge University Press, 1979; Metcalf, *A Borneo Journey into Death*.
15. Douglas, *Death in Murelaga*, p. 209.
16. Ibid., p. 19.
17. Simone de Beauvoir, *A Very Easy Death* (Harmondsworth, United Kingdom: Penguin Books, 1969).
18. Douglas, *Death in Murelaga*, p. 75.
19. Godfrey Wilson, *Nyakyusa Conventions of Burial* (Johannesburg: The University of Witwatersrand Press, 1939), pp. 22–23. (Reprinted from *Bantu Studies*.)
20. Ibid., p. 13.
21. In his survey of works on death published during the 1960s, for example, Johannes Fabian found that the four major anthropologi-

cal journals carried only nine papers on the topic, most of which "dealt only with the purely ceremonial aspects of death" (Johannes Fabian, "How Others Die—Reflections on the Anthropology of Death," in *Death in American Experience*, ed. A. Mack [New York: Schocken, 1973], p. 178).

22. Huntington and Metcalf, *Celebrations of Death*, p. 1.

23. Arguably, ritual works differently for those most afflicted by a particular death than for those least so. Funerals may distance the former from overwhelming emotions whereas they may draw the latter closer to strongly felt sentiments (see T. J. Scheff, *Catharsis in Healing, Ritual, and Drama* [Berkeley: University of California Press, 1979]). Such issues can be investigated through the notion of the positioned subject.

24. For a discussion of cultural motives for headhunting, see Robert McKinley, "Human and Proud of It! A Structural Treatment of Headhunting Rites and the Social Definition of Enemies," in *Studies in Borneo Societies: Social Process and Anthropological Explanation*, ed. G. Appell (DeKalb, Ill.: Center for Southeast Asian Studies, Northern Illinois University, 1976), pp. 92–126; Rodney Needham, "Skulls and Causality," *Man* 11 (1976): 71–88; Michelle Rosaldo, "Skulls and Causality," *Man* 12 (1977): 168–70.

25. Pierre Bourdieu, *Outline of a Theory of Practice* (New York: Cambridge University Press, 1977), p. 1.

Chapter 1

1. Ruth Benedict, *Patterns of Culture* (Boston: Houghton Mifflin, 1959 [orig. 1934]).

2. This generalization admits to exceptions, particularly during the 1920s and 1930s, when a "diffusionist" agenda in anthropology was giving way to a more "functionist" one. Diffusionists saw culture as a collection of "traits" that were borrowed and lent from one group to another; they asked about degrees of resistance and receptivity to borrowing, and about whether or not traits necessarily diffused in clusters ("necessary versus accidental adhesions"). The diffusionists saw that culture had porous boundaries, but downplayed questions of internal patterning. As functionalist theory took hold, inquiries into the degree of cultural patterning slipped into assumptions that were beyond question. For thoughtful historical critiques of the oversystematization of the concept of culture during the early classic period (1921–1945), see George W. Stocking, Jr., "Ideas and Institutions in American Anthropology: Thoughts toward a History of the Interwar Years," in *Selected Papers from the American Anthropologist, 1921–1945*, ed. George W. Stocking, Jr. (Washington, D.C.: American Anthropological As-

229 | Notes to Pages 28–35

sociation, 1976), pp. 1–49; James Clifford, "On Ethnographic Surrealism," in *The Predicament of Culture: Twentieth-Century Ethnography, Literature, and Art* (Cambridge, Mass.: Harvard University Press, 1988), pp. 117–51.

3. The distinction between cultural patterns and cultural borderlands, of course, closely resembles that drawn in the introduction between ritual as microcosm and ritual as a busy intersection.

4. My account of classic norms should not be conflated with the classic ethnographies themselves. The texts require more complex readings. See, e.g., Clifford Geertz, *Works and Lives: The Anthropologist as Author* (Stanford, Calif.: Stanford University Press, 1988).

5. The mythic form of my account imitates the mystique fieldwork holds for anthropologists. For a first person account that manifests the mystique, see Claude Lévi-Strauss, *Tristes Tropiques* (New York: Athenaeum, 1975). For a series of historical essays on fieldwork, see George W. Stocking, Jr., ed., *Observers Observed: Essays on Ethnographic Fieldwork* (Madison: University of Wisconsin Press, 1983). For a comprehensive account of anthropology during the nineteenth century, see George W. Stocking, Jr., *Victorian Anthropology* (New York: Free Press, 1987).

6. Sally Falk Moore, *Social Facts and Fabrications: "Customary" Law on Kilimanjaro, 1880–1980* (New York: Cambridge University Press, 1986), p. 4.

7. Although classic ethnographies often talked about "diachronic analysis," they usually studied the unfolding of structures, rather than open-ended processes. Among others, Bronislaw Malinowski introduced the so-called biographical method only to invent the composite life-cycle; Meyer Fortes studied households through time only to produce the developmental cycle of domestic groups; Edmund Leach lengthened his perspective beyond the lifespan only to construct the moving equilibrium of a political system. For the most part, so-called diachronic methods were used to study "structures of the long run" that revealed themselves only in periods of time more extended than the one- or two-year span of most fieldwork. Enduring social forms thus remained the object of anthropological knowledge. See Bronislaw Malinowski, *The Sexual Life of Savages* (London: George Routledge, 1929); Jack Goody, ed., *The Developmental Cycle of Domestic Groups* (Cambridge: Cambridge University Press, 1958); Edmund Leach, *Political Systems of Highland Burma* (Boston: Beacon Press, 1965).

8. T. O. Beidelman, *Moral Imagination of Kaguru Modes of Thought* (Bloomington: Indiana University Press, 1986), p. xi.

9. The political movements of the late sixties and early seventies more widely reshaped the intellectual agenda of American anthropology through the work of such figures as Laura Nader, Sidney

230 | NOTES TO PAGES 35-38

Mintz, Karen Sacks, Kathleen Gough, Sydel Silverman, Michelle Rosaldo, Gerald Berreman, Eric Wolf, Rayna Rapp, June Nash, Dell Hymes, Joseph Jorgenson, Louise Lamphere, and David Aberle. The tenor of the times can be discerned from Dell Hymes, ed., *Reinventing Anthropology* (New York: Random House, 1969); Rayna Rapp Reiter, ed., *Toward an Anthropology of Women* (New York: Monthly Review Press, 1975); Talal Asad, ed., *Anthropology and the Colonial Encounter* (London: Ithaca Press, 1973); Michelle Zimbalist Rosaldo and Louise Lamphere, eds., *Woman, Culture, and Society* (Stanford, Calif.: Stanford University Press, 1974). Ethnic minorities have thus far had less of an impact on mainstream anthropology than have women. French and British anthropology of the time also influenced American research programs. For example, Pierre Bourdieu developed a theory of practice and Talal Asad developed an analysis of colonial domination. The "reinvention of anthropology" was also influenced by broader trends in social thought, ranging from such writers as Antonio Gramsci and Michel Foucault, through Anthony Giddens and Richard Bernstein, to Raymond Williams and E. P. Thompson.

10. To be more precise, the dissatisfaction with objectivism's emphasis on pattern and structure reached epidemic proportions during the early 1970s. During the 1970s, "history" and "politics" were often invoked to describe what classic analysts had overlooked. Even during the classic period, however, certain critics voiced dissatisfaction with objectivism. Their articulate criticisms never became a dominant intellectual movement, and as a result could not become cogent programs of research. For relatively early critical works, see, e.g., Kenelm Burridge, *Encountering Aborigines* (New York: Pergamon Press, 1973); Roy Wagner, *The Invention of Culture* (Chicago: University of Chicago Press, 1975). For a historical assessment of such alternative views, see Dan Jorgenson, *Taro and Arrows* (Ph.D. dissertation: University of British Columbia, 1981).

11. Richard Bernstein, *The Restructuring of Social and Political Theory* (Philadelphia: University of Pennsylvania Press, 1978), p. xii.

12. Clifford Geertz, "Blurred Genres: The Refiguration of Social Thought," in *Local Knowledge: Further Essays in Interpretive Anthropology* (New York: Basic Books, 1983), p. 34.

13. Within anthropology a number of works on "ethnographies as texts" have appeared during the 1980s. See George Marcus and Dick Cushman, "Ethnographies as Texts," in *Annual Review of Anthropology* 11 (1982): 25–69; James Boon, *Other Tribes, Other Scribes: Symbolic Anthropology in the Comparative Study of Cultures, Histories, Religions, and Texts* (New York: Cambridge University Press, 1982); James Clifford and George E. Marcus, eds., *Writing Culture: The Poetics and Politics of Ethnography* (Berkeley:

University of California Press, 1986); George E. Marcus and Michael
M. J. Fischer, *Anthropology as Cultural Critique: An Experimental
Moment in the Human Sciences* (Chicago: University of Chicago
Press, 1986); Clifford Geertz, *Works and Lives;* James Clifford, *The
Predicament of Culture.* For related works from other disciplines,
see, e.g., Hayden White, *Metahistory: The Historical Imagination in
Nineteenth-Century Europe* (Baltimore: Johns Hopkins University
Press, 1973); Richard H. Brown, *A Poetic for Sociology: Toward a
Logic of Discovery for the Human Sciences* (New York: Cambridge
University Press, 1977); Dominick LaCapra, *Rethinking Intellectual
History: Texts, Contexts, Language* (Ithaca, N.Y.: Cornell University
Press, 1983); John S. Nelson, Allan Megill, and Donald N. Mc-
Closkey, eds., *The Rhetoric of the Human Sciences: Language and
Argument in Scholarship and Public Affairs* (Madison: University of
Wisconsin Press, 1987).
14. George E. Marcus and Michael M. J. Fischer's *Anthropology as
Cultural Critique* (Chicago: University of Chicago Press, 1986) at
once celebrates anthropology's "experimental moment" and claims
that it neither should nor will last very long. Although they favor
experimentation, Marcus and Fischer concede that over the long
run the excesses of eclecticism and the free play of ideas could well
prove debilitating to the discipline. Their mechanical reading of
Thomas Kuhn's *Structure of Scientific Revolutions* (Chicago: University of Chicago Press, 2d ed., 1970) leads them to assert that
anthropology's current experimentation is destined to end when
the advent of a new paradigm ushers in the discipline's next extended period of "normal science." Not unlike an unruly child, according to them, anthropology will soon outgrow its current phase,
and order will win out over chaos. Their message appears designed
to reassure the antiexperimentalists. Why bother to combat experimental writing when Kuhnian prophecy has promised a new reign
of stable ethnographic forms? I do not think that the "experimental
moment" is a flash in the pan because the discipline's new project
demands a wider array of rhetorical forms than were used during
the classic period.
15. To appreciate its range, Clifford's list should probably be cited
in full: "This blurred purview includes, to name only a few developing perspectives, historical ethnography (Emmanual Le Roy
Ladurie, Natalie Davis, Carlo Ginzburg), cultural poetics (Stephen
Greenblatt), cultural criticism (Hayden White, Edward Said, Fred-
ric Jameson), the analysis of implicit knowledge and everyday
practices (Pierre Bourdieu, Michel de Certeau), the critique of hegemonic structures of feeling (Raymond Williams), the study of scientific communities (following Thomas Kuhn), the semiotics of exotic worlds and fantastic spaces (Tzvetan Todorov, Louis Marin),

and all those studies that focus on meaning systems, disputed traditions, or cultural artifacts" (James Clifford, "Introduction: Partial Truths," in *Writing Culture*, ed. Clifford and Marcus, p. 3).

16. Mary Louise Pratt, "Fieldwork in Common Places," in *Writing Culture*, ed. Clifford and Marcus, p. 33.

17. Victor Turner, "Dramatic Ritual/Ritual Drama: Performative and Reflexive Anthropology," in *From Ritual to Theater: The Human Seriousness of Play* (New York: Performing Arts Journal Publications, 1982), p. 89.

18. Ibid., p. 100.

19. Jerome Bruner, *Actual Minds, Possible Worlds* (Cambridge, Mass.: Harvard University Press, 1986), p. 123.

20. Ibid.

21. Edward Said, *Orientalism* (New York: Pantheon Books, 1978).

22. E. E. Evans-Pritchard, *The Nuer* (Oxford: Oxford University Press, 1940), pp. 94–95. Also see Renato Rosaldo, "From the Door of His Tent: The Fieldworker and the Inquisitor," in *Writing Culture*, ed. Clifford and Marcus, pp. 77–97.

23. Louis A. Sass, "Anthropology's Native Problems: Revisionism in the Field," *Harpers* (May 1986), p. 52.

24. The contrast between the museum and the garage sale, of course, resembles that drawn early in this chapter between cultural patterning and cultural borderlands. The former distinction articulates on a geopolitical level what the latter expresses on the plane of social analysis. My claim is that changes in the world have conditioned changes in theory, which in turn shape changes in ethnographic writing, which return to raise new theoretical issues.

Chapter 2

An earlier version of this chapter appeared as "Where Objectivity Lies: The Rhetoric of Anthropology," in *The Rhetoric of the Human Sciences: Language and Argument in Scholarship and Public Affairs*, ed. John S. Nelson, Allan Megill, and Donald N. McCloskey (Madison: University of Wisconsin Press, 1987), pp. 87–110.

1. Américo Paredes, "On Ethnographic Work among Minority Groups: A Folklorist's Perspective," in *New Directions in Chicano Scholarship*, ed. Ricardo Romo and Raymund Paredes (La Jolla, Calif.: Chicano Studies Monograph Series, 1978), p. 2.

2. Ibid.; emphasis in original.

3. To top it off, a team of anthropological researchers in south Texas even failed to notice the emergence during their research period of a locally powerful political movement called La Raza Unida Party.

4. Paredes, "On Ethnographic Work among Minority Groups," p. 5.

5. Ibid., p. 28.

6. Talal Asad has made a similar argument in "The Concept of Cultural Translation," in *Writing Culture: The Politics and Poetics of Ethnography*, ed. James Clifford and George Marcus (Berkeley and Los Angeles: University of California Press, 1986), pp. 141–64. Also see Renato Rosaldo, "When Natives Talk Back: Chicano Anthropology since the Late Sixties," in *The Renato Rosaldo Lectures, 1985* (Tucson, Ariz.: Mexican-American Studies and Research Center, 1986), pp. 3–20.

7. Horace Miner, "Body Ritual among the Nacirema," *American Anthropologist* 58 (1956): 503–7.

8. My distinction between everyday and technical language is borrowed from Clifford Geertz, who expressed this distinction in the terms "experience-near" and "experience-distant" (which he in turn had borrowed from the psychoanalyst Heinz Kohut). In his words, "An experience-near concept is, roughly, one that someone—a patient, a subject, in our case an informant—might himself naturally and effortlessly use to define what he or his fellows see, feel, think, imagine, and so on, and which he would readily understand when similarly applied by others. An experience-distant concept is one that specialists of one sort or another—an analyst, an experimenter, an ethnographer, even a priest or an ideologist—employ to forward their scientific, philosophical, or practical aims" (Geertz, "From the Native's Point of View," in *Local Knowledge*, p. 57).

9. A. R. Radcliffe-Brown, *The Andaman Islanders* (New York: Free Press of Glencoe, 1964), p. 241.

10. In their writings on North American culture, the economist Thorstein Veblen and the sociologist Irving Goffman proved themselves masters at using distanced, normalizing discourse in an analytically effective satirical mode. In a representative example, chosen more or less at random, drinking and drug use appear under the following description: "The ceremonial differentiation of the dietary is best seen in the use of intoxicating beverages and narcotics. If these articles of consumption are costly, they are felt to be noble and honorific" (Thorstein Veblen, *The Theory of the Leisure Class* [New York: Random House, 1934], p. 70). Also see Irving Goffman, *The Presentation of Self in Everyday Life* (New York: Anchor, 1959).

11. *San Jose Mercury News*, January 17, 1984.

12. Among the Toraja of Sulawesi, Indonesia, for example, death is an elaborated cultural focus. For a recent ethnography, see Toby Alice Volkman, *Feasts of Honor: Ritual and Change in the Toraja Highlands* (Urbana: University of Illinois Press, 1985).

234 | NOTES TO PAGES 56-73

13. Jack Goody, *Death, Property and the Ancestors* (Stanford, Calif.: Stanford University Press, 1962), p. 87.
14. Ibid.
15. Ibid., p. 88.
16. Ibid., p. 91 (my emphasis).
17. Ibid. (my emphasis).
18. See Renato Rosaldo, "The Story of Tukbaw: 'They listen as He Orates'," in *The Biographical Process: Studies in the History and Psychology of Religion*, ed. F. E. Reynolds and Donald Capps (The Hague: Mouton, 1976), pp. 121–51; Renato Rosaldo, "Ilongot Hunting as Story and Experience," in *The Anthropology of Experience*, ed. Edward Bruner and Victor Turner (Urbana: University of Illinois Press, 1986), pp. 97–138.
19. Claude Lévi-Strauss, *Totemism* (Boston: Beacon Press, 1963), p. 70.
20. Ibid.
21. Ibid.
22. Clifford Geertz, "Ritual and Social Change: A Javanese Example," *The Interpretation of Cultures* (New York: Basic Books, 1973), p. 154.
23. Ibid., p. 156.
24. Loring Danforth, *The Death Rituals of Greece* (Princeton, N.J.: Princeton University Press, 1982), p. 11.
25. Ibid., p. 13.
26. *Chicago Tribune*, October 21, 1984.

Chapter 3

1. Fred Davis, *Yearning for Yesterday: A Sociology of Nostalgia* (New York: Free Press, 1979), pp. 1–2. See also, David Lowenthal, *The Past Is a Foreign Country* (New York: Cambridge University Press, 1985).
2. Allen Batteau, "Romantic Appalachia: The Semantics of Social Creation and Control" (1986, book typescript).
3. Richard Slotkin, *Regeneration through Violence: The Mythology of the American Frontier, 1600–1860* (Middletown, Conn.: Wesleyan University Press, 1973), p. 551.
4. Marshall Berman, *All That Is Solid Melts into Air: The Experience of Modernity* (New York: Simon and Schuster, 1982), p. 60.
5. My mode of analysis parallels that of Michael Taussig in his work on the culture of terror in Colombia entitled *Shamanism, Colonialism and the Wild Man: A Study in Terror and Healing* (Chicago: University of Chicago Press, 1987). For a review of classic modes of studying ideology plus a critique partially related to mine—that such studies do not attend sufficiently to what ideologies actually

say—see Clifford Geertz, "Ideology as a Cultural System," in *The Interpretation of Cultures* (New York: Basic, 1973), pp. 193–233.
6. Wilfrid Turnbull, "Among the Ilongots Twenty Years Ago," *Philippine Magazine* 26 (1929): 262–63, 307–310, 337–38, 374–79, 416–17, 460–70, at p. 262.
7. Ibid., p. 263.
8. Ibid., p. 469.
9. Ibid., p. 376.
10. Ibid.
11. Ibid., p. 378.
12. Wilfrid Turnbull, "1909 Report of an Inspection Trip through the Ilongot Rancherias and Country on and near the Cagayan River," typescript, Philippines Studies Library, Chicago, 1909, p. 8.
13. Wilfrid Turnbull, "Return to Old Haunts," *Philippine Magazine* 34 (1937): 449, 460, 462–64, 546–47, 557–58, at p. 449.
14. Ibid., p. 462.
15. Ibid., p. 464.
16. Turnbull, "1909 Report of an Inspection Trip," p. 13.
17. Sarabelle Graves, "Old Things Are Passed Away," *Island Challenge* (May 1956).
18. Bronislaw Malinowski, *Argonauts of the Western Pacific* (New York: E. P. Dutton, 1961), p. xv.
19. James Clifford, "On Ethnographic Allegory," in *Writing Culture: The Poetics and Politics of Ethnography*, ed. James Clifford and George Marcus (Berkeley and Los Angeles: University of California Press, 1986), pp. 98–121.
20. Ibid., p. 114. The social critic Raymond Williams generalizes about this pattern by documenting the historical persistence of nostalgic feelings toward the epoch about a generation in the past. He argues, however, that not all nostalgias are the same; under different historical circumstances, they mean quite different things. "What seemed a single escalator," he says, "a perpetual recession into history, turns out, on reflection, to be a more complicated movement: Old England, settlement, the rural virtues—all these, in fact, mean different things at different times, and quite different values are being brought into question" (Raymond Williams, *The Country and the City* [New York: Oxford University Press, 1973], p. 12).
21. Henry Milner Rideout, *William Jones: Indian, Cowboy, American Scholar, and Anthropologist in the Field* (New York: Stokes, 1912), pp. 200–1.
22. For a discussion of North American "innocence" and the ideological character of visions of individualism in the Wild West, see Garry Wills, *Reagan's America* (New York: Penguin Books, 1988), pp. 93–102 and 448–60.

23. William Jones, *Diary, 1907–1910*, entry of June 27, 1908, Field Museum of Natural History, Chicago.
24. Ibid., entry of July 26, 1908.
25. Renato Rosaldo, *Ilongot Headhunting, 1883–1974: A Study in History and Society* (Stanford, Calif.: Stanford University Press, 1980), p. 46.

Chapter 4

Portions of this chapter appeared in an earlier version as "While Making Other Plans," *Southern California Law Review* 58, no. 1 (1985): 19–28.
1. After learning about the saying, I found that it is quite widespread. Members of a Social Science Research Council Committee often jokingly invoke the saying to "explain" missed deadlines. A recent article in *Life Magazine* attributes the saying to John Lennon. Like all good proverbial wisdom, the saying is doubtless used so often precisely because it readily applies to so many contexts.
2. Joan Vincent, "System and Process, 1974–1985," *Annual Review of Anthropology* 15 (1986): 99–119, at p. 100.
3. A member of the Manchester school of anthropology, Victor Turner was part of a larger group that made the case method its cornerstone. Indeed, the term used below, *processual analysis*, is identified primarily with the Manchester school. For a representative methodological statement from this school, see A. L. Epstein, ed., *The Craft of Social Anthropology* (London: Tavistock, 1967).
4. Although I stress the similarities uniting Geertz and Turner, significant differences also divide them. If Geertz's Weberian heritage makes "culture" his master concept, Turner's Durkheimian legacy gives primacy to "society." The former stresses institutionally central cultural conceptions (such as statehood, kingship, and the market), and the latter focuses on the creative potentials of social marginality (such as monkhood, hippiedom, and the dispossessed). One emphasizes the unique qualities of particular cultures, and the other highlights the universal characteristics of social processes. Yet, for my present purposes, the similarities that unite them reveal more than their differences. The conceptual difficulties discussed below probably find their fullest expression in the more objectivist areas of cognitive science and artificial intelligence. My discussion focuses on Geertz and Turner in order to explore a point of contradiction in their work, rather than to discover the best example of the "control mechanisms" viewpoint.
5. Clifford Geertz, "Thick Description: Toward an Interpretive

Theory of Culture," in *The Interpretation of Cultures* (New York: Basic Books, 1974), pp. 3–30.

6. Ibid., p. 9.

7. Victor Turner, *Schism and Continuity in an African Society* (Manchester: Manchester University Press, 1957).

8. Ibid., p. 89.

9. Victor Turner, *Dramas, Fields, and Metaphors* (Ithaca, N.Y.: Cornell University Press, 1974), p. 36.

10. Clifford Geertz, "The Impact of the Concept of Culture on the Concept of Man," in *The Interpretation of Cultures*, pp. 33–54, at p. 44.

11. Ibid., p. 49.

12. Harry Stack Sullivan, *The Interpersonal Theory of Psychiatry* (New York: Norton, 1953), pp. 213–14.

13. Emile Durkheim, *The Division of Labor in Society* (Glencoe, Ill.: Free Press, 1964), pp. 203–4.

14. Ibid., p. 3.

15. *The Day After* was a television show that aired over the ABC network on November 20, 1983, at 9:00 P.M. (Eastern Standard Time).

16. *San Jose Mercury News*, January 5, 1984.

17. *San Jose Mercury News*, April 22, 1984.

18. Carl O. Sauer, *Seeds, Spades, Hearths, and Herds: The Domestication of Animals and Foodstuffs* (Cambridge, Mass.: MIT Press, 1969), p. 15.

19. Kenneth Burke, *The Philosophy of Literary Form* (New York: Vintage Books, 1957), pp. 95–96.

20. My phrasing of this matter most closely follows social theorist Anthony Giddens. See, for example, *Central Problems in Social Theory: Action, Structure and Contradiction in Social Analysis* (Berkeley and Los Angeles: University of California Press, 1979). Within anthropology, Sherry Ortner has provided an illuminating overview of the remaking of anthropology since the late 1960s. "For the past several years," she says, "there has been growing interest in analysis focused through one or another of a bundle of interrelated terms: practice, praxis, action, interaction, activity, experience, performance. A second, and closely related, bundle of terms focuses on the doer of all that doing: agent, actor, person, self, individual, subject" (Sherry Ortner, "Theory in Anthropology since the Sixties," *Comparative Studies in Society and History* 26 [1984]: 126–66, at p. 144).

21. Marx, Karl, *The 18th Brumaire of Louis Bonaparte* (New York: International Publishers, 1963), p. 15.

22. E. P. Thompson, *The Making of the English Working Class* (New York: Vintage Books, 1966), p. 9.

23. Raymond Williams, *Marxism and Literature* (Oxford: Oxford University Press, 1977), p. 132.
24. Pierre Bourdieu, *Outline of a Theory of Practice* (New York: Cambridge University Press, 1977), p. 10.

Chapter 5

1. E. P. Thompson, "Time, Work-Discipline, and Industrial Capitalism," *Past and Present* 38 (1967): 56–97, at p. 90.
2. Max Weber, *The Protestant Ethic and the Spirit of Capitalism* (New York: Charles Scribner's Sons, 1958), pp. 59–60.
3. Susan Philips, "Warm Springs 'Indian Time': How the Regulation of Participation Affects the Progression of Events," in *Explorations in the Ethnography of Speaking*, ed. Richard Bauman and Joel Sherzer (New York: Cambridge University Press, 1974), pp. 92–109.
4. Ibid., p. 94.
5. Charles O. Frake, "A Structural Description of Subanun 'Religious Behavior'," in *Language and Cultural Description* (Stanford, Calif.: Stanford University Press, 1980), pp. 144–65, at p. 145.
6. Charles O. Frake, "How to Enter a Yakan House," in *Language and Cultural Description*, pp. 214–32, at p. 214.
7. Renato Rosaldo, *Ilongot Headhunting, 1883–1974: A Study in Society and History* (Stanford, Calif.: Stanford University Press, 1980), pp. 66–79.
8. Michelle Rosaldo, *Knowledge and Passion: Ilongot Notions of Self and Social Life* (New York: Cambridge University Press, 1980), p. 43.
9. Ibid.
10. Hugh Brody, *Maps and Dreams* (New York: Pantheon Books, 1982), p. 37.
11. Renato Rosaldo, "Ilongot Hunting as Story and Experience," in *The Anthropology of Experience*, ed. Victor Turner and Edward Bruner (Urbana: University of Illinois Press, 1986), pp. 97–138.
12. Renato Rosaldo, *Ilongot Headhunting, 1883–1974*, pp. 103–4.
13. Ibid., p. 36.
14. Such Ilongot commands, called *tuydek*, have been studied in Michelle Rosaldo, "The Things We Do with Words: Ilongot Speech Acts and Speech Act Theory in Philosophy," *Language in Society* 11 (1982): 203–37.
15. Pierre Bourdieu, *Outline of a Theory of Practice* (New York: Cambridge University Press, 1977), p. 7.

Chapter 6

1. Deepening a process initiated by natural historians in the early nineteenth century, classic norms altered the ratio between description and narration. They elevated distanced, normalizing de-

239 | Notes to Pages 128–36

scriptions (present tense, third person), and subordinated histori-

239 | Notes to Pages 128–36

scriptions (present tense, third person), and subordinated historical narrative (past tense, third person) and personal discourse
(present tense, first person). Their descriptive practices produced
visions of culture as unchanging entities, which, by the scientific
standards of the day, were the only proper objects of knowledge.
My classification parallels that of literary theorist Gerard Genette,
who distinguishes narrative (third person, past), description (third
person, present), and discourse (first person, present). He characterizes the relations between narrative and description in two ways
that are particularly pertinent to this book's argument. First, one
can more easily describe without narrating than the reverse, hence
the tendency for the former to assume hegemony over the latter.
Second, description gives primacy to spatial modes of perception,
and narrative privileges temporal ones (Gerard Genette, "Boundaries of Narrative," *New Literary History* 8 [1976]: 1–13). Also see his
Narrative Discourse: An Essay in Method (Ithaca, N.Y.: Cornell University Press, 1980).
2. Richard Borshay Lee, *The !Kung San: Men, Women and Work in
a Foraging Society* (New York: Cambridge University Press, 1979),
p. 211.
3. Renato Rosaldo, "Ilongot Hunting as Story and Experience," in
The Anthropology of Experience, ed. Victor Turner and Edward
Bruner (Urbana: University of Illinois Press, 1986), pp. 97–138.
4. Jerome Bruner, *Actual Minds, Possible Worlds* (Cambridge, Mass.:
Harvard University Press, 1986), pp. 42–43.
5. Hayden White, *Metahistory: The Historical Imagination in Nineteenth-Century Europe* (Baltimore: Johns Hopkins University Press,
1973), p. x.
6. Louis Mink, "The Autonomy of Historical Understanding," in
Philosophical Analysis and History, ed. William H. Dray (New York:
Harper and Row, 1966), p. 178.
7. W. B. Gallie, *Philosophy and the Historical Understanding* (London: Chatto and Windus, 1964), p. 21.
8. Ibid., p. 43.
9. Ibid., p. 47.
10. J. H. Hexter, "The Rhetoric of History," in *Doing History*
(Bloomington: Indiana University Press, 1971), p. 30.
11. Ibid., p. 39.
12. Ibid., p. 45.
13. Paul Ricoeur, *Time and Narrative*, vol. 1 (Chicago: University of
Chicago Press, 1984), p. 3.
14. Ibid., p. 215.
15. Ibid., p. 178.
16. Louis Mink, "Narrative Form as a Cognitive Instrument," in
The Writing of History: Literary Form and Historical Understanding,

ed. Robert H. Canary and Henry Kozicki (Madison: University of Wisconsin Press, 1978), pp. 129–49, at p. 142. See also, Richard T. Vann, "Louis Mink's Linguistic Turn," *History and Theory* 26 (1987): 1–14.

17. Ibid., pp. 145–46.

18. E. P. Thompson, *The Making of the English Working Class* (New York: Vintage Books, 1966), p. 20.

19. Benedict Anderson, *Imagined Communities: Reflections on the Origin and Spread of Nationalism* (London: Verso, 1983).

20. Peter Brooks, *The Melodramatic Imagination: Balzac, Henry James, Melodrama, and the Mode of Excess* (New Haven, Conn.: Yale University Press, 1976), p. ix.

21. Thompson, *The Making of the English Working Class*, p. 19.

22. Ibid., p. 135.

23. Victor Turner, *Schism and Continuity in an African Society* (Manchester: Manchester University Press, 1957), p. 148.

24. A. L. Becker, "Text-Building, Epistemology, and Aesthetics in Javanese Shadow Theater," in *The Imagination of Reality: Essays in Southeast Asian Coherence Systems*, ed. A. L. Becker and Aram A. Yengoyan (Norwood, N.J.: Ablex Publishing, 1979), pp. 211–43, at p. 224.

Chapter 7

Portions of this chapter appeared in an earlier version as "Politics, Patriarchs, and Laughter," *Cultural Critique* 6 (1987): 65–86.

1. Américo Paredes, *"With His Pistol in His Hand": A Border Ballad and Its Hero* (Austin: University of Texas Press, 1958). All further references to the book appear in the body of the paper, cited by page number.

2. Ernesto Galarza, *Barrio Boy* (New York: Ballantine Books, 1972). All further references to this book appear in the body of the paper cited by page number. For another reading of *Barrio Boy*, see José Saldívar, "Caliban and Resistance: A Study of Chicano-Chicana Autobiography," paper delivered at the Chicano Colloquium Series, Stanford Center for Chicano Research, March 22, 1986.

3. Sandra Cisneros, *The House on Mango Street* (Houston: Arte Público Press, 1986). All further references to this book will appear in the body of the paper, cited by page number.

4. The political potential of juxtaposing multiple discourses has most recently been confirmed in the distinctively Filipino carnivalesque overthrow of the seemingly all-powerful Marcos dictatorship. In one moment, Filipinos wept in fear for their lives as they stood firm before tanks; in the next moment, they turned to buy ice cream or joke with friends. On the role of humor in the

politics of Chicano culture, see Américo Paredes, "The Problem of Identity in a Changing Culture: Popular Expressions of Culture Conflict along the Lower Rio Grande Border," in *Views across the Border: The United States and Mexico*, ed. S. R. Ross (Albuquerque: University of New Mexico Press, 1978), pp. 68–94; José Limón, "Agringado Joking in Texas-Mexican Society: Folklore and Differential Identity," *New Scholar* 6 (1977): 33–50. For a fuller list of their pertinent works, see Renato Rosaldo, "Chicano Studies, 1970–1984," *Annual Review of Anthropology* 14 (1985): 405–27.

5. See José Limón, "The Return of the Mexican Ballad: Américo Paredes and His Anthropological Text as Persuasive Political Performance," SCCR Working Paper no. 16 (Stanford Center for Chicano Research, 1986). See also, José Limón, "Américo Paredes: A Man from the Border," *Revista Chicano-Riqueña* 8 (1980): 1–5. The intensity of anti-Mexican prejudice among Anglo-Texans in the late 1950s appeared to call for a male hero capable of agonistic combat. One should add that the reputation of south Texan Anglo-American prejudice against Mexicans remains legendary, at least among its recipients.

6. For a less idealized view of primordial south Texas Mexican society, see David Montejano, *Anglos and Mexicans in the Making of Texas, 1836–1986* (Austin: University of Texas Press, 1987).

7. This reflexive comparison of Paredes's scholarly production with the deeds of the warrior hero deepens when one considers the beginning scholar's successful resistance to the University of Texas Press editor who initially refused to publish his manuscript unless he removed the critique of Walter Prescott Webb. See Limón, "The Return of the Mexican Ballad," p. 29.

8. José Limón compares the form of Paredes's narrative with the ballad form itself. See Limón, Ibid.

9. Mary Louise Pratt, "The Short Story: The Long and the Short of It," *Poetics* 10 (1981): 175–94.

10. Along with the story entitled "A House of My Own" (p. 100), this passage invites comparison with Jean Briggs's retreat to "a tent of her own." The allusion to Virginia Woolf probably speaks for itself.

11. For an earlier reworking of the warrior hero from a woman's point of view, see Maxine Hong Kingston, *Warrior Woman: Memoirs of a Girlhood among Ghosts* (New York: Vintage Books, 1977).

Chapter 8

1. Max Weber, "Science as a Vocation," in *From Max Weber: Essays in Sociology*, ed. H. H. Gerth and C. Wright Mills (New York: Oxford University Press, 1958), p. 136.

2. Max Weber, "Politics as a Vocation," in *From Max Weber*, Gerth and Mills, eds., p. 115.
3. Weber, "Science as a Vocation," p. 137.
4. Ibid., p. 155.
5. Clifford Geertz, "Thinking as a Moral Act: Dimensions of Anthropological Fieldwork in the New States," *Antioch Review* 28, no. 2 (1968): 139−58, at p. 156.
6. Lévi-Strauss, for example, says, "The ethnographer, while in no wise abdicating his own humanity, strives to know and estimate his fellow-men from a lofty and distant point of vantage: only thus can he abstract them from the contingencies particular to this or that civilization. The conditions of his life and work cut him off from his own group for long periods together; and he himself acquires a kind of chronic uprootedness from the sheer brutality of the environmental changes to which he is exposed. Never can he feel himself 'at home' anywhere: he will always be, psychologically speaking, an amputated man. Anthropology is, with music and mathematics, one of the few true vocations; and the anthropologist may become aware of it within himself before ever he has been taught it" (Claude Lévi-Strauss, *Tristes Tropiques* [New York: Criterion Books, 1961], p. 58).
7. Geertz, "Thinking as a Moral Act," p. 157.
8. Ibid., p. 153.
9. Jean Briggs, *Never in Anger: Portrait of an Eskimo Family* (Cambridge, Mass.: Harvard University Press, 1970). For more recent reflections on *Never in Anger*, see Jean L. Briggs, "In Search of Emotional Meaning," *Ethos* 15 (1987): 8−15.
10. Briggs, *Never in Anger*, pp. 237−38.
11. Ibid., p. 272.
12. Ibid., p. 259. The place of the typewriter in ethnographic discourse clearly merits more extended exploration. The machine appears as often as food and novels. It often symbolizes partially successful, partially frustrated efforts to maintain an academic identity by creating an imaginary "office" while doing fieldwork.
13. Ibid., p. 229.
14. Weber, "Science as a Vocation," p. 137.
15. Briggs, *Never in Anger*, p. 298.
16. Briggs's account formally resembles works where the anthropologist appears as fall guy, such as in Geertz's typewriter incident, the preface to Evans-Pritchard's classic, *The Nuer*, and Castaneda's *Teachings of Don Juan*. Readers without fieldwork experience often respond to the fall-guy figure with fantasies of "if only I'd been there, I'd have done it right." Such readings both miss the near-parodic conventions that have formed the fall guy and underestimate the powerful effects of deprivation, anxiety, and disorienta-

tion often undergone by field-workers. Culture shock consists not only of the confrontation with an alien reality but also of an overwhelming sense of loss, produced by the interruption of one's intimate relations and familiar patterns of love and work.

17. Ibid., p. 286.
18. Ibid., p. 234.
19. Ibid., p. 242.
20. Ibid., p. 247.
21. Dorinne Kondo, "Dissolution and Reconstitution of Self: Implications for Anthropological Epistemology," *Cultural Anthropology* 1 (1986): 74–88, at p. 74.
22. Ibid., p. 80.
23. Because oppressed groups emerge from different social formations, with distinctive cultures and histories, their political visions also differ. Yet a number of otherwise perceptive social thinkers persist in attributing universal goals to such movements. Ernesto Laclau and Chantal Mouffee, for example, posit liberty and equality, deriving from the French Revolution, as the only conceivable programs for modern radical democratic movements. Hence they find themselves forced to argue, among other things, that present-day Moslem revolutionary movements are neither radical nor modern. See Ernesto Laclau and Chantal Mouffee, *Hegemony and Socialist Strategy: Towards a Radical Democratic Politics* (London: Verso, 1985).
24. Michael Walzer, *Interpretation and Social Criticism* (Cambridge, Mass.: Harvard University Press, 1987).
25. Ibid., p. 22.
26. E. P. Thompson, *The Making of the English Working Class* (New York: Vintage Books, 1966).
27. Ibid., p. 832.
28. Harold C. Conklin, "Shifting Cultivation and Succession to Grassland Climax," *The Proceedings of the Ninth Pacific Science Congress, 1957* 7 (1959): 60–62.
29. Ibid., p. 60.
30. Walzer, *Interpretation and Social Criticism*, p. 50.
31. So-called Third World social critics (such as Fanon, Gayatri Spivak, and Edward Said) often are dismissed, in a gesture of white supremacy, because of their elite educations. Should one infer that social mobility "whitens"? Are only the poor and illiterate truly people of color? In my view, such critics derive their sense of entitlement, such as it is, not simply from their phenotype or social origins but from their participation in social movements. The same doubtless holds for other social critics, whether progressive or conservative, whether they speak about gender, sexual orientation, the environment, nuclear weapons, or imperialism.

32. Frantz Fanon, *Black Skin, White Masks* (New York: Grove Press, 1967), pp. 111-12.
33. Floyd H. Flake, "Blacks Are Fair Game," *New York Times*, June 19, 1987.
34. Jerrold Seigel, *Marx's Fate: The Shape of a Life* (Princeton, N.J.: Princeton University Press, 1978), p. 113.
35. Karl Marx, "On the Jewish Question," in *Karl Marx: Selected Writings*, ed. David McLellan (Oxford: Oxford University Press, 1977), pp. 39-62, at p. 58.
36. Ibid., p. 61.
37. Robert E. Hemenway, *Zora Neale Hurston: A Literary Biography* (Urbana: University of Illinois Press, 1980), p. 22. Although widely recognized in literary circles, largely through Alice Walker's efforts, Hurston remains relatively little known to anthropologists. For an illuminating recent discussion of her work by a literary person writing in an anthropology journal, see John Dorst, "Rereading *Mules and Men:* Toward the Death of the Ethnographer," *Cultural Anthropology* 2 (1987): 305-18.
38. Zora Neale Hurston, *Dust Tracks on a Road* (1942; reprint, New York: Arno Press, 1969), p. 177.

Chapter 9

Portions of this chapter appeared in an earlier version as "Ideology, Place, and People without Culture," *Cultural Anthropology* 3, no. 1 (1988): 77-87.

1. Gonzalo Aguirre Beltrán, *Regiones de Refugio* (Mexico City: Instituto Indigenista Interamericano, 1967).
2. See Renato Rosaldo, "The Rhetoric of Control: Ilongots Viewed as Natural Bandits and Wild Indians," in *The Reversible World: Symbolic Inversion in Art and Society*, ed. Barbara Babcock (Ithaca, N.Y.: Cornell University Press, 1978), pp. 240-57; "Utter Savages of Scientific Value," in *Politics and History in Band Societies*, ed. Eleanor Leacock and Richard Lee (Cambridge: Cambridge University Press, 1982), pp. 309-25.
3. Frances FitzGerald, *Cities on a Hill: A Journey through Contemporary American Cultures* (New York: Simon and Schuster, 1986).
4. Ibid., p. 218.
5. Ibid., p. 219.
6. For an extended treatment of Ilongot notions of *tuydek*, see Michelle Rosaldo, "The Things We Do with Words: Ilongot Speech Acts and Speech Act Theory in Philosophy," *Language and Society* 11 (1982): 203-37.
7. Renato Rosaldo, "The Story of Tukbaw: They Listen as He Orates," in *The Biographical Process: Studies in the History and Psy-*

chology of Religion, ed. Frank Reynolds and Donald Capp (The Hague: Mouton, 1976), pp. 121–51.

8. James Clifford, "Power and Dialogue in Ethnography: Marcel Griaule's Initiation," in *The Predicament of Culture: Twentieth-Century Ethnography, Literature, and Art* (Cambridge, Mass.: Harvard University Press, 1988), pp. 55–91, at p. 76.

9. Surprisingly, discussions of the "native point of view" tend not to consider that so-called natives are more than reference points for cultural conceptions. They often disagree, talk back, assert themselves politically, and generally say things "we" might rather not hear. See Renato Rosaldo, "When Natives Talk Back: Chicano Anthropology since the Late Sixties," in *The Renato Rosaldo Lectures, 1985* (Tucson, Ariz.: Mexican-American Studies and Research Center, 1986), pp. 3–20.

10. Robert Reinhold, "Illegal Aliens Hoping to Claim Their Dreams," *New York Times*, November 3, 1986.

11. Ibid.

12. Ibid.

13. Brandon Bailey, "Sophisticated Cocaine Rings Moving into the Bay Area," *San Jose Mercury News*, October 26, 1986.

14. Ibid.

15. By now the reader can better gauge the probable reaction of Anglo-American functionaries to their verbal Mexicanization by Ernesto Galarza, as depicted in chapter 7. The anxiety about Mexicanization recently surfaced in the academic homeland, where the transcript of a University of Arizona Faculty Senate meeting recorded a Spanish professor who, after protesting too much about having been called a racist, went on to say, "Despite my devotion to Hispanic civilization, I find that that culture has two institutions well worth avoiding—its forms of government and of higher education. The truth of the matter is that my unfortunate department was thoroughly Mexicanized back in the sixties. The university's president and provost apparently would like to make that mistake universal. I call upon all my colleagues with the least care for scholarly integrity to extirpate a deep rooted evil in one department to prevent its spread through the entire institution" (mimeographed transcript, January 20, 1986, p. 4). A briefer passage from the same text has also been cited in Scott Heller, "Language, Politics, and Chicano Culture Spark Battle at U. of Arizona," *Chronicle of Higher Education* 31, no. 22 (February 22, 1986): 1, 24–26, at p. 26. Whatever qualities of Hispanic civilization the Spanish professor may admire, they do not extend to placing Chicanos in positions of authority in government and education. Here, the professor puts up an invisible sign that says "No Mexicans allowed."

16. For a seminal, sophisticated essay in the extensive critical

discussion of "El Louie," see Arturo Madrid-Barela, "In Search of the Authentic Pachuco: An Interpretive Essay," *Aztlán* 4, no. 1 (1973): 31–59.

17. José Montoya, "El Louie," in *Literatura Chicana, Texto y Contexto*, ed. Antonia Castañeda et al. (Englewood Cliffs, N.J.: Prentice-Hall, 1972), pp. 173–76. Reprinted by permission of José Montoya.

18. Gloria Anzaldua, *Borderlands/La Frontera: The New Mestiza* (San Francisco: Spinsters/Aunt Lute, 1987), p. 79.

Epilogue

1. Fred Barnes, review of *A Conflict of Visions* by Thomas Sowell, *New York Times Book Review*, January 25, 1987, p. 14. See also, Thomas Sowell, *A Conflict of Visions: Ideological Origins of Political Struggles* (New York: William Morrow, 1987).

2. Ibid.

3. Clifford Geertz, "Distinguished Lecture: Anti Anti-Relativism," *American Anthropologist* 86, no. 2 (1984): 263–78, at pp. 263–64.

Index

Academic warfare, 218–24
American Anthropological Association, 35
Andaman Islanders, 52–53, 172
Anderson, Benedict, 138
Anglo-American(s), 26; culture, death in, 55–58; and Ilongot dogs, contrast between treatment of, 26–27
Anglo-Texans, Paredes's narrative about, 150–55, 156
Anti-Semitism, 190–92
Anzaldua, Gloria, *Borderlands/ La Frontera*, 216–17

Arnold, Matthew, 98
Athabascan hunters, 120, 122

Balinese, 26, 196
Barthes, Roland, 166
Basque society, 13, 26
Batteau, Allen, 71–72
Beauvoir, Simone de, 13
Becker, A. L., 142
Beidelman, T. O., 33–34
Beltran, Gonzalo Aguirre, 199
Benedict, Ruth, 192; *Patterns of Culture*, 27
Berman, Marshall, 72–73
Bernstein, Richard, *The Re-*

247

Bernstein, Richard (*continued*) *structuring of Social and Political Theory*, 36
Blake, William, 137, 183
Boas, Franz, 192
Bourdieu, Pierre, 105, 108, 126; *Outline of a Theory of Practice*, 107
Braudel, Fernand, 135
Briggs, Jean, 180, 193–94; *Never in Anger: Portrait of an Eskimo Family*, 176–79
Brody, Hugh, 120, 122
Brooks, Peter, 138
Bruner, Jerome, 41–42, 129
Buhari, Mohammed, 100
Burke, Kenneth, 104
Bushmen. *See* !Kung San

Calvin, John, 171
Case history, 139–41
Chaos: culture, control, and, 96–102; space between order and, 102–5
Chicago Tribune, 65
Chicano(s), 45, 49–50; movement, 35–36; narratives, 148–50 (*see also* Cisneros, Sandra; Galarza, Ernesto; Paredes, Américo); poetry, 215–16, 217. *See also* Warrior hero, Chicano
Cisneros, Sandra, 160–61, 166; *The House on Mango Street*, 148, 160, 161–66
Civil rights movement, 35, 187, 222
Class formations, 105–6
Clifford, James, 38–39, 81–82, 205–6
Colombian cocaine peddlars, 213–14
Conklin, Harold, 187, 192, 194; "Shifting Cultivation and

Succession to Grassland Climax," 184–86
Control, and culture and chaos, 96–102
Cooper, James Fenimore, 84
C.P.T. (colored people's time), 110
Cultural patterns, and cultural borderlands, 26–30
Cultural visibility and invisibility, 198–204
Culture(s): in borderlands, 207–14, and control and chaos, 96–102; learning about other, 25–26
Cushing, Frank Hamilton, 179

Danforth, Loring, 61
Dante, 43
Davis, Fred, 71
Death: anthropological studies of, 12–16, 19; emotional force of, 2; in North American culture, 55–58
Dickens, Charles, 138
Dobie, J. Frank, 154
Dogon, 205–6
Douglas, William, *Death in Murelaga*, 12–13
Du Bois, Cora, 44
Durkheim, Emile, 32–33; on enduring character of society, 103–4; his theory of social order, 98–100, 101–2

Eliot, George, *Middlemarch*, 81
Eskimos, study of, 176–79, 193–94
Ethnography, 31–34, 43–45, 105; remaking, as form of social analysis, 38–43
Ethnomethodology, 104–5
Evans-Pritchard, E. E., 42–43
Exchange theory, 3–4

187, 190, 193,
ck Skin, White
89
houghts and,

FitzGerald, Frances, 203
Flake, Floyd H., 189, 195
Force, notion of, 2
Frake, Charles, 115
Frontier mythology, 72

Galarza, Ernesto, 155–56, 166;
    Barrio Boy, 148, 155, 156–
    60; compared with Cis-
    neros, 161
Gallie, W. B., 132–33, 134, 135,
    141, 223
Geertz, Clifford, 60, 96, 176,
    179, 180, 193; on culture
    and control, 97–98; inter-
    pretive approach of, 7, 94;
    and processual analysis,
    93–95; on refiguration of
    social thought, 37; on rela-
    tivism/antirelativism, 223–
    24; "Thinking as a Moral
    Act," 173–74; typewriter in-
    cident of, 174–75
Goethe, Johann Wolfgang von,
    Faust, 72
Goody, Jack, 56–57
Graves, Sarabelle, 79–80,
    86, 87
Griaule, Marcel, 205–6
Grief, and rage, 1–12; Ilongot
    headhunting and, 16–19
Guadalupe, Treaty of, 152

Hanunoo agriculture, 184–86
Hardy, Thomas, 137, 138–39
Headhunting, 1–2, 62–63, 64,
    65; celebration, 5–6; end of,
    79, 80; explanations for,
    3–4; grief, rage, and, 1,

2–7, 11, 16–19,
    rium on, 4, 5, 6
Hegel, G. W. F., 189
Heilbroner, Robert, 12.
Hemenway, Robert, 192
Hempel, Carl, 130, 132
Hexter, J. H., 133–34, 135,
Hobbes, Thomas, 98, 101
Holocaust, 191
Homer, 44
Homophobia, 35
Huntington, Richard, *Celebra-
    tions of Death* (with P. Met-
    calf), 12
Hurston, Zora Neale, 192–
    93, 195

Ifugaos, 9, 123–24, 200
Illegal aliens, 210–11, 213
Ilongot(s): adultery among,
    101; and Anglo-American
    dogs, contrast between
    treatment of, 26–27; cul-
    tural analysis of, 197, 200;
    cultural changes undergone
    by, 208–9; headhunting by,
    1–7, 11, 16–19, 62–63, 64,
    65; hunting by, 128–29; and
    imperialist nostalgia, 85–
    87; William Jones's writings
    on, 83–85; language of,
    204–5; missionaries' im-
    pact on, 79–81; perceptions
    of modern warfare of,
    63–64, 65–67; rage in grief
    of, 1, 2–7, 16–19; relations
    of, with anthropologists,
    206; Wilfrid Turnbull's writ-
    ings on, 74–79; visiting,
    tempo, and social grace
    among, 112–26
Immigration, 214; process of,
    209–11
Impartiality, 21

ᴉ, 31, 41; intensifi-
ᴉf, 34, 35, 38, 44; and
alism, 42
alist nostalgia, 68–69,
207; and civilizing mis-
on, 74–81; mourning pass-
ing of traditional society,
81–86; mourning what one
has destroyed, 69–74
Indianapolis Star, 65
Indian Time, 110, 124; indeterminacy of, 111–12
Inquiry, value-free, 169–73
Interpretive method, 7
Iowa Writers Workshop, 161

James, Henry, 138, 176, 177
Javanese shadow theater, 142
Jonah (prophet), 187
Jones, William, 82–85, 87;
murder of, 74, 76, 78

Kluckhohn, Clyde, 8
Knowledge, relational, 204–7
Kondo, Dorinne, 180–81, 194
!Kung San, 128
Kwakiutl, 43

Landers, Ann, 91–92, 102
Latino population, increas-
ing, 214
Lee, Richard Borshay, 128
Lévi-Strauss, Claude, 59; *Tris-
tes Tropiques*, 81
Limón, José, 150
Listowel Banner, The (Ontario),
116–17
Locke, John, 187
LoDagaa, 56–57
Lofton, John, 66, 67

Malinowski, Bronislaw, 81,
85, 180
Manchester School, 139

Mang, Jessica, 56
Mang, Pamela, 56
Marcos, Ferdinand, 4
Marx, Karl, 193, 195; *The 18th
Brumaire of Louis Bona-
parte*, 105; "On the Jewish
Question," 190–92
Metcalf, Peter: *A Borneo Jour-
ney into Death*, 12; *Celebra-
tions of Death* (with R. Hunt-
ington), 12
Mexicans, 49–50, 214; nar-
ratives about, 150–55,
156–60
Mexican Time, 110
Mexico, cultural visibility and
invisibility in, 198–201
Miami Vice, 212–13, 214
Microcosmic view, 17
Miner, Horace, "Body Ritual
among the Nacirema,"
51–52
Mink, Louis, 131–32, 136, 142
Montoya, José, "El Louie,"
215–16, 217
Monumentalism, 31, 33, 34,
43–44
Monumentalist-objectivist
coalition, 219–21, 223
Moon, Rev. Sun Myung, 66
Moore, Sally Falk, 32
Multivocality, 2

Nader, Laura, *To Keep the Bal-
ance*, 82
Nagel, Ernest, 130, 132
Narrative(s), 127–30, 147–48;
Chicano, 148–50 (*see also*
Cisneros, Sandra; Galarza,
Ernesto; Paredes, Américo);
as form of social analysis,
130–36; and point of view
in social analysis, 137–43
National Enquirer, 66–67

Native Americans, 71, 81
Navahos, 196
Ndembu, 39, 96, 97, 140–41
Negritos, 81, 199–200
Neutrality, 21
New Left, 35
New Tribes Mission, 79–80
Norms, classic: erosion of, 28; rise of, 30–34; theory as reification of, 59–62
Nostalgia. *See* Imperialist nostalgia
Nuer, 42–43
Nyakyusa, 14, 26

Objectivism, 31, 32, 33, 34, 54
Objectivist-monumentalist coalition, 219–21, 223
Objectivity, 21
Order and chaos, space between, 102–5
Orientalism, 42

Parades, Américo, 49–50, 51, 150, 155, 166; compared with Cisneros, 161, 165; compared with Galarza, 155, 156, 159, 160; *"With His Pistol in His Hand": A Border Ballad and Its Hero*, 148, 150–55
Participant-observation, 180
Philippine Magazine, 74–76, 77–78
Philippines: cultural visibility and invisibility in, 197, 198–201; imperialist venture in, 72, 74, 83; Negrito groups in, 81, 199–200. *See also* Ilongot(s)
Philips, Susan, 111–12
Point of view, in social analysis, 137–43
Polysemy, 2

Positioned subject, 7, 8, 19, 207
Pratt, Mary Louise, 40, 161
Predestination, doctrine of, 6
Processual analysis, 92–93, 105; dilemmas of, 93–96; and narrative, 127, 131, 134–35
Pueblos, 81

Race relations, 212–13
Racism, 35, 71, 188, 189
Radcliffe-Brown, A. R., 52–53, 54, 58, 172
Rage and grief, 1–12; Ilongot headhunting and, 16–19
Reagan, Ronald, 65, 214
Reichard, Gladys, 192
Relational knowledge, 204–7
Repositioned subject, 7
Richness, 2
Ricoeur, Paul, 134–36
Rituals: and bereavement, 20; as busy intersection, 17, 20; death and, 12–16; exorcism, 16–17; failure to perform, 6; feelings aroused by, 9; and Ilongot headhunting, 16
Roosevelt, Teddy, 83
Rosaldo, Manny, 29, 204
Rosaldo, Michelle, 2, 4, 5–6, 85, 87, 197; on changes undergone by Ilongots, 208–9; death of, 9, 10, 11, 19, 29; and Ilongot visiting, 113, 118, 119, 120; and imperialist venture in Philippines, 74; writings of, 18, 74, 82, 86, 208
Rough Riders, 83

Said, Edward, 42
Sass, Louis A., 44

Sauer, Carl, 103
Seigel, Jerrold, 190
Sexism, 35
Shakespeare, William, 43, 44, 220
Sharp, William, 137
Sinhalese, 45
Slotkin, Richard, 72
Social analysis, 100; multiplex personal identities and, 179–81; narrative as form of, 130–36; new subjects of, 214–17; point of view in, 137–43; politics of remaking, 34–38; remaking ethnography as form of, 38–43; subaltern, 186–89; wit as weapon in subaltern, 190–93
Social criticism and multiplex communities, 181–86
Social grace, 112; tempo, and Ilongot visiting, 112–26
Sowell, Thomas, A Conflict of Visions, 221–23
Spanish-American War, 83
Stanford University, 65, 66; Campus Report of, 64–65, 66
Sullivan, Harry Stack, 98
Sun City (retirement village), 203–4
Systems thought, 93, 94

Tempo: of everyday life, 105, 107–8; in other cultures, 109–10, 111–12; social grace, and Ilongot visiting, 112–26
Tewas, 45
Texas, University of, at Austin, 150
Texas Rangers, 150, 153–54, 210
Texture, 2

Thick description, 2
Thompson, E. P., 107, 108, 187, 194; The Making of the English Working Class, 105–6, 137–39, 183–84, 186; on "time-discipline," 109–10
Time: cultural construction of, 109; -discipline, 110; Indian, 110, 111–12, 124; Mexican, 110
Trobriand Islanders, 43
Turnbull, Wilfrid, 86, 87; writings of, on Ilongots, 74–79
Turner, Frederick Jackson, 151
Turner, Victor, 40–41, 97, 98; and processual analysis, 93–94; use of case history by, 139–41

Unification Church, 66
Universities, conflict in American, 218–24

"Vanishing savage," notion of, 81–82, 85, 86
Vietnam War, 63, 72; mobilization against, 35, 65
Vincent, Joan, 93
Visiting, Ilongot, 112–26

Walzer, Michael, 194, 195; Interpretation and Social Criticism, 181–82, 186–87
Warfare, Ilongot perceptions of modern, 63–64, 65–67
Warrior hero, Chicano, 148–49; Cisneros's fading, 160–65; Galarza's mocking of, 155–60; Paredes's, 150–55
Washington, George, 210
Washington Times, 66
Webb, Walter Prescott, 154
Weber, Max, 110–11, 177; critique of masculine heroics

of, 166, 167, 169–73, 193; "Politics as a Vocation," 170; *The Protestant Ethic and the Spirit of Capitalism*, 6, 171; "Science as a Vocation," 170
White, Hayden, 130–31

Williams, Raymond, 105, 106, 107, 108
Wilson, Godfrey, 14–15

Zapotec Indians, 82
Zuni secret societies, 179